BLOODAXE CRITICAL ANTHOLOGIES: 2

DARK FATHERS INTO LIGHT:
BRENDAN KENNELLY

Books by Brendan Kennelly

The Penguin Book of Irish Verse (Penguin, 1970; 2nd edition 1981)
The Boats Are Home (Gallery Press, 1980)
Cromwell (Beaver Row, 1983; Bloodaxe Books, 1987)
Moloney Up and At It (Mercier Press, 1984)
Mary (Aisling Press, 1987)
Landmarks of Irish Drama (Methuen, 1988)
Love of Ireland: Poems from the Irish (Mercier Press, 1989)
A Time for Voices: Selected Poems 1960-1990 (Bloodaxe Books, 1990)
The Book of Judas (Bloodaxe Books, 1991)
Medea (Bloodaxe Books, 1992)
Breathing Spaces: Early Poems (Bloodaxe Books, 1992)
The Trojan Women (Bloodaxe Books, 1993)
Journey into Joy: Selected Prose, edited by Åke Persson
    (Bloodaxe Books, 1994)

AS CO-EDITOR
Ireland's Women: Writings Past and Present, with Katie Donovan &
    A. Norman Jeffares (Kyle Cathie/Gill & Macmillan 1994)
Dublines, with Katie Donovan (Bloodaxe Books, 1994)

BLOODAXE CRITICAL ANTHOLOGIES: 2

DARK FATHERS INTO LIGHT:
BRENDAN KENNELLY

EDITED BY
RICHARD PINE

BLOODAXE BOOKS

ISBN: 1 85224 275 2 hardback edition
       1 85224 276 0 paperback edition

First published 1994 by
Bloodaxe Books Ltd,
P.O. Box 1SN,
Newcastle upon Tyne NE99 1SN.

Bloodaxe Books Ltd acknowledges
the financial assistance of Northern Arts.

Cover printing by J. Thomson Colour Printers Ltd, Glasgow.

Printed in Great Britain by
Bell & Bain Limited, Glasgow, Scotland.

This book is dedicated with
gratitude and affection to the
Tyrone Guthrie Centre at Annaghmakerrig
where I have passed many of
my happiest and most rewarding days

RICHARD PINE

CONTENTS

9   MICHAEL D. HIGGINS: Foreword

11   RICHARD PINE: Preface

13   Notes on Contributors

15   RICHARD PINE: Introduction

27   GABRIEL FITZMAURICE: 'Becoming Song':
     The Translated Village

36   AUGUSTINE MARTIN: Technique and Territory in
     Brendan Kennelly's Early Work

50   TERENCE BROWN: Kennelly as Novelist

59   GERALD DAWE: 'And Then – the Spring!':
     Brendan Kennelly's *Breathing Spaces*

66   JONATHAN ALLISON: *Cromwell:* Hosting the Ghosts

91   ANTHONY ROCHE: *The Book of Judas:*
     Parody, Double Cross and Betrayal

114   KATHLEEN McCRACKEN: Rage for a New Order:
      Brendan Kennelly's Plays for Women

148   ÅKE PERSSON: The Critic: Towards a Literary Credo

168   'The Roaring Storm of Your Words':
      BRENDAN KENNELLY in conversation with RICHARD PINE

187   Notes

194   ÅKE PERSSON: Select Bibliography

MICHAEL D. HIGGINS

FOREWORD

I am only one of those who have benefited from the generosity of the human spirit that is manifested in Brendan Kennelly.

That generosity extends beyond the patience of the poet offering scarce time to the unfinished image of another or the granting of time to those striving to make a shape of words, of dreams, or voices from the dark or light.

Brendan Kennelly continues to break so many rules including those that have invaded aesthetics and the space of creativity that have immiserated so much of our times. He has discarded the neat rational use of polarities that might suffice in the academy or in the shadowland where critical thought is reputed to live.

Instead, in the integration of the life and work he has sung and screamed the pain of contradiction as well as the precious moments of celebration.

I am so pleased that the task of locating Brendan Kennelly's work has been attempted. The terrain that he has covered makes the effort admirable but also certain of uncertainty in its conclusions. Kennelly has grazed on the grass of the long acre. The pastoral categories are clearly insufficient.

Neither the life nor the work acknowledges the walls of arbitrary academic proprietorship, yet he has brought to the road he has chosen the finest flowers of the meadows into which he has broken.

Time and place offer no restrictions either. Myths and symbol, sound and artifact are presented to us in vessels we are meant to recognise and broken in front of our faces with a laugh that at once shocks and also reminds us of our unfreedom.

I see him laughing as he places the sacral and the sexual on the same altar. I hear his voice as clear as water and as unpredictable as a mountain stream.

I often worry for the darker side that reason suggests as the price for such a dazzling light. I am reminded that the polarity has been rejected. We are not asked to choose between the darkness and the light.

Brendan Kennelly's act of integration between heart and head, the known and the unknown, the male and female, the tragic and the comic is almost unique. Who else could write of Judas as the

Bowsie that is the Everyperson of our shattered century? Who else could introduce his personal ghost to the demons of others? Who else could let all the voices scream from him in unrestricted beauty and awful terror?

There is a swagger in the works that goes beyond the gimp of a fine poet or the memory of a parish victory in merry football. The personal journey across the plays, the novels, the essays reminds us that the price of pain has been paid, and for the truth of the thing, for ourselves and others, is best expressed, not hidden. For that truth, the connection between 'the word, the gasp, the laugh, the line, the poetry, so many are and will be grateful. Through Brendan Kennelly's work we are reminded that authenticity continually threatens to assert itself.

MICHAEL D. HIGGINS, TD
Minister for Arts, Culture and the Gaeltacht

RICHARD PINE

PREFACE

Critics from three generations, and from a variety of cultural backgrounds and perspectives, have assembled here to judge and commend the work of Brendan Kennelly. The warmth and readiness with which they responded to my invitation is a mark both of their friendly esteem for Kennelly himself and of their professional regard for his work.

There is always a danger, when the academic world turns its attention to living poetry, that the work will be veiled by considerations of method. This is not the case with the present collection: the fact that three of the authors are themselves established poets, and that each of us is in some measure intimately concerned with the creative process, has given the book as a whole an imaginative thrust which anticipates, as well as records, Kennelly's own kinetic energy. The fact that he is himself a member of this academic community, making an increasingly productive fusion of poetry and criticism, is evident, too, in our responses to his work. He is seen from within, and this allows the criticism to live on the page.

As if by natural, implicit consensus (but not by editorial design), contributors have provided more extended commentary on the later work, to some extent leaving the earlier collections greater space in which to speak for themselves. In any age concerned conspicuously with the nature of difference and otherness, with fear and doubt, it is perhaps understandable that works of anxiety should require examination more than those of certainty and joy. Despite the undeniable force to which Kennelly has submitted the sonnet form in *Cromwell* and *The Book of Judas*, however, my personal admiration for sequences such as *Love Cry* is undiminished and perhaps enhanced. But it is probably unwise and unnecessary to be certain on such a point.

In presenting these essays on all facets of Kennelly's work, I realise how rich is the seam from which they have been quarried. This is the first collection of its kind, but it will certainly not be the last: it opens up a body of work for wider scrutiny and appraisal, and I am confident that it will be rewarded with the monographs which that work undoubtedly deserves.

It has been an especial pleasure to me to gather respected friends and colleagues for this occasion, and to find new ones. A particular word of thanks is due on behalf of us all to Geraldine Mangan, of the English Department, Trinity College, Dublin, for her valuable practical support over many years for Brendan Kennelly's work and its students. Finally, Brendan Kennelly himself has been characteristically ingenuous and resolute about the book, as he has indeed been during our friendship of more than twenty-five years, and this is evident in the interview with which it closes.

Annaghmakerrig,
New Year's Day 1994.

NOTES ON CONTRIBUTORS

Richard Pine, critic and broadcaster, writes on cultural studies, including communications, music and post-colonial literature. He is a Governor of the Royal Irish Academy of Music, and a former Chairman of the Media Association of Ireland, Secretary of the Irish Writers' Union and Co-Editor of the *Irish Literary Supplement*. His publications include: *Oscar Wilde* (1983), *The Dublin Gate Theatre 1928-1978* (1984), *The Dandy and the Herald: manners, mind and morals from Brummell to Durrell* (1988), *Brian Friel and Ireland's Drama* (1990), *Lawrence Durrell: The Mindscape* (1994) and *The Thief of Reason: Oscar Wilde and Modern Ireland* (1995).

Gabriel Fitzmaurice teaches in the National School in his native village of Moyvane, County Kerry. A former Chairman of Listowel Writers' Week, he has published many volumes of poetry including *Rainsong* (1984) and most recently *The Father's Part* (1992) and *The Space Between* (1993), and has been widely translated; he has edited several anthologies, including *Irish Poetry Now: Other Voices* (1993) and (with Declan Kiberd) *An Crann Faoi Bláth / The Flowering Tree* (1991).

Augustine Martin is Professor Anglo-Irish Literature and Drama at University College, Dublin. Director of the International James Joyce Summer School, he has represented the National University of Ireland in the Irish Senate. Author of *W.B. Yeats* (1983/90) and *Anglo-Irish Literature* (1982) and editor of *James Joyce: The Artist and the Labyrinth* (1990), he is currently working on the official biography of Patrick Kavanagh.

Terence Brown is Professor of Anglo-Irish Literature at Trinity College, Dublin. His publications include *Louis MacNeice: Sceptical Vision* (1975), *Ireland: A Social and Cultural History* (1985) and *Ireland's Literature* (1988) and, as co-editor, *Tradition and Influence in Anglo-Irish Poetry* (1988); he is currently working on a critical biography of W.B. Yeats, and is series editor of Gill's Studies of Irish Literature.

Gerald Dawe, poet and critic, lectures in Literature and Drama at Trinity College, Dublin. His collections of poetry include *Sheltering Places* (1978), *The Lundys Letter* (1985) and *Sunday School* (1991). He has also published three books of criticism, *How's the Poetry Going* (1991), *A Real Life Elsewhere* (1993) and *False Faces* (1994), and is founder-editor of *Krino: the review*. His collected essays on Irish poetry, *Against Piety*, will be published in 1995.

Jonathan Allison, a graduate of the Queen's University, Belfast, University College, London, and the University of Michigan, is currently assistant professor at the University of Kentucky and is editor of *Yeats's Political Identities* (University of Michigan, forthcoming). He has published articles on Yeats, Heaney and Paul Muldoon, and is working on a book on Heaney.

Anthony Roche lectures in the Department of English at University College, Dublin, and has written and broadcast widely on Irish writing in English. A former Chairman and Secretary of the Irish Writers' Union, Co-Editor of the *Irish Literary Supplement* and Associate Director of the Yeats International Summer School, he is the author of *Contemporary Irish Drama* (1994).

Kathleen McCracken lectures in English and American Studies at the University of Ulster at Jordanstown. She has published four collections of poetry, the most recent of which, *Blue Light, Bay and College* (1991), was nominated for Canada's Governor-General's Award. Her critical study, *Radical Vision: The Poetry of Paul Durcan*, is due from Bloodaxe Books in 1995.

Åke Persson, a graduate of the universities of Karlstad, Hull and British Columbia, Vancouver, is completing his Ph.D. thesis on the work of Brendan Kennelly at the University of Gothenburg. From 1986 to 1993 he taught Swedish at Trinity College, Dublin. He has published extensively on the work of Brendan Kennelly, and is the editor of Kennelly's critical essays, *Journey into Joy* (1994). He is currently preparing a second selection of Kennelly's prose.

RICHARD PINE

INTRODUCTION

The poet is a maker of images which speak to our minds, our affections, our bowels; the poet's sensibility a place of conflict, a place of contending voices urgent to be heard. Only when the identities have been resolved, the chimera pacified, the past revisited and acknowledged, the sexes reconciled, ghosts appeased and the future grasped, will the act of surprise, the poem, the metaphor, become possible. On the journey, brief spots of time illuminate this possibility, dispelling the poet's despair and feeding his hope.

The writing of Brendan Kennelly, as poet, playwright, novelist, critic, translator has, since the late 1950s, followed a trajectory of emergence from tribal, prehistoric darkness, from the known places of childhood, into the uncertainties of an uneven, challenging world. His natural gift of honesty to himself, his faith in life, has marked the inner quest for love and identity. His natural charisma as a personality and as a poet – often identical in their expression – has fuelled the public career. Personal triumphs and adversities, sureness and dismay, have played their part in equal measure. The sense of a kind of joy has been the compelling motive in his movement from darkness into light; he embraces the notion that even in the darkest and most obscure places one can hear laughter, or the echo of laughter.

The purpose of this Introduction is to describe to the reader the themes of love, violence, betrayal, joy and hope on which Kennelly's work rests. I want to suggest some of the images from which these themes spring, such as the village, the playing-field, the river and the house, and to make a preliminary exploration of Kennelly's view of poetry.

Born in Ballylongford, County Kerry, in 1936, and educated in Tarbert and at Trinity College, Dublin, and Leeds University, Brendan Kennelly has published twenty-one individual volumes of poetry ranging from slim collections to the massive *The Book of Judas* (1991) and six volumes of selections; two volumes of verse translations from Irish; two novels in the 1960s; four plays; critical introductions to collections of poetry, prose and drama and a volume of critical essays. Since 1973 he has held a Professorship of Modern Literature at Trinity College, Dublin, where he is a Senior Fellow and where he has also fulfilled several administrative functions; he has lectured at universities throughout the world, including terms as visiting Professor at universities in the United States and in Holland. Chairman of the Cultural Relations Committee of the Department of Foreign Affairs, he raised some eyebrows in polite society with a series of automobile commercials for television and radio in 1991-94, the chief irony perhaps being the fact that Kennelly himself cannot drive a car. In all of these roles, Kennelly's humour, warmth, compassion and sense of mischief have been evident as unifying features.

But within this apparently simple private quest and monolithic public career is a complexity of competing and contradictory forces. The act of making begins with the act of making sense, of examining the materials to hand and acknowledging their qualities: making a poem and making a life are natural pursuits, yet they contain all the difficulty, all the anguish, pain and perplexity contained in nature itself. Kennelly's worlds – the home place of childhood to which he constantly returns and which has provided the affective base of his poetry, the world of teaching in a great university, where he has acted out that poetry and developed his critical insight, and the international forum of academe and poetry where he has achieved further distinction. These places set up the tension between public and private personae, between poet and orator. They suggest the discontinuities which can occur between what is promised and what is excluded.

Furthermore, the fact that the observer inevitably disturbs the field of observation, turns the relationship between the poet and his worlds into a series of indeterminate experiences: action and reaction intensify the complex uncertainties of even the most pacific, well-tempered house, creating resonances and antinomies to confuse and trouble the psyche.

For the poet, the act of singing is internally polyphonic even when the emergent song has a single voice. The critic's assiduous commentary, by creating and participating in the world on which he comments, makes his aesthetic world political. However mundane – music, the cut throats of pigs, swimming the Shannon – life in Kennelly's poetic world is local, intimate and visceral, and at the same time universal, grand and concerned with *la politesse*. Root and branch are interdependent: the pagan voices resonate in the court society; in Kennelly's words, poetry 'finds its life in these feelings'[1] and becomes, as Åke Persson calls it, 'a literature of feelings'.[2] The emotions feed on the rhythm and periodicity of nature – providing what Kennelly sees as 'a whole imaginative world...a nodal community'. From this springs what in 1970 he called 'the Irish mind [which] delights in simple, direct, lively expression'[3] yet is bedevilled by problems of communication because words are the means by which we discover our differences. In a thoroughly happy, integrated world, words and writing would be unnecessary; in a fragmented, uncertain world the song sings the singer.

*   *   *

The themes which we so readily associate with the plays of his fellow Kerryman, John B. Keane – violence, greed, dishonesty, simple virtues, innocence, inborn dignity and sham respectability – are also the hinterland from which Brendan Kennelly derives his poetry. They inform the dialogue between himself and his community – the same landscape of North Kerry with its extraordinary network of towns and villages, its mountains and, as its northern boundary, the powerful force of the Shannon – and they provide the daily commerce which Kennelly, almost as a form of automatic writing, shapes into the love-children of his poetry.

The factors which hold such a society together are reverence and irreverence, trust and distrust, likeness and difference, nearness and distance; the disparate units of men which mesh to make a town: the storyteller, fortune teller, diviner, priest, drunkard, whore, fornicator, recluse, blacksmith, silversmith, pig-killer, bodhran maker, singer, man in pursuit of 'a mortaller';[4] the commerce between the living and the dead, between now and history, between poetry and rhetoric; the digging, reaping, hammering, crafting, despatching, celebrating, which represent the forms of life.

All of this is implicit in the single word 'house': Kennelly says 'we do not ever escape from a certain house'. For the child of the Ballylongford bar, finding a life amid a forest of adult legs, becoming a scholar in the tradition of the hedge-schools, a footballer, an observer and participant in acts of violence – the inter-village 'battles' with the animation of their 'wonderful intensities' – the interrelationship of people becomes a mosaic of images seeking transfiguration and wholeness: 'poetry is written by blind men, groping for some kind of light'. Poetry is also the record of the fact that we 'cannot leave people alone', that we are continually interfering in each others' lives, making joyful and tragic, welcome and rejected appearances in each others' narratives – all of them inevitable.

In this society Kennelly bears witness at once to the struggle for survival of its folk and to their spontaneity. He sings because it is first an oral tradition. When he refers to 'my native flaw' as the problem of translation into a written tradition, the term becomes ambiguous: the flaw for the modern, urban critic is the difficulty of transference, but the flaw resides also in the acquired, written tradition. The oral tradition is not the less articulate or cohesive for being unlettered – the continuity and antiquity which Kennelly has emphasised [5] is cognate with that of the Finnish *Kalevala* with its archetypal figures of wisdom, authority and song, its celebration of rivers, gods and men, a mythology which Yeats admired as a model for the re-creation of the Irish poetic psyche.[6] The impeded speech atoned and celebrated in 'The Stammer' – 'lips pumping silent cries' (*BS* 17) – is part of Kennelly's childhood, as is the figure of Jane Agnes McKenna, his teacher, to whose memory *Breathing Spaces* is dedicated.

This celebration is a voice both for the 'nodal community' and for the self. That voice describes what happens when one steps outside that community, and begins to flounder; it insists on the need for 'boundary-breakers...limit-smashers' and, ultimately, for 'betrayal as a principle' of poetry. Within the breakable limits of poetry lies the capacity for 'ecstatic self-destruction' which has on occasions brought Kennelly to the edge of existence itself: 'I feel like a battle-ground in which there is this fight between intelligent, enlightened surviving and loving, and a kind of black desire to fuck it up'. This in itself imposes a dual obligation on the poet: 'a genuine violation of inherited prejudices' and 'the struggle of a work to survive its own stages'.[7]

                              *   *   *

There are times in his poetry when Kennelly looks around him with childish glee and naïveté. Innocence and wonder do not, however, exclude wisdom: the child's role, like the struggle of the poem to survive, is to explore and unravel the complexities of the life woven by those who have come before him, to resolve the apparent difficulty presented by the manner in which they come between him and life itself – the problem of nostalgia, the painful homecoming to self, to truth, to love. The naïf and the canny are held together in the lives of what George Fitzmaurice once called 'wicked old children'.[8]

Kennelly's express intention is 'to define love'. To do so he must investigate what we are not, in order to discover what we are, and to find that both 'I' and 'Not-I' inhabit the same skin, compose the same integer. 'Emotional maimings have something to do with it, they're part of it, of the ultimate fluency we can achieve in our life'. The notion of metaphor as understanding, as equivalence, is vital to this act of definition. Throughout Kennelly's early work the equation, the transference of affection between signifier and signified, between sexual partners, even between the butcher and the pig, was achieved with facility. The relationship of man and land – rock, clay, hillside and river – of man grounded in place, was accepted: word and gesture together intimately express and extend the community which gives them life. As the painter Tony O'Malley puts it: 'painting is the need to express that place, *which also includes myself*'.[9]

The poem is both mantic and semantic in its confirmation of history and, thereby, the creation of a new day. Even though the 'dark fathers' lived an 'intolerable day' (*ATFV* 18-19), it could be celebrated because it contained the seeds of a miracle. The enemy of poetry is time – time before and time after – and therefore 'the only agelessness/ Is yes' (*ATFV* 24). If poetry, then, is affirmation, it can only be born of a battle between hope and despair, as intense and unrelenting as the battles of rivalry between the Kerry villages: 'hope or grit, survival, coming from the brutality of life ... Hope is an achieved thing, an earned thing...the one thing on which my poetry rests.'

In the first of his two novels, *The Crooked Cross*, Kennelly depicts with the intensity of the *mezzogiorno* the struggle to maintain the equilibrium of the village of Deevna. Employing it as a symbol for the whole of Ireland, he encompasses and transcends this brutality, encouraging the reader to accept simultaneously the ugly and the beautiful, the sacred and the profane, as they co-exist in this village of rhymers and liars. If, as the novel suggests, the poet sits at the right hand of God (*CC* 14), then we should add that he sits also at the left hand of the Devil.

Everything in Kennelly's work derives from the pursuit of the marvellous, and is to be measured against the achievement or loss of hope. Reading his work chronologically, we might reasonably regard the point of his life at which he began to write more public poetry, in *Cromwell* and *The Book of Judas*, and to explore the feminine psyche more severely in his versions of the Greek tragedies, as a sea-change, catalysed by his own experiences of a collapsed marriage and treatment for alcoholism. In his version of *Medea* he has referred explicitly to the circumstances in which he first began to hear the voices of women's rage (*Medea* 7). But equally, he has told us that his knowledge of women's strength, portrayed in *The Trojan Women*, was pushed along by an echo of that strength from his childhood.[10] Kennelly's own insistence on this point – that, despite the apparent caesura in his work around the early 1980s, there is a discernible continuity in his approach to love – demands exploration. The lyricism and wistfulness of the earlier work, the rhythmic elegance, even the ingenuous humour, set against the earthy *chiaroscuro* of that Kerry hinterland (in *Love Cry*, for example), has indeed given way to a more gritty, resolute and yet carefree writing, but the vigour is aboriginal.

The vitality of poetry springs from the struggle which lies at the heart of metaphor. This is the trellis around which the vocabulary and syntax of love-poetry can grow, and in a sense, in Kennelly's terms, all poetry, perhaps all writing, is love-poetry. But while the trellis may be sturdy, the tendrils of hope are fragile and vulnerable. In *Medea* we witness the death of the future, the death of hope.[11] The murder of one's own children and the slit throat of the pig are equally plausible in Kennelly's work: they lie there in strange proximity, because beneath the known soil of everyday habit is the layer of the unpredictable, the element of surprise which belongs equally to everyday.

The powerful moment of connection, the point at which the metaphor is achieved, can occur only when this unpredictability comes into play. In the village of Deevna there is a relationship between men and God which seems very special but is in fact ubiquitous, ordinary: 'if the good Christ came on earth again, He'd be crucified right here...The only mistake God ever made was when He made this place' (*CC* 9). Intimacy between the natural and the supernatural, physical and metaphysical, depends on the notion of constant surprise which is rooted in assumptions, in received wisdom. The fulcrum of the village, as it is of the larger world, is the wonder which resides in the word 'if'. Thirty years later we find Kennelly still pursuing this state of wonder in *The Book of Judas*, asking 'If Christ came in today...' Would we recognise him? Would we betray him? How can one betray with the symbol of love – the kiss?

The pursuit of betrayal as a quality resident in human commerce is as compelling as the pursuit of violence. We make daily incursions into each other's lives and psyches in order to confirm our own need for solitude. Only by knowing the other can we possess the self. Thus, in the same moment when we retreat from that other, we colonise the world with images of our own psyche. To return to Kennelly's 'Yes':

> I am always beginning to appreciate
> The agony from which it is born.
> Clues from here and there
> Suggest such agony is hard to bear
> But is the shaping God
> Of the word that we
> Sometimes hear, and struggle to be.   (*ATFV* 24)

In the beginning was God, shaping the word, and it is the word that we 'struggle to be'. Such an act of faith is bound to be both painful and precarious because Kennelly knows, with Byron, that while 'poetry is the expression of an excited passion...there is no such thing as a life of passion'.[12] This sense of instability and impermanence, of seeking what must be called miraculous because it is beyond possibility, beyond reality, is at once the fuel and the stumbling-block of poetry. Poetry is natural, it shares its texture and resonance with the 'real' world, yet it is defeated by the very mystery which it pursues. This difficulty stands in the way of the storytelling which in Kennelly's case informed his childhood and lies behind everything he writes.[13] When he says 'you can make a poem out of your horror' he knows that the story is always provisional, because although the goal is 'yes', the affirmation sought in homecoming, there is always the problem and the possibility of 'if'. In the case of writing *Judas* it became the problem of finding the Judas within himself.

How, in this condition, does one write? Perhaps Kennelly began to confront this question with the arrival of unpredictable difficulties in his own life: the question had been there from the beginning, implicit in the villager of Deevna who 'liked comparing his life to things' (*CC* 12), but unvoiced. The first *agon* of 'My Dark Fathers' may have appeared to be simply stating the position, setting out the pieces, yet merely by articulating the darkness, announcing his provenance ('Since I am come of Kerry clay and rock' *ATFV* 19), Kennelly was taking leave of its shelter and moving towards an unstable position beyond his first house. He carried within him the search for love – love of family, love of friends, love of women, love of place – and the culture of song which is its own intoxicant.

Out on his own, the poet can make liaisons which are disastrous or miraculous. As time crashes on, the need to 'give a voice to the unthinkable' increases, because we thereby come nearer to 'creating your own morality'. This is the 'push towards your honesty', towards the *éclaircissement* of knowledge: 'until your chaos is formed it has no meaning'. Until we can find a place in our everyday lives for the gift of surprise, it will have no power to move us towards

the ultimate miracle. This vulnerability compels the poet to revisit
old certainties, the bases of hope and assumption. Thus while in
his early work Kennelly relied on identities implicit in the act of
naming people ('the thatcher', 'the tippler', 'the prisoner'), the tools
of their trade ('the knife', 'the leather apron', 'the stick') and their
places ('in Moynihan's meadow', 'the tent in the blacksmith's field',
'Nolan's Hill'), the certainties shade into new forms of discovery as
he examines the need to seek identities beyond the names. Meeting
the Cromwell and the Judas within himself began, perhaps, in 1977
when he encountered 'The Islandman' as an extension of the self,
and realised that 'to see...the essential humanity of people and
therefore to come into contact with what I hope is my own' (BS
102) is an increasingly complex undertaking. It means to seek 'an
essentially moral imagination',[14] 'to transform loud facts into quiet
metaphors, to find the still centre of significance in the booming
muddle'.[15]

For Kennelly, the pre-requisite of poetry is to empathise, to find
oneself within another, and thence to derive vitality.[16] In this sense
the difficulty of relation became acute when he began to address
the question of difference between man and woman. 'The attempt
to be imaginatively a woman' became the new experience of his
work in the late 1980s, with versions of Sophocles' *Antigone* and
Euripides' *Medea* and *The Trojan Women*, and of Lorca's *Blood
Wedding*. If there was any turning point in Kennelly's public persona as a poet and critic, it was in the disruption and discontinuity
of his private mind which was brought to the surface by this experience. More than purely emotional or intuitive, it sees Kennelly
encountering the difference of *mind* which had not previously been
evident – the way in which woman's rage and madness, her laughter, her knowledge of her children, her approach to 'love', to 'house',
are qualitatively different to man's rage and madness, yet organic-
ally related to him and he to her.

Thus the violence and tenderness of love itself, the act and
emotion of loving, the possession and submission, give way to an
affirmation of a different kind of difference, of the need for feminism, of the necessity of opening the gates in man's heart, as in his
city, to the woman who already resides there. He once wrote of
Synge that he 'looks at life across an abyss. The fact that he cannot
cross this abyss makes his observations all the more moving.'[17] The
sea-change in his own work indicates that never again, in Kennelly's
imagination, will woman suffer the indignities depicted in the cycle
A Girl. The image has been transmuted, and thus the epicentre of

his poetry has shifted. In emancipating the woman in his mind and heart, the affective woman in his psyche, Kennelly crossed the abyss of himself.

*   *   *

It remains to discuss the increasing importance of Kennelly as a public figure, making poetic statements which are expressions of his privacy but also of his sense of citizenship. In the evolution of his poetry he has moved beyond history into an engagement with the matter of Ireland: his new decisions about womanhood have a counterpart in the public sphere, in the issue of women's affairs, while his concerns for identity have resulted – in *Antigone*, for example – in what might be construed, in the Irish context particularly,[18] as a trenchant view on civil rights.

In this development of parallel lives, Kennelly has indicated his imaginative reliance on the treasury of Gaelic poetry both in the original and in translation, which was the subject of his own Ph.D. thesis in the 1960s.[19] The influences on his poetry, however, are so few as to be explicit. As a playwright, he creates echoes more extensively than elsewhere – even Shakespeare and Eliot put in an appearance and the dispossessed Gaelic singers of the seventeenth century (*an duanaire*) are recalled in *The Trojan Women* ('Havoc and death she brought/ And ruin to me and mine').[20] But the presence of Ferguson and Yeats, the two dominant personalities in his treasury, is scarcely noticeable. We find allusions to the former in 'The Scholar's Retreat' ('I am no stranger here')[21] and to the latter in 'Traffic Lights, Merrion Road, Dublin 4' ('Poets calculate the sacrifice that turns the heart to stone')[22] but the overriding impression of Kennelly's work is that he is a poet without handles, without edge.

If we accept discontinuity as a central feature in the Irish experience, then its evolution into Irish writing must be seen as internal and organic, even unconscious, rather than shaped from without and by design. Kennelly's own discontinuities, therefore, may have been sublimated into this larger sense of time and status. His own private conversation with himself can, at certain points, be identified with that of his country. But as a poet he transcends nation and becomes a member of a larger community: 'unless each poet discovers and explores a personal mythology, his work will degenerate into fragmented utterance and transient comment';[23] as a critic, his judgements have been unequivocally Irish, yet have embraced and exemplified a European humanism which locates Ballylongford somewhere near the parish of Athens. By accepting poetry as a gift, Kennelly (like Seamus Heaney)[24] agrees to carry within him its burdens and joys.

Thus while, chronologically, there is a point at which the work as a whole seems to move decisively from the private into the public mode, thematically and conceptually this distinction will not hold up. Even if we impose the Yeatsian definition that 'we make out of the quarrel with others, rhetoric, but of the quarrel with ourselves, poetry',[25] the predominant aspect of Kennelly's work has been struggle with self, to which he has given expression in the form of poetic bulletins. The state of health may have fluctuated, but the epiphanies have been consistent. He has resolutely lived his life in public.

We can therefore appreciate that while there have been certain milestones in Kennelly's transition – and many poems which he has chosen to discard or rewrite along the way – the general tenor of the work has been smooth and even predestined. The benchmark remains his first major poem, 'My Dark Fathers', which until recently was the poem most likely to be encountered by the general reader. The appearance of Cromwell, with the public discussion which ensued, changed that, even though Buffún, in whose head the poem takes place, might stand as the narrator or observer of all the previous work.[26] The fabric of the poetry thereafter has been woven with extra threads; designs were changed, but not discarded. Many readers dismissed the rewritten Moloney Up and At It, unable to accept the sheer jovial indecency of a man gay with lusts and a world full of gamey women to match them. How could this stand beside the noble dignity of tragic woman as depicted in Kennelly's Hecuba? Moloney's notion that 'Faith in a woman is all we need',[27] irreverent and scatological though the specific context might be, contains the answer. The quality residing in each of us, man and woman, is passion, and passion is without dimension. To find the place of ecstasy – to stand outside oneself – is the same contumescent motive whether the coition be physical or intellectual.

The most difficult metaphor is the transformation of the muddle of love into some satisfactory stillness which will reflect the change inherent in the act of loving, and re-fashion, re-integrate the partners in their new relationship. Kennelly would like to 'spend his lifetime praising certain women and count that life well spent' (TW 5), and that is in itself inherently a beautiful thought and a magnificent pursuit. But the projection of private passion onto a public canvas becomes an emotional and psychic minefield:

What man
Knows anything of women?
If he did
He would change from being a man
As men recognise a man.[28]

With the understanding of woman comes another kind of maturity
– 'there will be/ womansongs in answer to the false/ songs of men'
(*Medea* 34). The 'why?' of dismay which entered his world in 'The
Hurt' (*A Kind of Trust: ATFV* 53-4) extends to the point of love
itself:

How can murder so easily take the place of love?
Women who dare to love, what sort of evil
do you create in men? What sort of evil
do you discover in yourselves? This thing called love,
how much of the world's evil has it created?   (*Medea* 71)

Men may go to war, but women are the victims. Their tragedy is
private, until their dismay becomes despair, their inner fury an outward rage, and war takes on a new meaning as revenge, the woman's
prerogative, becomes the order of the day. Not until this point is
reached in the evolution of an individual heart or of a nation on
the march, does war become three-dimensional, and when it does,
the meanings of love and life are transformed.

We find this in Kennelly's continuing 'play about women', his
versions of Sophocles, Euripides and Lorca. But we also find it in
Judas, where the action of warfare is inverted and the war takes
place in the mind and heart; the private tragedy is transferred into
the public space. Kennelly brings Judas, the man whose kiss, the
symbol and act of love, identified and condemned his friend and
mentor, into the heart of Irish life, into politics, the family, the
love-bed, the courts of law, the market place, and shows how he is
indelibly present in all our transactions: 'this scapegoat, critic of
self and society, throws chronological time out the window. Before
his ancestors arrived on the scene, he was. After the unborn will
have ceased to exist, he'll be' (*BOJ* 12).

The other important lesson to be learned from *Judas* concerns the
nature of poetry itself: that a book, or a poem, or a fleeting thought
is not complete until it has canvassed, parsed and resolved the onus
of its own thought. Nothing in the act of writing is external. Nothing in the act of reading is forgivable. Slowly we become aware not
only of the facts of history repeating themselves at every gallows, at
every hearth, at every committee meeting, but also of the beauty
inherent in every lie, the fact that 'At the heart of nothingmatters,
love is born' (*BOJ* 58).

If you had not betrayed me
How could I ever have begun to know
The sad heart of man?   (*BOJ* 156)

The essential Kennelly, who has shown us in his plays that he can
see further than most into the 'sad heart' of both men and women,
is ultimately honest enough to tell us that he has no answers, only
questions. If a poem is about love, if it can establish the shortest
metaphor in the world – the single-word poem, 'yes' – then its
privacy can only be expressed between poet and reader if they are
one. If the poem cannot find the metaphor, if it only approximates,
by means of simile, to the equation, then its expression will be inadequate and it were best not uttered. Answers are not enough:
'there are small moments when all I care to do/ Is praise the lone-
liness/ I cannot understand' (*BOJ* 161). The man who can ask these
questions, without demanding answers, is the man who can live with
the idea of 'if', not as a wish but as a condition – and *The Book of
Judas* is Brendan Kennelly's proof that 'if' is a gerund which can
engender laughter and tears, pouring from the eyes and mouths of
wise men and fools, virgins and whores.

GABRIEL FITZMAURICE

'Becoming Song': The Translated Village

Brendan Kennelly was born in Ballylongford, County Kerry, on 17 April 1936, the son of Tim Kennelly, publican and garage proprietor, and his wife Bridie Ahern, a nurse. Ballylongford is a small village like the other villages in the hinterland of Listowel in North Kerry. To understand Kennelly and his poetry, you have to come to terms with the traditional culture of North Kerry – its sports, pastimes and lifestyle – which Kennelly has translated into poetry which is both intimate and epic. It's flat land touching the River Shannon and the Atlantic. For the most part pastureland, it was, in Kennelly's youth, mainly a farming community – mixed farming, milch cows, pigs for the table and for commerce, poultry likewise, tillage – potatoes, cabbage, turnips, carrots and parsnips for the table, mangolds for the animals. The farmers, small farmers mostly, were generally not well off. But they loved to sing. At night they'd go to the local pub on bicycles or on foot (this was before the general availability of the car), drink 'small ones' (whiskies) and pints of Guinness and swap stories, news, songs and 'recitations'.

Memory, in particular the poet's memory, gathers these moments together. Kennelly's was, and remains, a public house – Brendan heard these songs, stories and recitations regularly in the pub – not just imported songs (from the gramophone and radio – there was as yet no television) but local ballads too, 'Charming Carrig Isle' and others. Later the young poet would make his own ballads. Later still, the mature poet would write affectionately of this in his poem 'Living Ghosts', of

> ...men in their innocence
> Untroubled by right and wrong.
> I close my eyes and see them
> Becoming song. (*BS* 43)

Three elements which largely constitute the mystical body of Kerry are football, politics and religion. Indeed it is often said that football (Gaelic football, at which Ballylongford excels) is the religion of Kerry. A small boy in Ballylongford dreams of playing for his parish – to don the blue-and-white of Ballylongford is to become flesh of your tribal soul, the incarnation of your native place. Brendan Kennelly became flesh of his native place – he played for his street, his parish, his county. He was a very good footballer – to have played minor, junior and senior football for Kerry as he did, is a distinction achieved by few. But Kennelly came from a family of footballers – all six boys (including Alan, who now runs the pub and garage, John, a priest, Paddy and Kevin, both teachers) played for their County at minor, junior or senior level, while one, Colm, now Kerry County Engineer, won senior All Ireland football medals with Kerry in 1953 and 1955. The Kennellys were robust footballers when football was a robust game. Brendan was the gentle one.

Football in Kennelly's time was an epic affair. Whereas all the villages belonged to the mystical body of Kerry (which they passionately believed, and still believe, in), they were tribal, too. When Ballylongford took on Tarbert, the neighbouring village, war was declared. Tarbert, the neighbour, is the old enemy: I once asked Kennelly why he hadn't included Thomas MacGreevy, the modernist poet, born in Tarbert, in his *Penguin Book of Irish Verse*. No doubt he had his reasons, but the one he gave me, half jokingly, was 'MacGreevy was a Tarbert man!'

Football then, especially, had an epic, mythical quality. The game originated from *caid* which was played between two parishes, started midway between the two, and the winner was the parish which carried the ball into the opponents' parish – hence the phrase, until recently used in local derbies, 'we bate 'em home'. This was the game where the playing field was invaded regularly by spectators, men and women, and a glorious fracas would ensue, a fracas which would end as suddenly as it began as passion, sated, spent itself. John B. Keane tells the story of a rainy day on a waterlogged pitch when a player was sent off in a North Kerry derby for the 'attempted drowning' of an opponent. Football was, and is, larger than life.

Ballylongford, as I've said, were, and are, superb footballers. At their best, they play thoughtful, skilful football with a quiet passion. Kennelly was a half-forward – a winger. He liked playing there. It gave him scope, he could create out there, away from the centre of things. The centre players, backs, midfield and forwards carried the responsibility of the game; the winger could create on his own

– now in the thick of things, now in space, observing, calculating, now receiving the gift of a ball passed to him, now passing it on, defending, attacking according to the flow of the game. This early involvement in football epitomises Kennelly the poet.

*   *   *

After football, politics came next. North Kerry is republican country. During the Long Kesh hunger strike of 1981 in which Bobby Sands, and others, died, there was a black flag on every telegraph pole from Tarbert to Tralee. In the struggle for independence (1919-21) all Republicans fought together against the British, Ballylongford so prominently that part of it was burned by the Black and Tans. Then came the Treaty. The united republican movement divided into anti-Treaty ('Republicans') and pro-Treaty ('Free Staters'). Literally (for instance in my own village of Moyvane) brother fought against brother. The one thing which united people around here, healing the wounds of the Civil War, was football – quickly, the memories of the atrocities of the Civil War were put aside and Free Staters and Republicans united on the playing field – the sight of John Joe Sheehy of Tralee (a Republican) and Con Brosnan of Moyvane (a Captain in the Free State army) playing together on the County team in the 1920s and early 1930s was an example to all. The Kennellys were pro-Treaty, later Fine Gael. Ballylongford was, and is, strongly divided in its loyalties. When Kennelly supported Charles Haughey as a statesman and patron of the arts, his sister-in-law wrote to him enquiring 'What about the corkscrew?' Brendan, baffled, replied 'What corkscrew?' only to be reminded that his father used to opine that de Valera (founder of Fianna Fáil, Haughey's party) was so crooked that if he swallowed a nail, he'd shit a corkscrew. But Kennelly is a winger – he follows his own lights, playing the ball as it comes to him.

Religion is central to the life of rural Ireland. I say this in the full knowledge that religion plays a part in the lives of urban dwellers too. But it's different in the country. Everyone knows what everyone else is doing – there's not much hidden in a small village. Ballylongford, the 'Crooked Cross' of Kennelly's first novel (and the Kennellys lived at the intersection of that cross) is no different. The school system worked hand in hand with the Roman Catholic Church – faith was taught as if knowledge was belief. Pupils in Kennelly's day had their heads full of the big (theological) words, which he has written about in his poem 'The Big Words', words that would protect against the 'evil', 'Godlessness' and 'worldliness'

of England, particularly, and the United States of America – Ireland
was educating its youth for emigration then. The word that would
protect, the sanctuary of the word, the sacredness of the word.
Kennelly learned the big words, learned them very well. When he
began to question them, they yielded up a necessary alternative
theology. The case of Francis Xavier Skinner, in his poem 'The
Sin', is instructive. Skinner (Kennelly?) realises that sin flatters his
own vanity, that in reality he is only a puny little human trying to
measure up to God in the belief that his sin is important, original
and hurtful to God. It is, of course, no such thing. It is an insult
to love, no more and no less. Later Skinner, having prayed to his
maker 'To give [him] the vision/ To commit a significant sin', will
become Judas and the nightmare begins. I mentioned to Kennelly
after I had read *The Book of Judas* that I had profound difficulties
with the book, with the spirit of the book. When asked by him for
an instance I mentioned what I felt to be the naked hatred of women
I had picked up here and there in the book. I had no problem with
the straightforwardness of *Cromwell*, where Kennelly writes:

> Drag the rat out here into the square.
> Does he think he can write a book like this
> And get away with it?
> Christ Almighty, is there anything he won't say?
> How can we protect ourselves against him?   (*C* 153)

But I found *Judas* offensive. Kennelly replied: 'Is it because you
think I hate women? I hate myself.' I believe that Kennelly's sensibility is a fairly traditional Catholic one, part of which is obsessed
with sin and guilt. John Berryman, likewise afflicted, once told a
story of a girl whose sense of sin he envied – she said prayers of
thanksgiving after making love; Berryman could only feel guilt. The
misplaced sense of sin is manifestly destructive. But Catholicism
isn't entirely about sin – the true purpose of the confessional is to
get rid of sin. The downside of confession is not its orthodox spiritual tyranny but the absolution from responsibility some expect
from 'confessors/ Who would forgive [them] anything' as John
Liddy has pointed out in his poem 'Southern Comfort'.[1]

*   *   *

But the central problem for Kennelly is not sin or Cromwell or
Judas. It is the problem of language, how to say himself. 'In the
beginning was the Word,' Kennelly often quotes, for, like many
poets, he is obsessed with words. He wrote, I think in the *Sunday
Independent*, some years ago that it is as important to know where

the words in your mouth come from as to know where the food in your mouth comes from. The word, the *logos*, is an abstract, intellectual concept, the mouth is not: it is physical, passionate, primal, the instrument of satisfying our need for living, speaking and loving, primal things. To Kennelly words are physical. Irish, up to shortly before Kennelly's birth, had been the first language of North Kerry (the Census of 1901 shows that in Moyvane, neighbouring Ballylongford, there were still a few native Irish speakers). The Irish language went into decline for mainly economic reasons, which, allied to a failure of nerve, a lack of confidence in the native language (the fact that it would be unable to translate itself on the streets of London or Liverpool, New York or New Orleans), was the death knell of spoken Irish throughout Ireland, except in the Gaeltachtaí where Irish remained the spoken language of the people.

But a language, in a sense, never dies. Though Kennelly's Buffún moans (in *Cromwell*):

> I had a language once.
> I was at home there.
> Someone murdered it
> Buried it somewhere.
> I use different words now
> Without skill, truly as I can.
> A man without a language
> Is half a man, if he's lucky   (*C* 39)

he does not

> ...believe this language is dead.
> Not a thousand years of hate could kill it,
> Or worse, a thousand years of indifference.
> So long as I live my language will live
> Because it is mine...
> ...Someone, somewhere, will learn.   (*C* 41)

Seán Ó Ríordáin (1917-77), the Irish-language poet, wrote of the echo that is heard even in places which have abandoned the native dialect (in his poem *Ceol Ceantair* [Local Music]).[2] This is true of villages like Ballylongford and the other North Kerry villages. The language of the people was not Irish, it was not English, it was not Hiberno-English. It was a language whose accent, vocabulary and syntax were a translation from the Irish. Words were taken from the Irish and "Englished" – for instance 'kippen' from *cipín*, a twig, a little stick. Someone would ask you to go out and bring in 'a gu-awl of kippens' – a *gabháil* (armful) of twigs. Inevitably, some things had names then which have no names now. I think of the word *scrá* (nearest English equivalent, a clod). Boys would throw 'scraws' at

each other for fun. They still do occasionally, but now they have
no name for what they are throwing. Kennelly learned standard
Hiberno-English in Ballylongford National School (where one of
his teachers was Johnny Walsh, the great Kerry footballer) and
later at Saint Ita's Secondary School in Tarbert. Saint Ita's, and its
founder and guiding spirit, the teacher Miss Jane Agnes McKenna
must be considered as the significant event of Kennelly's early
education. Jane Agnes McKenna was an enlightened teacher, strict
but enabling, who recognised the potential of the young Kennelly.
She facilitated him in every way and became, I suspect, the role
model for Kennelly the teacher. In Saint Ita's, Kennelly encountered French and Latin, the one a 'modern' language, the other
providing him with the etymology he so desperately needed – and
which informs him to this day.

Kennelly was a good student and was awarded a sizarship to
Trinity College, Dublin, but because of shyness and a lack of confidence in himself, he left. He worked at various jobs – in the pub
in Ballylongford, in the Electricity Supply Board, as a bus con-
ductor in England, before re-entering Trinity, from which he grad-
uated in 1961. In 1963 he was appointed to the Department of
English there, was made a Fellow in 1967, Associate Professor in
1969 and was appointed to the newly created Chair of Modern
Literature in 1973. English, Irish, his local dialect, French and
Latin – words to discover, to savour and create. This is Kennelly
the communicator who insists that what he says (and writes) is well
said, memorable, catchy. A deeper voice insists that it is profound,
spiritual, searching. These tributaries converge in the ballad/lyric
of his 'mainstream poems'.

*   *   *

The ballad is vital to the life of North Kerry. No team wins a football final that is not sung – it is as if winning the Final is insufficient
– the stuff of mere mortals, temporal and temporary – until it is
immortalised in song. Everything in North Kerry was celebrated
in balladry in Kennelly's youth – love lost and found, martyrdom
(the martyrs of the War of Independence and Civil War), sport
(football and greyhounds mainly), emigration... The poet 'made' a
ballad – 'writing' or 'composing' were not the terms. He (or she)
made the ballad and all the ballads had mythical qualities, for the
men in them were not mere men but heroes, larger than life, the
only limits on them what one could entertain. The ballad bound
the tribe together. This is where Kennelly comes from – he is a

balladmaker, first and last. He extends the ballad by coupling it with the lyric, and the love-child is born in the ear, sings in the ear and is translated by the ear. This is the territory of passion, of the heart, of the force of personality where *how* a thing is said (rhythmically, rhetorically, dramatically, even melodramatically, but above all musically) is as important as *what* is said. This is no puritan territory, but Catholic in its exuberance – symbol, image, bell and candle. To reduce it is to kill it. Kennelly's poetry is like a ritual – the ritual of the Church, or of the pub. It involves more than the mind, more than the intellect, as a ballad insinuates itself with its music and hyperbole into an area of consciousness undreamed of by the reductive mind.

But let us not forget Moloney, a character as devious and cunning as Buffún, but, unlike Buffún, a hero. Indeed, Kennelly chastised me when I identified him with Buffún in my review of *Cromwell* in *The Kerryman* newspaper [3] but blithely signed my copy of *Moloney Up and At It* as 'Moloney'. Who is Moloney? Judas is Moloney gone wrong. Moloney is the life force who witnesses the resurrection (of Kate Finucane), who enters death (he hops into bed with a corpse), who makes love on his mother's grave, who receives the dust of the cremated Mike Nelligan courtesy of a '...tricky hoor of a Shannon wind', who in so doing takes death into himself and possesses it. If he will not, ultimately, triumph over death, he uses his wits to cheat death, to come to terms with it, to possess it. Death and life are one in Moloney. Moloney knows the place of sin in his life – that's his salvation – Judas doesn't and is damned. Moloney is, in many ways, the archetypal North Kerryman – worldly-wise, cute (i.e. 'cunning'), fun-loving, anecdotal, with flashes of the profound and otherworldly, but above all he doesn't take life (or sin) too seriously. He is rooted in himself and in his place.

Kennelly is rooted in two places – Ballylongford and Dublin. At home in both, they are, for him, places of permanent beginning, places of revelation. There is a sense that Kennelly exists in language – that without words there is no Kennelly. All his translation is a translation of Ballylongford. Time and again he returns to the happenings of his youth. His *Antigone, Medea* and *The Trojan Women* have their roots in the Ballylongford of his youth. He lives, for instance, with the memory of the local woman who railed at her dead husband to get up out of his coffin because his death betrayed her. There is too, as Peter Levi has pointed out (in *The Lamentation of the Dead*),[4] a Greek dimension to *Caoineadh Airt Uí Laoghaire* (the *Cry for Art O'Leary* so lovingly translated by Kennelly) – the keening of the dead unbroken from Biblical times, from Homeric times right up to Eibhlín Dhubh Ní Chonaill's lamentation of her dead husband in the late eighteenth century. 'With this poem,' Levi concludes, 'a world ended; we had not known that it had lived so long.' Its vestiges were to be found, until quite recently, in places like Ballylongford. What Kennelly translates is experience, the feel of a thing. He translates the spirit of a poem or play; he is no slave of the literal. Yet this approach is faithful and powerful as mere imitations are not – to render a poem or play word by word is to lose sight of the whole. Poetry is made in the translation, too. He can, on occasion, remain quite close to the text – as he often does in the shorter Irish lyrics which he has published in *A Drinking Cup* and *Love of Ireland* which are faithfully translated in sound and sense.

Seán Ó Ríordáin wrote that poetry was to be *fé ghné eile* (under another aspect, to enter the other).[5] Translation is for Kennelly one such vehicle. But then, Cromwell and Judas are translations too. Becoming the other, giving voices to the other... For, like all poets, Kennelly is both himself and other. He once wrote to me that 'There's nothing musical that isn't a deepdown war'. It started, perhaps, with his 'Blackbird':

> I scarce believe his murderous competence
> As he stabs to stay alive,
> Choking music
> That music may survive   (*BS* 42)

and continued in other ballad/lyrics where the objective world of the ballad enters the personal world of the lyric; it was furthered in translation – entering the other. But there is an end to that road. It is, then, no wonder that he eventually exploded into the epic mode. Some things are too big for ballads and lyrics. They must be all-inclusive, they must howl and sprawl. Kennelly's epics translate him into the other, not just his alter ego but to aspects of his early epiphanies in Ballylongford. Kennelly, like all poets (and wingers) writes his own rules – at its best this is a revelation, at its least it's merely 'to shake the hoors up' as he has said more than once. Like his second cousin, Robert Leslie Boland (1888-1955), 'The Poet-Farmer of Faranastack' whose poems were published in book form for the first time in 1993,[6] he can be sublime or vulgar – but never ridiculous. He carries Ballylongford, his Crooked Cross, with him as he carries his alter egos, his deities and his demons, his passions and his depressions, his alcoholism. The demons he sees in his loved ones terrify him, the demons in himself do not. He confronts his obsessions aggressively, even violently as a man goes for a ball; he can also, like a good footballer, create his own space as he goes for the goal. Tender and violent, loving and fearful, a rooted man, he has absorbed his childhood and early years. The boy who saw

> ...the darkness and the shame
> That could compel a man to turn his face
> Against the wall, withdrawn from light so strong
> And undeceiving, spancelled in a place
> Of unapplauding hands and broken song   (*ATFV* 19)

now says it all and hides nothing. He exists in language. He is because he says. He is what he says.

AUGUSTINE MARTIN

Technique and Territory
in Brendan Kennelly's Early Work

The first restless decade of Brendan Kennelly's work begins with
a small book of verse, *Cast a Cold Eye* (1959) and ends with his
edition of *The Penguin Book of Irish Verse* (1970). My survey stops
just short of *Bread* (1971) where I feel he had definitively found his
poetic voice. There are eleven volumes of original poetry between
these dates as well as two novels. I read most and reviewed some of
these volumes as they appeared, but didn't, as far as I can recall,
meet the poet. My witness therefore is that of a contemporary looking back, and trying to recapture that decade when a generation of
poets succeeding Clarke and Kavanagh explored their options.

An initial assertion may be risked: that Kennelly was recklessly
prolific during those early years; and that his publishers' faith in
his precocious talent together with the user-friendly popularity of
the poetry itself may have constituted a mixed blessing for his
reputation, if not indeed for that talent itself. Now that his place
is secure in the first rank of contemporary Irish poets, it may be
forgivable to rehearse his sallies and retires during those formative
ten years.

It will help if we glance at the field into which Kennelly first
advances his standard. In 1959 Kavanagh's *A Soul for Sale* (1947),
highly prized but out of print, could not be had in the bookshops
for love or money. Kavanagh's iconoclastic personality still enlivened
the Dublin scene, but few expected from him that poetic impact
which *Come Dance with Kitty Stobling* was to deliver in 1960. Clarke's
literary personality was muffled by his bumbling book reviews in
the *Irish Times* every Saturday and his cosy, if highly professional,
weekly poetry talks on Radio Éireann. In 1955 he broke a long
silence with *Ancient Lights* – a slow fuse leading to the detonation
of *Flight to Africa* (1963). I recall the late fifties as a dead time.

Apart from the sporadic appearances of *Irish Writing* there were no literary magazines to speak of; the Abbey was in its Babylonian exile at the old Queen's cranking out popular comedies – nothing much was happening, or so it seemed.

Then Liam Miller's Dolmen Press began to engender what we sensed might be a new stirring of imaginative life. Thomas Kinsella, six years Kennelly's senior, after a careful apprenticeship in translation from the Irish, produced his first substantial volume, *Another September* (1958). It struck a note of such authority that no young contemporary could look on it without dismay. John Montague, five years Kennelly's senior, published *Forms of Exile* (1958) a sophisticated book, quite free from the embarrassment of juvenilia.

Kennelly's first two volumes were also published by Dolmen, *Cast a Cold Eye* (1959) and *The Rain, The Moon* (1961), both collaborations with Rudi Holzapfel. They did not look like Dolmen publications, and they still don't. Kennelly made two more joint volumes with Holzapfel – a poet still publishing regularly who deserves more critical attention than he receives. Kennelly then proceeded alone, with the Dublin firm of Allen Figgis as his chief publisher. By 1963 Kinsella had produced his magistral *Downstream*, Montague his formidable and original *Poisoned Lands*. Both writers, while maintaining their link with Dolmen, were taken up by British and American publishing houses. Richard Murphy – Kennelly's senior by nine years – whose first booklet, *The Last Galway Hooker* (1961), had appeared from Dolmen, now published, with Faber, *Sailing to an Island* (1963). The movement was under way.

Kennelly, loyal to his Dublin publisher and producing at a rate of knots, was still floundering gallantly among false starts: three books of verse – *Green Townlands, The Dark About Our Loves, Let Fall No Burning Leaf* – and a novel, *The Crooked Cross*, appeared in the years 1962-63. When Seamus Heaney, three years his junior, arrived on the scene with *Death of a Naturalist* (Faber, 1966), Kennelly had at last published a slender volume of poems, *My Dark Fathers*, which could hold up its head in that rigorous company. It was the sixth of his poetry volumes. His first 'collected' was already in press, *Collection One: Getting Up Early* (1966). Everyone was saying that Brendan Kennelly was publishing too much, and from where I now sit it looks as if everyone was right. But these things are not simple.

Kennelly has always had more gifts than were good for him. He was cursed from the start with a ready eloquence, a natural sense of rhythm, a mercurial range of sympathies and interests, a gener-

ous susceptibility to influence, inexhaustible energy and a Kerryman's conviction that there is nothing he can't do. His original
master, as the title of his first volume attests, was Yeats. He could
pull a Yeatsian stroke – with a touch of Pearsean top-spin – without sweating: this is how 'The Mother' opens:

> I have sent them out beyond the gaunt ridge
> Of black stones above the thorny glen;
> I have watched them go, my sons
> Walking with the terrible strength of men
> Who hated what they did. [1]

The control of rhythm in these lines is impressive. The poet is
using the sonnet form and refusing its ready iambics. The movement of the thought is paced with admirable deliberation. But
tone, idiom and image are incorrigibly derivative. Kennelly has
not yet sensed the immense struggle with technical difficulties in
which Yeats had engaged to achieve the rhythmic life of his poetry – the initial prose versions, the oral incantations, the slow curbing of easy eloquence in the successive drafts. Kennelly seems still
to feel that a poet can write in 1961 of gaunt ridges, black stones,
thorny glens and mothers sending sons out to break their terrible
strength, and hope for the traditional poetic dividends. It is the
strenuous conquest of that illusion over these early years that makes
his development so fascinating.

But his virtuosity is endless. With a down-turn of the wrist he
could produce another type of sonnet, energised apparently by the
challenge of new subject and speech rhythm:

> The negro smiled. His teeth showed white as snow,
> His eyes stirred like the depths of muddy wine
> He said, 'Back in Jamaica, I use' go
> Pick coconut every mawnin'. Sun shine
> Early, five, six o'clock maybe, an' we
> Spend all day hackin'. Jus' hackin', man. fine
> Time we have, though. Sometimes under a tree,
> I sleep during day; always watch for sign
> Of sun. Man, it was warm. At night I lie
> On sand with girl. Toss her hair. Laugh. And we
> Sing a li'l. Now, she have ten chil'ren. I
> Know she ugly now, like my mother.' He
> Paused and smiled again. 'My mother fine. But
> Man, she think whole world made of coconut.' [2]

Few writing then or now could manage such a *tour de force* – Holzapfel maybe, but that's another story. Take the playful impudence
of the rhymes throughout, and especially the rhymes of the sestet,

lie/we, I/He – this is a sonnet! – and the delicious thump of the couplet. With the brisk ebb and flow of the negro's speech, the achieved presence of his personality, the reader is scarcely aware that the sonnet's formal demands are being nonchalantly fulfilled to the letter. We can only marvel at the versatility of the talent that produced this one-off prototype of a line immediately to be abandoned. The sonnet form, however, he never abandons. It remains one of the staples of Kennelly's mature art, coming on with magnum force ten years later in *Love Cry* (1972).

Among the many possible modes open to Kennelly in the late fifties was that of the *poete doctus* or university wit. The campuses of the English-speaking world were swarming with clever young dons producing well-turned ambiguities in the manner of William Empson or W.H. Auden. He tried his hand at it and produced poems for the reader and lessons for himself which were to stand him in good stead when he came finally upon his own special mode and idiom. I often regret, for instance, that he has dropped 'Marlowe' from his later selections:

> There was a quarrel about a bill
> Of reckoning, not paid until
> Kit Marlowe, knifed above the eye
> By Ingram Frazier, finally
> Settled everything with his blood,
> The whole account was closed for good. [3]

Many of the later virtues are deployed here as two registers of language are deftly counterpointed: the cool implications of bill, reckoning, settled, and account, nicely played off against the hotter importunities of knife and blood; the well-judged tension between syntax and metre as the single sentence moves to its routine yet appalled conclusion. In the third stanza there is a moment of sententiousness when Marlowe's spilt blood becomes 'the rich flux, preserved in art'. But it steadies itself and ends as a formidable poem. If Kennelly had gone on writing poems like 'Marlowe', picking his subjects coolly from the furniture of his academic day, he would have certainly achieved a respectable fame and a modest place in the anthologies. But he was playing for bigger stakes, and beginning to sense what they might be. But to distinguish purposeful beginning from energetic dawdling is very difficult in the early Kennelly. What, for instance, made him write in 1963 what I myself dismissed then as a 'sour little fable' of his native Kerry, *The Crooked Cross*?

A tentative answer is not far to seek. He wanted to compose an allegorical tale on the state of Ireland, characterising the country

as a spiritual desert, enervated by unemployment, drained by emigration, sick with futility and self-hatred. So he invented a Kerry
village called Deevna, shaped like a crooked cross – suitably recog-
nisable as his home place, Ballylongford – where the people are
crucified with a summer-long drought. After many failed stratagems
they call in a sort of saviour figure called the Pope, Larry the Lad
O'Gilligan. He has a passion for bottled stout and a gift for water-
divining. He finds water, a shaft is drilled, the water spurts, and
hope returns to Deevna – 'they marvelled at it as a thinking sinner would marvel at the prospect of finding his soul drenched in
the grace of god' (*CC* 137).

The allegorical intention is easy to understand. The 'flight of
earls' theme with its various threnody on the decay of rural Irish
life in song, ballad, play and fiction was everywhere in the early
sixties – from Bridie Gallagher's 'Goodbye, Johnny Dear' to John B.
Keane's *Many Young Men of Twenty* and Brian Friel's *Philadelphia,
Here I Come!* I wonder, however, if there wasn't a deeper personal
exigency at the back of Kennelly's move, what might be termed
the territorial interdiction. Harold Bloom has accustomed us to
think of young poets struggling with giant predecessors in their
genre in an attempt to get from out of their shadow and win personal space for their own developing art. Yeats was, and still is,
the commanding precursor for every modern Irish poet and we've
seen a little of his impact on Kennelly. Later, as we shall see, it
will be Kavanagh.

But precursors can be even more troublesome when it comes to
landscape and territory. When, for instance, will a young English
poet venture again into the Lake District after Wordsworth? a novelist into Wessex, after Hardy? an Irish poet into the drumlins of
Monaghan, after Kavanagh? or into the boglands of County Derry
after Heaney? For how many centuries are Ben Bulben and Knock-
narea to be no-go areas? And isn't it significant that Padraic Fallon
could only re-inter Loughrea and Gort in order to challenge the
poetic expropriations of Yeats?

It is here we have to reckon with the figure of Bryan MacMahon.
A decade before *The Crooked Cross*, MacMahon had published an
idyllic account of a Kerry village entitled *Children of the Rainbow*
(1952), a novel which may well have been in turn a rebuttal, in
terms of cultural nationalism, of Brinsley MacNamara's fierce indictment of the Irish rural parish in *The Valley of the Squinting Windows*
(1918) a generation before.

With hindsight we can trace in Kennelly's early work a homing back towards Kerry, the landscape of his birth, the real home of his imagination, only to find the place crowded with characters from Maurice Walsh, George Fitzmaurice, Eamon Kelly the seancháí, but above all, the totemic figure of MacMahon with his plays, novels, short stories and ballads. MacMahon had written the priests, the tinkers, the fishermen, the publicans, the mountainy men and the townies of Friary Lane. I suspect that Kennelly was in near despair of securing a firm foothold on this territory when he thought of *The Crooked Cross*, a counter-truth showing the gangrenous under-belly of *Children of the Rainbow*.

As in MacMahon there is a cast of rural humours in *The Crooked Cross* with weirdly exotic names – Sheila Dark, Mickey Free, Goddy O'Girl, Naked Cully, Paddyo, All-or-nothing, the Dwarf and the One-eyed Palestine. As with MacMahon's Cloone the community is bound together with ties of kinship, avocation and trade. Like Cloone it even has an eccentric – Naked Cully – who never leaves his house. And like MacMahon, Kennelly provides a good deal of mating, drinking and brawling. There the resemblances end.

With MacMahon's characters there is an inner nobility, a roman-tic energy which is sensed to derive from a continuity with the past. This past at times assumes the status of a golden age, symbolised by song, dance, story, love of place, nature, religious faith, the poetry of an ancestral language. Under that ancestral pressure the present is characterised by neighbourliness, respect for the aged, a com-munal affection which embraces the crippled, the eccentric, the illegitimate, the retarded. In Kennelly's counter-truth the calamity of drought calls forth the antimonial voices in full cry. Here's the womaniser, All-or-nothing, brooding on his illegitimate offspring:

> Everybody in the village knew who they were, knew they would grow up known to all and sundry as 'the three livin' bastards of All-or-nothing'. That would be hard on them. And, as surely as he stood there, All-or-nothing knew what would happen to them. They would grow up dressed in shame; as children playing with other children they would hear their names bandied about as bastards... (*CC* 43)

And MacMahon's noble peasants suffer strange transmogrification in Kennelly. The drunken Dwarf walking down the street stumbles over an old mange-eaten sheepdog: 'The Dwarf kicked viciously at the creature's head, swore explosively and stumbled on, mumbling' (*CC* 58). In the next pub he visits he finds himself in a trial of strength with the One-eyed Palestine:

> They presented an odd, frightening sight as they sat facing each other on the floor of the public-house, the sweating Dwarf with his long yellow fangs and red face, and Palestine, eyes shut as he strained with all his

drunken strength. A lacey ribbon of brown spittle lay on the Dwarf's
chin as he heaved and struggled with body and soul... (*CC* 64-65)

There are admittedly more life-affirming spectacles in *The Crooked
Cross* than these, but Kennelly's vision is closer to *Tobacco Row* –
a contemporary American best-seller banned from sale in Ireland
– than to *Children of the Rainbow*. And the air is, of course, cleansed
in the final chapters by the Pope's miraculous gift of water. But the
author's creative exertion is barely redeemed by the book's merits.
The heavy social and moral commentary at the end, leaning on a
theme of emigration, is hardly justified by the novel's episodic
central action:

> Youth will never live long enough with total apathy, which is nothing
> less than a surly melancholy in the face of joy. The vital impulses of
> youth tend towards an exuberant robust gladness...The tragic fact now
> was that nearly all the young people had left the village, turning their
> backs on their birthplace with a sigh of relief and a sense of hope...The
> laws of nature sternly proclaim... (*CC* 134)

These are the gestures of a writer impatient to wrap up his fable
and get back to something that really interests him. The blunt
authorial intervention with its parade of verbal cliché and moral
platitude does not bespeak a writer deeply interested in the craft
of fiction. But *The Crooked Cross* has broken the territorial interdiction. It has planted the flag of his imagination in Kerry on his
own terms.

MacMahon has a story, 'Chestnut and Jet', of a man and a stallion walking the streets of a Kerry town. It is a celebration of male
power, of the stallion's 'chaotic blood', the 'treasured violence of his
haunches'.[4] The people come out of their houses 'to see the grand
man and the grand stallion'. A couple of years after writing *The
Crooked Cross*, Kennelly writes one of his most assured poems, 'The
Tamer', upon the same scenario, but curbing the inevitable mach-
ismo to the demands of a new emphasis: that of the power struggle
between man and beast:

> The light rein links him to the brute;
> His head held high
> (As the stallion's is, the white
> Star splendid on the forehead),
> His hands stretch forth as though
> Supplicating the animal blood. [5]

But the man's supplication is his devious way to power and mastery. The poem as it proceeds subverts the romantic balance of
MacMahon's 'grand man'/ 'grand stallion' to a ritual of taming and
mastery:

'Hi, beast! Hi, beast!' – on many a road
These words are said
Gently to pacify the blood
Unsubmissive still
To the hand that soon bends power and pride
To its own will.

In its nervous control of rhythm, its emotional restraint and its exactness of observation 'The Tamer' is, in its own right, a considerable poem. In a sonnet simply entitled 'The Stallion' the tone is pure Kennelly. Worshippers after Mass change from 'prayer to admiration' as they gaze on the splendour of 'the great champing brute' outside the chapel gate; they then change to calculating the animal's worth, before shifting into a final, contemplative gear in which 'many a farmer there'

Forgetting life and death and everything,
Thinks of the stallion spraddled on a likely mare. [6]

Perhaps it was *The Crooked Cross* that enabled Kennelly's first great Kerry poem, 'My Dark Fathers', published in a volume of that name in the following year. There are Yeatsian echoes in the poem – of 'cold Clare rock and Galway rock and thorn' – and its first line seems to recall the opening of Kavanagh's 'Shancoduff' in tone and rhythm – 'My black hills have never seen the sun rising'. This may indeed be, consciously or otherwise, part of the project. What matters is that the poem is unmistakably a Brendan Kennelly poem, as well as being a formal claim to ancestral territory.

I have suggested elsewhere [7] that while Joyce's hero, Stephen Dedalus, saw history as a nightmare from which he was trying to awaken, the Kennelly persona habitually sees history as a nightmare which he must re-inhabit; as his Shelley does in Part VI of *Shelley in Dublin*:

Who am I
To have this pity for these damned
Who lurch and sway
In the light and dark of nightmare? [8]

There is indeed a sense in which everything in his early work is leading towards *Cromwell* (1983) when the challenges of history, myth and identity are taken on in a sustained frontal assault. 'My Dark Fathers' is the first formal plotting of this historical retrospect.

My dark fathers lived the intolerable day
Committed always to the night of wrong,
Stiffened at the hearthstone, the woman lay,
Perished feet nailed to her husband's breastbone.

> Grim houses beckoned in the swelling gloom
> Of Munster fields where the Atlantic night
> Fettered the child within the pit of doom,
> And everywhere a going down of light.

In a shrewd prosodic strategy the general, apocalyptic theme is consigned to the regular iambics; while the particularity of the old couple's death is rivetted in the powerful trochaic chords which open lines three and four. The event to which these lines apply are from Peadar O Laoghaire's autobiography *Mo Scéal Féin*: an old couple cannot bear the segregation of men from women in the famine workhouse; they escape to a country hovel so as to die together; and are found dead with the woman's feet clutched for warmth to her husband's breast. Thus the beckoning grim houses of line five is more specific than at first glance, referring to workhouses; the 'pit of doom' is the mass grave and the rotting potato-pit; the going down of light recalls that the sun rarely broke through the rain-haze during the worst famine years. Stanza two:

> And yet upon the sandy Kerry shore
> The woman once had danced at ebbing tide
> Because she loved flute music – and still more
> Because a lady wondered at the pride
> Of one so humble. That was long before
> The green plant withered by an evil chance;
> When winds of hunger howled at every door
> She heard the music dwindle and forgot the dance.

Again the reference is precise. The woman dancing on the shore, Kennelly notes in *New and Selected Poems* (1976), is recorded in the travel writings of Mrs Asenoth Nicholson. Kennelly is now at the centre of MacMahon country, confident in possession of his own magniloquence. The dying fall of 'withered', 'winds' and 'dwindle' prepares us for the tragic consequences for a culture when a people 'forgot the dance'. The apocalyptic horror of the famine – we think more of Mangan than of Yeats in this context – is registered in the third stanza as the woman with her 'innocent appalling cry' searches the sky for a sign. And in the fourth the poet's 'dark fathers' try to comprehend the 'The giant grief that trampled night and day, / The awful absence moping through the land' while dance and music cease.

The third particular image in the poem, maybe more grievous than that of the dead pensioners or the girl by the sea, occurs in the final stanza. While asserting his kinship with the intolerable past, Kennelly invokes what used to be a common sight in rural Ireland within his own memory – that of a shy man facing the wall while he entertains the company with a song.

> Since every moment of the clock
> Accumulates to form a final name,
> Since I am come from Kerry clay and rock,
> I celebrate the darkness and the shame
> That could compel a man to turn his face
> Against the wall, withdrawn from light so strong
> And undeceiving, spanceled in a place
> Of unapplauding hands and broken song. (*ATFV* 18)

The image of the clock brings Kennelly's fable dramatically into the personal here and now, preparing us for his definitive poetic utterance. The symbolism of dark and light, which has carried his thought through the historical nightmare, returns in that remarkable cultural image of the singer who cannot face the reality of his liberation. The historical *via dolorosa* which begins with the nailed feet of the first stanza, through the 'thorny savage furze' of the third, accumulates in the traumatised, 'spanceled' immobility of the last lines.

Yet the poem is heroic in its ambitious sweep as well as in the earned bravado of its stance, its declaration of artistic faith. I suspect that it is the poem he had been looking for through so many experiments with time and place, with character and landscape, with history, myth and geography. He can now be accounted one with Mangan, who is commemorated in another poem in the same volume, as 'Scrupulous poet of a people's loss'.

Yet by no means is the ground gained, the energies released in 'My Dark Fathers', put to the most valuable account. *Up and At It* (1965), that celebration of footloose randiness, is to my mind a dubious departure, though the poet prizes it enough twenty years later to republish it as *Moloney Up and At It* (1984). Before considering it as a poetic sequence, a glance at his second, and less successful novel, *The Florentines* (1967) may help our perspective.

Re-reading *The Florentines* after a twenty-five year interval I find myself wondering why Kennelly took time off from his poetry to write it at all. Its model is Boccaccio's *Decameron* in which a group of worldly people spend a time telling tales, insulated, like Kennelly's postgraduates, from the world. Its hero is named Gulliver – so Kennelly gives notice that there is really no comparison that he is not willing to invite. Pitched in the convention of the picaresque, with the young hero setting out for his year's postgraduate study at the University of Barfield, the story is obviously based on a year the author spent in Leeds on graduate research. On the Liverpool boat Gulliver Stone encounters a boozy little Tipperaryman with a hurley-stick who sings rebel songs and shouts 'Up Tipp!', and a woman named Concepta McGillicuddy who gives his overtures the cold shoulder.

Gulliver's stay in Barfield is told in a deadpan prose which seldom rises to any sense of narrative excitement. The events are presented as a set of journalistic set-pieces – a street fight, a student booze-up, a student demonstration, an attempt at seduction aborted by the hero being drowned in the puke of the beloved, the sea-journey home. The characterisations are perfunctory and inconsequent. Above all, we don't get a single insight to the hero's heart or conscience. The one feature it shares with *The Crooked Cross* is its refusal to give anything away about its author. Swift's Gulliver is a character of subtlety and nuance by comparison with his lapidary successor in *The Florentines*.

There is significance, however, of a negative character in the events described in Gulliver's return to Ireland on the same Liverpool Boat. The little Tipperaryman is present again, this time singing nationalist songs in competition with an Ulsterman singing Orange ballads. He notes that the years had 'modified ancient bitterness', and that the boat had only one destination, Ireland.

> Two little islands in a world of trouble, and they were best who travelled from one to another with a song on their lips...Gulliver thought of the island behind him. Busy turbulent, frequently unhappy, and the island ahead, gay mocking, secretive. He looked about him at the men, women and children, who were kin to the island waiting for them in the darkness. What could one do but drink their health. (*Flor.* 109)

With these thoughts Gulliver, who still retains his virginity, goes to his bunk below, only to find the hitherto untouchable Concepta MacGillicuddy waiting for him there:

> 'Do you mind?' she said, more in hope than in anger. In answer he laid his last bottle of Guinness reverently on the floor and sprang forward, echoing the little hurler's tribal battle cry...'Up Tipp!' (*Flor.* 109)

The author – for it is his, not Gulliver's, voice we hear in the narrative – is not to be blamed for his optimism about Northern Ireland; we all shared that complacency in 1967. But – even allowing for the fact that Kennelly is rounding off a story of temporary exile – there's no forgiveness for that sentimental reverie on 'Ireland-the-smile-and-the-tear-in-her-eye'. And the randy swagger of the final trope is not to be excused by the need for a romantic flourish and a happy ending. It's the self-conscious Kerryman at work, 'the likes of Owen Rua O'Sullivan and the poets of the Dingle Bay' as Pegeen Mike envisaged them in Synge's *Playboy*.

Kennelly approves of Patrick Kavanagh when the elder poet condemns what he calls 'buck-lepping' and 'gallivanting' in Irish poetry. The latter word was used by Kavanagh to indict the rollicking poetic gestures of F.R. Higgins in an essay he entitled 'The Gall-ivanting Poet '.[9] The danger of such writing, Kavanagh asserts, is two-fold: it tempts the writer towards faking an energy he does not feel; and it prevents him from looking sincerely into his own condition. It is a besetting temptation in the early Kennelly, and it finds its most sustained outlet in the Moloney persona whom he seems to have created for the purpose in *Up and At It* (1965).

These poems are widely, and perhaps justly, admired, for their rhythmic energy, their amoral extravagance, their *joie de vivre*. I am also aware that these tales of wandering rakes, and drunken hallu-cinations, of wakes where the corpse comes to life and wild men find themselves copulating on the graves of their mothers, have an honourable history in Irish folk tradition. What I distrust in the Moloney narratives is that they bespeak a sort of extrovert reck-lessness that is the opposite of what Kennelly feels most inwardly – an apprehension of existential terror, not unmixed with a sense of self-loathing, at the human condition.

This quality begins to come through with thrilling authenticity in the nightmare title poem of *Dream of a Black Fox* (1968) which opens

> The black fox loped out of the hills
> And circled for several hours,
> Eyes bright with menace, teeth
> White in the light, tail dragging the ground.
> The woman in my arms cringed with fear,
> Collapsed crying, her head hurting my neck
> She became dumb fear. (*ATFV* 63)

The beloved, I take it, does not see the black fox. She sees its men-ace reflected in the poet's terror; hers is a fear of fear. The ease with which the irregular lines register the loping motion of the inscrut-able monster is only matched by the pathos of the human lovers, reduced and vulnerable before its menace. In the last stanza the poet acknowledges that he had not just seen and felt fear, but 'Fear dispelled by what makes fear'. That is something permanent and central in his experience of living. Something that will re-appear with more dreadful particularity in 'The Black Fox, Again'.

The innocents in a poem of that name 'suffer martyrdoms, / Bleed invisible before / Our judges and centurions'. The tone is too close to confession not to communicate a shudder of sympathy, evoke an impulse to absolution:

> They create, but mostly hell
> For others and themselves;
> It can't be otherwise until

> We see that suffering remains,
> Consumes itself, devours its neighbours
> Always causes pain...   (*ATFV* 147)

In 'Nightmare' there is a marvellous, desperate play on the juxtaposed values of love and fear:

> And on your face was terror, love,
> The terror of knowing
> That the demon held our destiny
> And played with it... [10]

It would be comforting to think that 'love' was merely apposition-
al, but we know it's mostly vocative. These poems of terror are
rather like those of Mangan in a poem like 'Shapes and Signs'. The
ubiquity of the demon figure suggests that they may be about alcohol. What is certain is that they are about fear – which means that
the poet is finding his true courage. This theme finds its most intense expression in such late lyrics as 'The Pig', 'The Joke', 'The
Black Fox, Again', and in *The Book of Judas* where they are given
veritable orchestration.

I've been cutting a sort of single-minded furrow through this
first decade of Brendan Kennelly's prose and poetry, concentrating
on swerves, side-steps, false starts and blind alleys as much as on
the achievement itself which is of course the main event. One might
even adopt another phrase from Stephen Dedalus and declare that
these are not false starts at all, merely potholes of discovery. It is
in the nature of things, as James Stephens observed, that pens are
such as write too little or too much.

Before concluding I must confess to having neglected a number
of brilliant critical opportunities offered by Brendan Kennelly's
work over this first decade of his creative life in the work of this
decade. In pursuing the adventure of the poet's development in
time and space I have virtually ignored the question of artifact, the
poem itself, as manifest in the remarkable number of achieved
lyrics created by the way.

Had I chosen another approach and emphasis I would have lin-
gered, for instance, over 'The Gift' with its tentative delicacy of
movement, echoed by a sort of sister poem 'Girl on a Rope'. 'Johnny
Gobless', 'The Hunchback', 'The Dummies', 'The Blind Man',
might have been explored as poems of empathy and inscape that
James Stephens would not have disowned, troubling in the suggestion that they may be oblique self-portraits. There is the haunting city atmosphere of 'Light Dying', his moving elegy for a car-
dinal presence in his life, Frank O'Connor.

Then there are those curt, seminal images of rural life, 'A Far-mer Thinks of His Daft Son', 'The Thatcher', The Tippler', 'The Pig-Killer', balanced against such an exquisite suburban genre-piece as 'At the Party'. One might have reflected on theme and technique in his declaration of personal faith, 'The Good', or on the powerful narrative thrust of 'Night-Drive' where his poetry of terror may have had its first promptings – or on 'Ghosts', which comes immediately after it in *Selected Poems* (1969), and in which he defines his vocation:

> Respecting the definition of death
> And the sea's untiring style,
> Desiring the precision of birds
> That flash from black to white,
>
> I look within, without
> And write. [11]

Taken all in all, the sixties were for Brendan Kennelly a decade of astonishing productivity, of tireless experiment and genuine, various achievement. He keeps attacking on several fronts, apparently will-ing to take casualties with the same cheerfulness as when winning bridge-heads. Unlike Louis MacNeice's exasperated Mrs Carmichael in 'Bagpipe Music' he shows no sign whatever of being 'through with over-production'. And the direction of this ten years can now be seen as leading inexorably to the ambitious consolidations of *Cromwell* and *The Book of Judas*. There his great obsessions, historical, territorial, and personal have been elaborately rehearsed in a performance that shows no sign of closing.

TERENCE BROWN

Kennelly as Novelist

'Trouble is' Brendan Kennelly has Edmund Spenser remark in *Cromwell* 'sonnets are genetic epics. Something in them wants to grow out of bounds.' He might have been reporting on his own work, drawing attention to the fructifying generic impurity and instability of his own *œuvre*, its vital proliferation, its protean refusal to be bound by safe artistic taxonomies. Here is the writer as lyric poet, dramatist, social commentator, critic, essayist, performer, satirist, anthologist, whose public *persona* encompasses the university professor and the front-man for motor-car ads, the compelling lecturer and the newspaper columnist. Indeed it is almost impossible to discover in Kennelly's substantial body of writings any which do not bear some marks of an impatience with generic demarcations and a kind of exhilarated, voracious welcoming of the way works of art insist on their mongrel pedigree as they traffic with a world in which no motive can be entirely pure, no act uncontaminated by ambiguity and uncertainty, no utterance entirely true or false. For this is a body of writings which has to do with a social and psychic reality of hybrid, disorientating disequilibrium, which brings into its obsessive, iterative purview mythology and TV images, small-town life and the global village, archetypal order, momentarily celebrated in lyric intensity, and contemporary disintegration, dereliction, the flotsam and jetsam of a crazed consumerism of ideas, emotions, products. Its overall impact is dependent too on an impression of linguistic perviousness. Kennelly's language is characteristically assured, its syntax bold and confidently correct. Its vocabulary seems unhesitatingly available to the tongue, immediately apposite. On the page the poems look clean-cut, even, perhaps, buoyantly certain of themselves.

Yet the language of these eloquently energised verbal performances also finds itself invaded by the casual demotic of small-town and city life, by the clichés and slang of everyday gossip, the cant of the media-circus, the catch-phrases of journalese. Often, particularly in his later work, in *Cromwell* and in *The Book of Judas*, his effects are achieved by allowing the speech of the streets and the public bar to work against the grain of a rhetorical verbal trajectory which finds appropriate expression in a sense of inevitable poetic form. Here, for example is ' In the Stock Exchange', from *The Book of Judas*:

'Holy Jesus my whole neighbourhood is upset
Not a body can sleep at night
Because this red setter bitch is in heat
And scatters of dogs from Dublin and Meath

Smell her in the air and get
Randy as bejasus for the ride and set
Out to find her, sweaty bitch, you know what
I mean, pure female, drives males mad with

Her smell, Christ Almighty, the silky wet
Little bitch brings twenty dogs all hot
And panting into, Holy Jesus, the Stock

Exchange where they all try to screw her,
The little punter full of the readies takes the lot, ups
And out into the street. What's next, mate? Pups!'   (*BOJ* 177)

Such a poem has an unsettling quality of disequilibrium about it. The instinctive blasphemy and obscenity of the imagined speaker threaten to overwhelm the poetic form with scabrous informality, so that we seem to be present at a moment of artistic mutation when a new kind of writing is in the making – a hybrid of energised form and disruptive, levelling, anecdotal argot.

The ubiquitous presence of story as a generating force in Kennelly's art is, by contrast, a factor which tends to stabilise the heteroglossia of his variegated texts. Poems are frequently developed as anecdotes and gossipy narratives, his dramas are versions of the Greek with their roots in myths and legends. The history confronted in *Cromwell* is an oft-told Irish tale compact of 'biography, speeches, letters, legend, folklore, fantasy' (*Cromwell*, 6). as well as the official historical accounts. *The Book of Judas* has its origin in the story of the betrayal in the familiar gospel text. But for all the dependence on narrative and story there is clear evidence that Kennelly, addicted to generic impurity, has been loath as a writer to allow story a normative, privileged authority in his work. Accordingly, in his two major works, *Cromwell* and *The Book of Judas*, he has been at pains to direct the reader's attention to the ways he has sought to disrupt narrative conventions in works so rooted in primary narratives, that

of Irish history and that of the Christian gospel. It is as if even the
deep structure of story itself as a constituent of human consciousness cannot be allowed to predetermine how the writer will treat
what he experiences as radical discontinuity and incoherence in the
modern world even as he exploits its literary potential. Familiar
stories must be subjected, massively indeed, to techniques which
throw them out of shape, render them in terms which augment
the destabilising effects of the generic impurity which also marks
Kennelly's writings. In his note to *Cromwell* Kennelly insists 'The
method of the poem is imagistic, not chronological' (*Cromwell* 6).
In the preface to *The Book of Judas* he expands on the implication
of a non-chronological structure in a poem based on a primary
narrative. He reflects that 'there is something in Irish life which
demands that you over-simplify practically everything. This is
another way of saying that everybody must be labelled, made readily
accessible, explainable' (*BOJ* 9). In contrast to such ready stereotyping he invokes poetry as intimate with an energy which disrupts
and detonates, which allows the voice of an outcast like Judas his
terrifying say: 'But there is an electricity in the air that burns the
labels and restores the spirit of investigative uncertainty. Poetry
tries to plug into this electricity, to let it thrill and animate one's
ways of feeling and thinking and seeing' (*BOJ* 9). But to let this
current spark the poem into life, to permit Judas to step from a
familiar tale with all his radical interrogations of conventional consciousness, chronology must be eschewed:

> This scapegoat, critic of self and society, throws chronological time out
> the window. Before his ancestors arrived on the scene, he was. After the
> unborn will have ceased to exist, he'll be. As others arrive, exist and
> perish, he tholes. Time is merely a stage where his reticent yet theatri-
> cal spirit is repeated and refined as it continues to endure the stones of
> blame thrown by those who really know the score. If I'd stuck to chron-
> ology in this poem I'd have lost the voices of that spirit. By treating
> time in the ways a blamed person treats it, that is with the ceaseless
> nervous agility of the accused-from-all-sides, the poem became open to
> the stimulating effects of that electricity which saves most thinking people
> from the pornography of labels. (*BOJ* 12).

Intriguingly, Kennelly then associates the electricity into which
poetry tries to plug itself with, of all things, 'muttering' – the stray
phrases heard in the street, random, apparently meaningless, passionate nevertheless, which are a kind of freedom the poet would
wish to achieve in the free form of his atemporal, achronological
poem:

> I have always associated unbridled passionate muttering with freedom. There is something more attractively genuine in such mutterings than in most of the bland interchanges that go by the name of 'communication'. Wherever I see men and women furiously muttering to themselves in the streets of Dublin I am saddened by their loneliness, touched by their sincerity, awed by their freedom. (*BOJ* 12).

An art which pays obeisance to such muttering and which eschews chronology is by definition a long way not only from the simple consolations and deceptions of narrative but also from any kind of stable text or unmixed mode.

Two early works of this remarkably fertile writer supply telling evidence of how deeply rooted is this impulse to escape the limitations of any given form and to transcend even the less than obviously constricting implications of anecdote, narrative and chronology. They are the short novels which Kennelly published in the 1960s in the first phase of his literary career.

These two novels, *The Crooked Cross* (1963) and *The Florentines* (1965) both exhibit a marked attentiveness to the kind of social reality which is the focus of realist fiction. The first is concerned with the effects of emigration on the youth of Ireland in the period, while the second is pervaded by the slightly hectic atmosphere of the 1960s England when fear of nuclear holocaust was palpable in the wake of Nagasaki and Hiroshima. *The Crooked Cross* explores the sad dereliction of a modern Ireland, in which emigration is sapping the life-blood of the nation, through the metaphor of a village wracked by drought. The realist vision of George Moore in *The Untilled Field* and of Joyce in *Dubliners* seems close at hand to give authority to this more recent, bleak assessment of a land in the grip of paralysis (the text even refers to 'the paralysed Main Street' of the village). *The Florentines*, the story of a young Irishman's coming of age in a university town in the English Midlands, finds its place as an Irish-accented version of a familiar Sixties fictional kind, where the scholarship boy makes his way through a realistically-observed university milieu. Neither is remarkable for its originality of theme or focus. Nor can it be said that either exhibits Kennelly as skilled in plot construction or character portrayal. Both works are, in narrative terms, apparently simple constructs.

The one follows the course of events in the Kerry village of Deevna through a long hot summer until water is found; the other follows its hero Gulliver Stone from Dublin to Barfield University and back for an academic year, where all that really occurs is a series of encounters and eventual sexual initiation. What does give both of them their undoubted energy is the way the conventional

material and the very straightforward constructions are invaded by
a sense of completely different literary modes than the fictional realism to which the texts ostensibly aspire. For inherent in some of
the most achieved passages in these books are the charged intensities of the lyric and the supple force of epic narration. Both give
to these rather slight works a sense of a writer open to the exciting
potentialities of a mixed form.

   The Crooked Cross and *The Florentines* proceed episodically. In
composite this can seem too blatantly contrived a technique for
realist fiction to bear. The complex inter-relationships of character, motive and event can seem too obviously sacrificed to the
exigencies of a completed individual action, which Kennelly seems
to prefer to the detailed filiations of novelistic narration. But as
individual fictional moments they can have remarkable effect as they
demonstrate how Kennelly can open his realist prose to currents
which flow from other literary forms. And they do also suggest an
early suspicion of mere chronology, as the two works compose
themselves as discrete pulsations of fictional energy. So, although
both novels follow the predictable temporal progression implicit in
their subject matter, what the reader remembers is a series of powerfully recounted episodes which focus attention on representative
moments which begin to possess the implications of symbol or
allegorical instance. *The Crooked Cross* begins, for example, with a
beautiful tinker woman coming to the village, stirring the sexual
juices of many a frustrated male in a world about to be visited by
the drought which is the metaphoric equivalent of its own human
aridity. Then the drought takes hold, a child dies from fever and
her sexually profligate father determines to make his life anew in
exile at work in England as if the death observed in this episode has
been the death of a local future. In another graphically realised
incident an alcoholic brute of a man on a binge triumphs in fierce
physical combat in a public house but is humiliatingly whipped home
by an enraged son who resents the wastefulness of his father's
drunken excess, signalling generational war as the consequence of
a life where drink offers the only escape from boredom and frustration. This is a world, indeed, in which the village story-teller,
an old sailor, loved by the children and an image of the artist in a
deprived community, will be consumed in apocalyptic fire in one
terrible, symbolically charged episode. The water to save him cannot be found.

   At the heart of *The Crooked Cross* is a chapter entitled 'The Walk'.
It recounts how for an afternoon a village girl escapes the infected

heat and malicious gossip of her native village. Anne Dillon is the
only child of her widowed mother. She is forced by poverty to
work as a skivvy for several of the villagers. An employer is the
grocer Dan Wynne, who one fine day makes a crude pass at her,
which she disgustedly repels. Subsequently, she overhears his wife
pronounce her pregnant and Dan Wynne smears her as a promis-
cuous slut. She flees the village for the countryside in sick misery.
What follows is a powerful piece of poetic prose in which she
becomes one with nature, the sky, the fruit and flowers of the
countryside and with the river in which she bathes her naked
body in a ritual of redemption and renewal.

The episode is of course remarkable, in a volume marked by its
sense of Irish restriction and oppressiveness, for its celebration of
pagan sexuality, bodily freedom and female pleasure. The poetic
resources of image, symbol, and a charged metaphoric sense of
language are brought to bear on this ecstatic epiphany:

> As she watched, the river turned blue. The summer sky was suddenly
> there at the river-bed, projecting its blueness into the brown water and
> transforming it. The great blue bowl of the sky seemed somehow to
> have got under the water and to be holding it cupped in the alchemy
> of its blueness. It was a beautiful sight and it made the girl breathless.
> She dropped to her knees in the deep grass and, like a hare, sat back
> on her heels. She stayed looking at water and reflected sky and sun for
> more than half-an-hour.   (CC 88-89)

So instead of the cruel, dirty-minded world of the village with the
grocer's ferret-like lust, the girl enters a primal world of pagan lush-
ness, ripe blackberries which stain her mouth like an original innocence, animal images of vital sexuality and fertility, a river which
washes her clean and gives her the strength to decide her own fate:

> Then she gripped projecting pieces of rock with both hands and clam-
> bered up till she sat on the almost flat surface. The three white rocks
> were known locally as the Cow, the Bull and the Calf. The Bull was
> the centre one. Anne sat on it for a few moments, her wet naked body
> as white as a hound's tooth in the sunlight, her dark hair clinging wetly
> to her shoulders. Then she stretched out on her back and let the sun
> fall on her belly and legs. She closed her eyes. Under her back, the white
> surface of the rock was warm and she didn't mind the minute fragments
> of gravel which stuck to her wet skin from the rock-surface. It was all
> freshness and beauty; it was all clean water and warm sunlight, green
> grasses and yellowy flowers, berries and the blueness of the pool. Her
> closed eyes saw nothing but blueness of water and sky and her naked
> body exulted in the feeling of utter cleanliness. She was back in the
> morning of the world when the first light was breaking over undiscov-
> ered fields, and nothing was unclean or fallen.   (CC 93)

The writing here is, one senses, functioning imagistically, as the
world of the village – arid, venal and repressed – is juxtaposed with
the revivifying vitality and open eroticism of the river scene. What
results is a kind of prose-poem in which the central conflicts of
the novel itself – between youth and age, drought and abundance,
male and female, repressed individuality and free expression of the
self – find symbolic expression in an intensely realised lyrical description. It reminds indeed of that moment in *Dubliners* when the
style of scrupulous meanness which has been the instrument through
much of the work for Joyce's exacting realism is abandoned as 'The
Dead' concludes, for the haunting poetic meditation on the snow
which is general over Ireland and the work enters an imaginative
universe of symbolic, poetic import. 'The Walk' prepares us in fact
for the arrival of the diviner and the magical flow of water which
he brings to conclude *The Crooked Cross* – emblem of hope even
in Deevna where life 'seemed to be flowing away daily' (*CC* 144).

The central preoccupation of *The Florentines* is encounter: Gulliver Stone's encounter with England, with English university life,
with political commitment (it's the era of the ban-the-bomb marches),
with the mythology he is studying and with the opposite sex, with
English beer. This thematic orientation has its narrative equivalent
in the repeated fights, in the streets and in the pubs, which the hero
witnesses or joins. In fact no sooner has he arrived in Barfield than
he and a drinking companion are set upon by a gang of thugs as if
he must show his Irish mettle in a rite of passage which allows this
Irish youth to enter the English world. There is accordingly a
suggestion in the work that Gulliver (rather obviously named, one
feels) is undergoing a series of trials of strength and competence
like a hero in one of the myths or folk-tales he is studying during
his year abroad.

The writing in those passages where the violence of the town
erupts is supple, spare and direct. As such it contributes to the
sense that the novel is not simply a realist account of a social moment in the 1960s and of a young man's coming of age but a work
which owes some of its force to a quite different kind of writing: to
epic narrative and tales of heroic exploit. One of the most effective
episodes in the book is in fact the account of a judo match between
the local university hero and an Oxford man who has come to
challenge him. Their struggle is recounted like something from the
Táin, from an epic narrative:

> The Oxford man remained upright, almost motionless. Black Belt circled
> him and, within a minute of his fall, he leaped tigerously again. The

> Oxford man didn't expect this, he thought he'd completely winded Black Belt, but the stocky Barfield man was superbly fit and full of fight. In an instant, he gripped the blonde giant in precisely the same way as he'd done previously; the Oxford man again got his right hand around Black Belt's chest, and Gulliver was certain that his friend was about to be thrown heavily again. But then, with unerring speed, Black Belt caught the Oxford man's right hand, flicked it over his own right shoulder, and heaved like a young bull. Gulliver thrilled as he saw the blonde muscular figure of the Oxford man cleave the air, and thump noisily on the mat. He twisted his body as he fell to save himself from being injured. The noise of his fall was deceptive; it echoed sickeningly through the small hall. But the Oxford man was on his feet as quickly as Black Belt had been, and again he towered, blonde, almost motionless, over the crouched menacing figure of Black Belt whose face now held a thin coating of perspiration, and whose narrowed eyes darted like lightnings here and there, as he sought an opening for another leap. (*Flor*, 73)

What gives especial effect to this heroic episode in the book, adding to its air of having come down from an ancient text to find its place in a contemporary novel, is that Black Belt is gracious and gentle in defeat. The episode ends, as if to exemplify the magnanimity and virtue of the true epic hero, with Black Belt helping an old crippled man back to his humble lodgings where 'with great ease and tenderness, Black Belt set the old man down in his armchair' (*Flor*, 76-7).

In an insightful essay on the short stories of Liam O'Flaherty, published in 1979, Kennelly noted of that writer's prose that it has 'a genuine epic throb, an unpolluted primitive wonder, a strong purity of narrative line, which, by reason of its very strength, is more like verse than prose'. He argues that one of O'Flaherty's tales, which he quotes admiringly as a species of poetry, 'falls naturally into verse' and continues:

> If we listen to its rhythms, the varying cool impassioned flow of its sympathies, its unfolding of anticipation, conflict and resolution, we find ourselves in the company not of a modern writer of short stories but a bardic teller of tales... (*JJ*, 202)

Something similar can be said of Kennelly's own two early experiments in prose. These are the 'prentice work of an artist who was to remain throughout his career open to the hybrid possibilities of literary form, its fertile instability. Lyric intensity, symbolism, imagistic juxtaposition and epic directness of style enter their episodically fragmented realism as if to signal the author's impatience with any too univocal a text, anticipating the radical heteroglossia of his later achievements. And in both, the presence of an oral community as the text's originating source, in *The Crooked Cross* made present in the frequent incorporation of ballad material and gossipy anecdote, in *The Florentines* in the frequent outbreaks of student song and poetic recitation, charges the writing at its best moments with that democratically available electricity, the language on the tongue and in the mouth, which Kennelly believes is the source of true generic freedom.

GERALD DAWE

'And Then – The Spring!':
Brendan Kennelly's *Breathing Spaces*

> There is no audience in Ireland, though I have managed to build up
> out of my head a little audience for myself. The real problem is the
> scarcity of a right audience which draws out of a poet what is best in
> him. The Irish audience that I came in contact with tried to draw out
> of me everything that was loud, journalistic and untrue.[1]
>
> – PATRICK KAVANAGH

Much of what Brendan Kennelly has written is influenced, directly
or indirectly, by the problem so boldly stated by Patrick Kavanagh
in his *Self-Portrait* (1964). In particular, Kennelly's early poems,
most of which are collected in the volume *Breathing Spaces* (1992),
chart his growing unease and concern with making what he simply
calls 'connection':

> The sense of connection, when it occurs, feels like a stroke of great
> good luck. But with whom or what does it become even momentarily
> possible to connect?   (*BS* 129)

The need, to quote Kavanagh again, 'to build up a little audience
for myself' is taken over by Kennelly as both a personal and a cultural mission. Kennelly's poetry inhabits the artistic ground where
these two impulses collide.

Undoubtedly this provocative intersection accounts for the extraordinary commitment Brendan Kennelly has shown during the 1980s
and 1990s to give readings from his work, primarily throughout
Ireland, but also abroad. It may also account for his willingness to
speak on various moral and sexual issues which emerged in Ireland
throughout the same period.

This high-profile public persona was indeed consummated in
Kennelly's book-length poems, or epics, *Cromwell* and *The Book of
Judas*, and has certainly contributed enormously to Kennelly's vast
popular reputation in Ireland.

In the earlier work, such as *Love Cry* (1972), *Islandman* (1977), *A Small Light* (1979), *A Girl* (1981) and in the previous uncollected poems gathered in the title section, *Breathing Spaces*, one sees the extent to which Kennelly has been preoccupied with these polemical issues of audience and the poet's place in a society such as Ireland – so very traditional in ways, and yet brashly, almost aggressively, engaged by the new.

What makes *Breathing Spaces* as a volume particularly revealing is that, in the Introduction and 'Notes' accompanying each section of the book, Kennelly alludes to a deep anxiety about the fault-lines which run between the traditional, community life in Ireland and its demise. It is an anxiety Kavanagh would have well understood.

In a sense, Kennelly is to the Republic of the 1980s what Kavanagh was to the Republic of the forties and fifties. Both poets are haunted by bardic nostalgia; both suspicious of high-brow pretensions about 'Art'; both are mindful of the subversiveness of the comic spirit and both respect the rhetorical wisdom of anecdote and folklore. Indeed, while much has been made of Seamus Heaney's intellectual appropriation of Kavanagh's example, we should bear in mind the equally important cultural similarities which Brendan Kennelly shares with Kavanagh.

To take even the most obvious of examples: both poets come from a small-town/rural village background, the familiarity of which led to a sense of spiritual shock and personal difficulty when confronted by city-life. This breakdown is recorded in the poems with pathos, bitterness, and, sometimes, self-mockery.

Kavanagh's distaste for Dublin's literary life is, of course, legendary. 'I wasted what could have been my four glorious years,' Kavanagh recalls in *Self-Portrait*, 'begging and scrambling around the streets of malignant Dublin'.

The experience of leaving behind the known, identifiable world of Inniskeen for Dublin in 1939, and the kind of personal distortions and loss which this change seems to have brought about in Kavanagh's psyche is a dominant theme in his poetry. It is also the focus for *Self-Portrait* and provides the radical poignancy to Kavanagh's life and work as a poet:

> Round about the late nineteen-thirties a certain prosperity came through and foolishly enough that was the time I chose to leave my native fields. I had no messianic impulse to leave. I was happy. I went against my will. A lot of our actions are like that. We miss the big emotional gesture and drift away. Is it possible to achieve our potential grand passion? I believe so. Perhaps that has been my weakness.[2]

Kavanagh's Monaghan provided him with what he called 'the right simplicity' which he had to rediscover ('back to where I started') in order to achieve 'weightlessness' – the unforced, indifferent mystery which is the hallmark of true poetry.

The Kerry and Shannon where Kennelly grew up during the late 1930s, 40s and 50s provide him with rich local detail, landscape, stories and the very 'simplicity' of language which characterises *Breathing Spaces*.

Like Kavanagh, Kennelly records the transition of the individual from having a defined and definite place in a community, to another world of broken and fractured identities wherein 'the self' is effectively unknowable in the received and hierarchic terms of the parish. The self becomes instead the site of 'egotism', a deeply suspect force in Kennelly's lexicon.

Kennelly's uncertainty in addressing the self is matched by Kavanagh's reticence: 'I dislike talking about myself in a direct way. The self is only interesting as an illustration,' is how Kavanagh opens his *Self-Portrait*.[3] Similarly, Kennelly states in his note to *Islandman*:

> Through an act of sustained and deliberate indirectness, it is possible to say more completely whatever one has to say. It is one of the fertile paradoxes of poetry that one can be more candid by engaging less in frontalism and by listening more keenly to the voices of the personae in the wings. (*BS* 102)

Throughout his Introduction and in the Notes to the individual volumes of *Breathing Spaces*, Kennelly is troubled by 'the self'. It is a 'mobile, boggy swamp of egotism and dull confusion' (*BS* 10) – a phrase which he repeats – and he refers later to the 'monstrous yet magnificent energies of egotism' (*BS* 102). Other references include the mere self, the messy self, all by way of disentangling the one moral and artistic problem which Kennelly clearly sees as being paramount to his own identity as a writer: 'I sometimes think that poetry takes the mickey out of poets…The problem is to keep the egolife from mauling the poemlife' (*BS* 10).

Indeed, poetry threatens to become a *substitute* for the self, an alternative life almost, which bridges the past, and its known community (an inherited audience, in effect), with the present atomised reality.

Many of the poems in *Breathing Spaces* literally document, sociologically, anthropologically, the traditional community as in *Love Cry*, a sequence of forty sonnets. Most of the poems name a place or person, tell stories and document the passing of a way of life.

It is poetry as lament. While conscious of the brute realities of farming, Kennelly dramatises the beauty of the landscape wherein his
'characters' live out their lives. Little is gone into, but the suffi-
cient exterior of *Love Cry* reveals a terrifying cycle of acceptance,
tinged with regret and, often, curtailed rage, as in 'Spring' (*BS* 93).

> Curtin spent the winter in the County Home
> And drank and whored and gambled in the spring;
> I met him once, the black days coming on,
> He told me straight that he was going in.
> 'Last night,' he said, 'I left a farmer's house,
> The moon was up, a wicked light abroad,
> The innocent roads were turning treacherous
> And ice, you know, is the pure cruelty of God.
>
> Well, soon enough, I'll meet the men who fail
> At everything poor Christian men esteem.
> Down hearted villians! You should hear them sing!
> Homeless as crows, yet they keep body and soul
> Together. Just like me. Know what I mean?
> The winter within walls. And then – the spring!'

The poem displays the characteristic attributes of *Breathing Spaces*:
the encounter, the conversation, the voice, the closure – 'And then
– the spring!' What is so noticeable about *Breathing Spaces* is the
extent to which the poems, ranging over twenty years, are shad-
owed by death, pain and loss.

It were as if, deprived of the defined communal world, the poet
finds recompense in the language and social conditions of the past
only to realise that these no longer exist and that the worldview
they embody has fragmented and is, effectively, dead. How else is
one to account for the (almost) obsessive preoccupation of the poems
with death, dying, ghosts, and the adequacy of poetry to convey
such experience?

> The fields were strewn with dead metaphors.
> Language had fought a pitched battle and lost.   (*BS* 48)

Physical death is omnipresent in *Breathing Spaces*. There is too the
notion that failure, as another form of death, must be acknowledged
by the poetic imagination since nothing should be repugnant to the
poet. 'Failure is your daily bread' (*BS* 23). 'It is the source / of all
our celebration,' as Kennelly remarks in 'Failure' (*BS* 76) and concludes the poem:

> I will look at all this, loving it
> As I have always loved it,
> Feeling the failure rise like the tide,
> Waves wasting their perfection
> On my ignorant shores.

So the Poet becomes an icon of authentic life, taking everything 'in' and by that very fact celebrating Life in the teeth of denial, repression and insufficiency. This late-Romantic notion, conditioned by the joking, devilish quality in the poetic personae, finds straightforward endorsement in Kennelly's introductory note to *Islandman*:

> I want to love every heartbeat, every musical second of happiness and grief, boredom and fun and the usual no-man's-land of viable and reasonably rewarded half-being, permitted between stoneself and definite dust. Whatever forces help one to love this frequently muted music of time are to be welcomed by imagination and intelligence, body and soul. Whatever or whoever you are, be with me now. (*BS* 103)

The yearning here ('be with me now') does have a religious dimension to it because poetry becomes a form of secular mass, compensating for the deadliness of institutional spirituality. Kennelly's poetry, after all, depicts the lives of the victims of the Irish Catholic Church. Such failure hangs like a cultural fate against which the characters of Kennelly's poems sometimes rail, mock, but often accept with inarticulate cries from the heart.

> Ritchie screamed to see his chastised son
>
> So changed, as though the quick rebuke
> Had driven him to a world unknown.
> But now he lay there, still, beyond all pain;
> The village watched and wept while Ritchie shook,
> Two women pressed eager lips upon
> Blue lips, giving their kiss of life. In vain. (*BS* 90)

In this sense, then, the Poet is looked to as a figure who can strike back, if symbolically, at the forces of moral, sexual and political containment: 'Ireland,' Kennelly writes in his 'Introduction', 'is, above all, the land of the label, a green kingdom of clichés. To write poetry is to declare war on labels and clichés' (*BS* 11). The poem is a coded message which confirms in the reader's (or audience's) mind that the poet knows what is going on, because he has suffered the same kind of repression as his audience. The poem is a vehicle of this identification. Such knowledge is not, however, absolute and incontrovertible. As Kennelly remarks in the headnote to *Love Cry*:

> I showed some of these poems to an old man from the place in which most of the poems are set. He read them and said vehemently, 'Lies! Lies! Poetry is all bloody lies!' He paused, then added, much more gently, 'But a poet's lies can make a man look twice at himself and the world.' (*BS* 80).

What Kennelly has achieved in the poems of *Breathing Spaces* is to keep an accessible channel of communication open between himself and the wider public in whose name his poems are addressed. He has recreated that audience in the image of what they once were and he has been able to maintain this relationship by exploiting the language of church-ritual and common speech with total ease.

> I touch the stones.
> My mother smiles, my father dances,
> My daughter peppers me with questions,
> A swimmer finds his music, an ambulance screams
> In mercy, I build a bridge of love,
> The willow speaks, the lightning dreams,
> The blackbird sings, I make a wish, the gift appears
> To bless this art
>   that deepens friendship
>   through the years.   (*BS* 78)

The force of poetic personality, the telling accent of the spoken line, has meant that Kennelly's poems are essentially available as stories. In this he has kept faith with his forebears, a loyalty which marks almost every poem in *Breathing Spaces* and the ideological commitment which Kennelly declares in *A Small Light*:

> Today the idea of community is vanishing fast; what we witness for the most part, in the efforts of those who try to create them, are, however admirable the impulses behind the efforts, sad parodies of community. (*BS* 128)

Kennelly's poetry is painfully aware of the parody and the unavoidable reality that the idea of community which he re-imagines in his writing is literally *vanishing*. What exactly that idea of that community is will provide historians and cultural critics with a tantalising glimpse of an Ireland which might have been; elusively present in the voices, feelings and attitudes of Kennelly's countryfolk, 'the personae in the wings'.

For all the brash rhetoric and ebullience of *Breathing Spaces* there is a Lorca-like recognition of darkness and death and an anger at the modern world:

> Is the contemporary poet, by definition, a part-timer, one who with a grateful sigh settles down to try to write when the fierce trivialities have for the moment been coped with? He is so often a voice without an audience, an endured oddity, an articulate freak with oddball values, a stone, a severed head, a voice in a void. (*BS* 129)

This is plain as a pike-staff and it lays down Kennelly's just claim to be considered alongside those other poets in these islands, such as Tony Harrison, who attempt to restore the contemporary poet to some kind of public life.

Certainly Kennelly's unflagging energy in producing poetry which is popular (in the sense of being directed at the People) should only point out again his critical relationship with Patrick Kavanagh. As Kavanagh remarked in one of the finest passages of *Self-Portrait*:

> I had been assailing the myth of Ireland by which they were managing to beat the artistic rap. I had seen and shewn that this Ireland thing was an undignified business – the trade of enemies and failures. [4]

In the major poems which followed the collections gathered in *Breathing Spaces*, Brendan Kennelly assails 'the myth of Ireland' with a vengeance. The anticipations, echoes and soundings which one hears in *Love Cry, A Small Light* or *Shelley in Dublin* are, in retrospect, unmistakable preparations for the war of words, the operatic thunder and 'fabulous fact' (*BS* 128) of Kennelly's greatest poetic achievements to date – *Cromwell* and *The Book of Judas*.

JONATHAN ALLISON

Cromwell: Hosting the Ghosts

You ask what I have found and far and wide I go,
Nothing but Cromwell's house, and Cromwell's murderous crew.[1]
 — W.B. YEATS

The name of Cromwell even now acts as a spell upon the Irish mind,
and has a powerful and living influence in sustaining the hatred both of
England and Protestantism.[2]
 — W.E.H. LECKY

I sympathise with the ageing, disillusioned man who struggled on under
the burden of the protectorate, knowing that without him worse would
befall: who wanted to be painted "warts and all". But it is the boister-
ous and confident leader of the 1640s who holds my imagination, and
whose pungent, earthy truths echo down the centuries.[3]
 — CHRISTOPHER HILL

In the 1950s, the suggestion that a college in the University of Dur-
ham, which Oliver Cromwell had established, should be named
after him met with unexpectedly stiff opposition, and the University
decided in favour of the less inflammatory name of 'Grey College'.[4]
The memory of Cromwell, the republican parricide and strong arm
of the English Revolution, is not universally revered in England,
where the beneficent effects of his ideas on civil and religious liber-
ties have been most deeply felt. Posterity in general has been divided on the subject. Some historians have praised his devotion to
religious tolerance and his systematic opposition to the élite institutions of British Government and society, including the monarchy
and the aristocracy, while others have lamented his despotic Puritanism, and in popular legend he is remembered as 'a desecrator
of sacred places', in Christopher Hill's words, and as a ruthless
murderer of heretics.[5] Yet surely nowhere is Oliver Cromwell more
hated than in Ireland, where in his campaign of 1649-50 to scotch
Royalist support for Charles II (and to exact revenge on the Irish
for the 1641 rebellion), he put thousands to the sword, including

priests and civilians, and burned many churches and houses.[6] His sackings of Drogheda on 11 September 1649 and of Wexford in the following month are remembered with particular horror, and are most immediately associated with what is known in Ireland as 'the curse of Cromwell'. At least one historian has compared the sacking of Drogheda to the bombing of Hiroshima, a monstrous demonstration of strength in order to overwhelm and undermine enemy morale.[7] Lecky compared the sieges of Drogheda and Wexford to 'the most atrocious exploits of Tilly or Wallenstein, and they made the name of Cromwell eternally hated in Ireland'.[8]

It seems unlikely that this popular image of Cromwell as the angel of death will ever be fully revised, despite the fact that he was in his personal life more complex and humane than is usually thought – a fond father to his five children, a lover of mathematics, music and horses – despite the fact that painting, sculpture, literature and music flourished during the years when he was Lord Protector. It is speculated that he may have been manic depressive. He loved practical jokes. While Brendan Kennelly, in *Cromwell*, portrays the ferocity and brutality of Cromwell and his troops during his Irish campaign, he also insists on portraying that other side of Cromwell, the lover of horses (always thoughtful of his men's mounts, he insists in stabling them in Catholic churches when in Ireland), the concerned father (three poems are based on letters to his son, daughter, and brother), and the practical joker: ' "I love an innocent jest" Oliver purred' (*C* 87).

It is clear that Kennelly regards himself as a kind of historian-poet, who wishes to understand the complexity of the man behind the myths, and to open his imagination to one of the most reviled men in Irish history. Kennelly has described himself as a demythologiser, a hater of stereotypes and clichés, and a seeker of the veins of truth flowing beneath such static surfaces: 'There are few states as secure as living in the clichés and labels of religion and history. Ireland is, above all, the Land of Label, a green kingdom of clichés. Needless to say, I find I have more than enough in my own heart and head, not to mention my language. But I try to fight their muggy, cloying, complacent, sticky, distorting, stultifying, murderous and utterly reassuring embrace' (*BS* 11). We may not agree that an over-reliance on cliches is a peculiarly Irish problem, but we will admit that clichés are a prevalent feature of daily discourse everywhere. For Kennelly a cliché is 'distorting, stultifying', a myth in the negative sense of that word, expressive of tired truths, half truths, or comfortable lies. But what about Cromwell? If it is indeed

a 'cliché' that he was the scourge of the Irish in Drogheda, Wexford and elsewhere, isn't it true? Kennelly does not disagree with
this, but he wishes to understand the man behind the terrible legend, and to open his poetic voice to Cromwell's voice, as it can be
heard not merely through the poet's fantasy life, but in the body
of texts (letters, speeches, historical accounts) which survive him.
Indeed, opening his imagination to other voices is, for Kennelly,
one of the primary tasks of the poet (hence he titles his current
selection of poems *A Time for Voices*):

> I believe poetry must always be a flight from this deadening authorita-
> tive egotism and must find its voices in byways, laneways, backyards,
> nooks and crannies of self. It is critics who talk of an 'authentic voice';
> but a poet, living his uncertainties, is riddled with different voices, many
> of them in vicious conflict. The poem is the arena where these voices
> engage each other in open and hidden combat, and continue to do so
> until they are all heard. (*ATFV* 12)

This statement suggests a faith in the poet as a monitor of vying
and often contradictory impulses, as a locus of dialogue and conflict,
and as a negatively capable articulator of uncertainty, rather than
as the voice of faith and certainty. Kennelly sees the poet as dialogic, not monologic. He believes in poetry as drama, as a Yeatsian
quarrel with the self, and as an exploration and presentation of
alternative points of view; above all he has a notion of poetry as
non-judgemental, open to the voices of difference and of the other,
and as a democratic parliament of tongues, rather than a podium
where a single hierarchical voice speaks and speechifies.

When he writes about hearing voices and in his poetry articulating these voices, Kennelly refers recurrently to the words 'freedom' and 'liberating'; the poet is most free when most polyvocal,
or dialogic, and when the antinomies of experience find utterance,
rather than when one voice speaks for all the impulses within the
poet. The imagination, when multivocal, is 'democratic' he writes
(*ATFV* 12); poetry leads to 'liberating myself from my self' (*ATFV*
12); he seeks in his poetry a 'liberating expansiveness' (*BS* 11). It
may seem ironic that a poet of personal and internal freedom might
wish to give voice to such an oppressive figure as Cromwell (no
matter what the historians might say about Cromwell's 'religious
toleration', he showed none to Irish Catholics). The solution to
this problem, and indeed the poetic roots of the Cromwell book,
lie in his attraction to the figure of the outcast; the marginalised,
un-social or anti-social figure who has become reviled by society –
'a lot of people in Ireland need to be "contaminated" by these out-

cast energies', he has remarked (*BS* 11). That is, he finds imaginative contact with alterity personally liberating and imaginatively
nourishing: 'I'm very grateful for my historical and religious mon-
sters' (*BS* 11). The roots of Kennelly's interest in Cromwell also
lie in his fascination, as expressed in earlier poems, with the power
humans wield over one another, especially when wielded self-right-
eously in the name of some idea, cause or God. In the earlier poem,
'Six of One' (a sequence of six sonnets), Kennelly describes six
egotistical characters, each of whom is in love with his own sense
of power, and each of whom is also the object of the poet's gentle
but incisive satire (*ATFV* 133-35). Kennelly is deeply suspicious of
the powerful, and cynical about how they tend to use or abuse it.

One of these six, the Barbarian, believes in civilisation and education ('ignorance is a sin'), and in the final lines of the sonnet the
egotism of his seeming philanthropy is subjected to a subtle critique: 'He makes articulate the pitifully dumb,/ Dark souls lit with
the glow of his own soul' (*ATFV* 133). In 'The Expert', the protagonist's utter self-confidence reaches hubristic heights ('God's a
dunce') and the poet ridicules his ultimate preference for the 'authentic text' of the field of his expertise over living itself (*ATFV* 133).
The so-called 'warriors' of the poem of that name believe in systems
of their own making ('their comprehensive plan'), which they impose on the 'shabby towns' throughout the land, 'Thus re-discover-
ing heroic man / Pregnant with honour in service to The Cause'
(*ATFV* 134). Kennelly's contempt for these characters' conceptions
of heroism, honour and service is barely disguised in this grimly
sardonic closure. Yet if these poems, concerned as they are with
power and the self-righteous imposition of it upon others, may be
said to foreshadow Kennelly's subsequent interest in the Cromwellian campaign in Ireland, no character of the six in this poetic
sequence more resembles the Commander in Chief of the Army in
Ireland than the missionary, in the poem of that name (*ATFV* 134).
The missionary addresses his audience of potential converts ('Dear
souls'), in the condescending tones of the self-convinced. He is
God's representative ('My mind is made of His light'), and is certain that his audience of sinners must change their ways if they
should avoid damning ('all your gods must go'). They should develop humility and 'surrender to the true' (to him, that is). Here in
the use of an ironic persona who bases his power to impose his will
upon others on a claim to divine right, Kennelly has produced the
blueprint of the character of Cromwell as he is presented, or presents himself, in Kennelly's later book.

While Kennelly tends to express suspicion of the powerful, especially of the self-appointed, he has also at times voiced admiration
for the powerful persona who entertains no doubts and brooks no
opposition. The roots of his interest in Cromwell lie not merely in
hatred of the missionary English soldier but also in a sneaking and
even reluctant admiration for him:

> Powerful figures such as The Visitor and Cromwell attract me because
> they act as if they were intensely one in themselves, dramatically and
> passionately present to themselves and to others, sure of their own
> voices, capable of uniting fragmented people about them. Poems try to
> do that. Poems that know how to surrender to experience can achieve
> a tyrannical capacity to master it. (*ATFV* 13)

'The Visitor' is an early poem which portrays an unbelievably
confident, elegant, king-like visitor who overwhelms women and
children with his laughter. Ultimately he is likened to the force
and beauty of nature itself – 'He was all the voices/ of the sea'
(*ATFV* 43). The powerful figure in Kennelly's poems impresses
the author because he unifies the diverse, heals the wounded,
repairs the fragmentary. He has power over others, and embodies
a certainty which Kennelly has elsewhere said escapes the poet,
who gives voice to uncertainty in polyvocality. The powerful figure represents unity, and for Kennelly becomes an emblem of the
burnished poem itself, produced out of the flux of experience but
achieving a polish and fixity which experience lacks. The suggestion
here is that the controlling or ordering power of the masterful persona (including Cromwell himself) is related to the ordering power
of the artist, and thus the poet sees, even in the immoral imposition of control, a quality which he admires and desires for himself,
struggling as he is to control the materials of his own art work.

* * * *

Whereas the 1987 Bloodaxe edition of *Cromwell* displayed cartoon
figures of Cromwell and various Irish yokels and buffoons upon its
colourful and deliberately playful cover, the 1992 second impression
has a much graver feel to it (perhaps this is in response to the ser-
iousness with which the book has been received). The cover presents us with a detail from Robert Walker's (1607-60) portrait of
Cromwell. The right hand side of his face is illuminated, the left
faintly veiled in shadow. The dark, unshaven chin of Cromwell
contrasts with the white of his shirt collar. A streak of white paint
delivers the reflection of light upon his cuirass. Cromwell looks
composed, though tense. His mouth appears taut. He looks like he

hasn't slept for a few nights, which is appropriate enough for a book of bad dreams, which *Cromwell* might be thought to be. (The portrait would satisfy Cromwell's own request in Kennelly's poem 'Portrait': 'I am content that my face go forth/ full of sleepless nights, some remorse, long wars/...With public care written in all its lines' [*C* 143].) However, if the portrait suggests the brooding menace of the backbench Parliamentarian who rose through the ranks to kill a king, to crush the Levellers, and to suppress the Scots and the Irish, it also portrays an unexpected thoughtfulness, and a suggestion of the vulnerability which challenges the mythologised and demonised image of Cromwell which has been current in Ireland for centuries. (There is a striking contrast between this portrait and that attributed to G. de Crayer which is reprinted on the cover of Christopher Hill's important 1970 study, *God's Englishman*, in which the portrait sitter looks every inch the Lord Protector: inhumanly certain of his rectitude, and slightly mad.) The cover portrait suggests the complexity of Cromwell. The picture does not settle for a tired cliché about the religious fanatic, the bloodthirsty killer (although it does not exclude the possibility that the sitter is both of these); it suggests that a complicated figure sits among the shadows, and this is in part what Kennelly's book is about. As the cover portrait would suggest, this is a book about a historical figure, and, like all history books, it implicitly raises questions about how we know what we think we know about the past, mediated as it is by more or less subjective narratives, myths and fantasies. Kennelly has remarked elsewhere that his approach to writing history, or poetry based upon historical subjects, should not eschew the legends and myths which professional historians tend to dismiss, or attempt to deconstruct, but should embrace them wholeheartedly, since they constitute an integral part of how the memory of the past is communicated to the present; and this is in part what he does in *Cromwell*, juxtaposing extracts from Cromwell's speeches and letters with anecdotes from contemporary accounts, as reproduced by Lecky and other historians, and with legends about Cromwell and his men in Ireland. In this way, Kennelly deliberately merges fact with myth: 'It has always seemed proper to me to blend legend and history so that poetry is, literally, fabulous fact' ('A Small Light', *BS* 128). Although a history book of sorts, it is not a chronological narrative, nor does it appear to put forward a coherent argument about Oliver Cromwell. Its method is 'imagistic, not chronological', as Kennelly says in the preface to the book. At times, indeed, the lyrics appear to proceed in more or less haphazard fashion, though there is continuity at the level of image and theme, and at the more inscrutable level of association. For while this is a disjointed epic narrative, dominated by sonnets, and a history book, it is also a dream book, and a book of dreams, which take place in the mind of the character, the poem's 'little hero', in Kennelly's phrase, M.P.G.M. Buffún Esq. Kennelly writes:

> This poem tries to present the nature and implications of various forms of dream and nightmare, including the nightmare of Irish history. Just as Irish history is inextricably commingled with English history, so is this poem's little hero, M.P.G.M. Buffún Esq., helplessly entangled with Oliver Cromwell as the latter appears and disappears in history, biography, speeches, letters, legend, folklore, fantasy, etc. (C 6).

That is, the past is recollected in terms of Stephen Dedalus's well-known trope of history as inescapable dream; the past is witnessed by a consciousness (that of Buffún) submerged in a troubled sleep, in which the trauma of an entire country (and the triumphs of another) finds embodiment in the figure of Cromwell, and in the stories of revenge and rapine which are fixed to the memory of his Irish campaign. For Kennelly, the history of Ireland cannot be understood without considering its complex relations with England, and thus the study of Cromwell is integral to the study of Ireland itself. The poem's protagonist and fictional narrator is Buffún, whose name suggests his folly, although Kennelly clearly enjoys him; indeed he may be considered an aspect of the author himself, as well as an Irish Everyman persona. If the book's poems represent Buffún's dreams, then his dreamlife is pervaded by the image of Oliver Cromwell (sometimes represented by his own voice, at other times represented by historical and popular folklore narratives), as well as by a range of other historical characters, including Edmund Spenser and King William of Orange, and fictional characters, including the Hand, the Belly, Mummy (Buffún's mother, also appearing as Mother Ireland), and the Giant. These characters appear in Buffún's dreams, and may also be seen as aspects of Buffún himself, as voices within his consciousness: 'Buffún's nightmare is his own. Hence the fact that he is not a voice; he is many voices' (C 6). Kennelly attempts, therefore, at the outset, to frame the poem in such a way that its apparent diffuseness, its sprawling, associative exuberance and vigour, can be seen as unified by the monolithic, overarching character, Buffún, in whose mind these voices sound off. These are voices within the subjective life of the poem's 'little hero', who explains his complex, multivocal nature in 'A Host of Ghosts':

> I am slipping into the pit of my own voice,
> Snares and traps in plenty there
> If I ponder on shadows in the grass
> I will find Oliver, Mum, The Belly, Ed
> Spenser down in Cork, the giant, He, a host of ghosts... (*C* 16).

He might 'find' them, that is true, but he has already admitted, in 'Measures', that he has deliberately invited Cromwell, like some spirit of the Ouija board, to enter his imagination, his consciousness, his art work:

> I invited the butcher into my room and began a dialogue with him, suspecting that he'd follow a strict path of self-justification. Imagine my surprise when, with an honesty unknown to myself (for which God be thanked officially here and now) he spoke of gutted women and ashen cities, hangings and lootings, screaming soldiers and the stratagems of corrupt politicians with a cool sadness, a fluent inevitable pity. (*C* 15)

Cromwell's 'fluent' pity is surprising, considering his reputation for butchery, yet in the Cromwell poems in the collection, that note of pity and remorse is noticeably absent. When Buffún accuses Cromwell of 'following the most atrocious of humanity's examples' (Herod), and creating a dangerous precedent for posterity, Cromwell protests:

> I am not altogether responsible for the fact that you were reared to hate and fear my name which in modesty I would suggest is not without its own ebullient music. I say further that you too are blind in your way, and now you use me to justify that blindness. By your own admission you are empty also. So you invited me to people your emptiness. This I will do without remorse or reward. But kindly remember that you are blind and that I see.
>
> The butcher walked out the door of my emptiness, straight into me. (*C* 15)

Buffún feels 'empty', or lonely, invoking the ghost of Cromwell and others to people his dreams and to lighten his darkness. He feels vacant when dissociated from history, as if the present requires the infusion of the past in order to animate it. The past is thought to have a plenitude missing from the present. Like Buffún, the poet must invent characters in order to make his imagination come alive. The book is composed of poems in which Buffún's imagination plays host to ghosts, and in which Kennelly's imagination opens itself to their voices, articulated within the voice of the poet's mask or alter ego, Buffún. Cromwell and the others are personae Kennelly places upon the stage of his poetry. He explained the usefulness of poetic personae thus, in *Islandman* (1977):

> The use of a persona in poetry is not a refusal to confront and explore the self but a method of extending it, procuring for it a more imagina-

tive and enriching breathing space by driving out the demons of embarrassment and inhibition and some, at least, of the more crippling forms of shyness and sensitivity. A persona, though apparently shadowy and elusive, can be a liberating agent. It/he/she can provide friendly company in loneliness and give dignity to desolation. (*BS* 102).

The voice of the poem is not, as Yeats commented, the bare voice of the poet, that bundle of accident and incoherence that sits down at the breakfast table. Buffún extends the poet's voice, and provides multiple voices for the poet, within his own voice, which 'give dignity to desolation', and fill the silence of the poet's solitude. Yet if Buffún invites Cromwell to enter his dream, he feels very ambivalent about it; he wants to censure him, as in 'Measures'. In a poem appearing later in the book, 'A Relationship', Buffún describes his hatred for Cromwell, which persists despite the fact he knows it is inevitable to confront him, and to suffer the nightmare of what he was and remains:

> I hate and fear you like the thought of hell.
> The murderous syllables of your name
> Are the foundations of my nightmare.
> I can never hate you enough. That is my shame.
> Every day I pray that I may hate you more. (117)

Kennelly's urbane and sympathetic Cromwell tells Buffún to get it off his chest: 'I sympathise with your plight'. Buffún knows, however, that Cromwell is part of his own personal nightmare, and is essential to Ireland's history. Like any nightmare, the only escape is to wake from it, but that cannot be done without experiencing it from beginning to end, like a harrowing journey through the underworld. Buffún is resigned to suffer the dream in its entirety. He fantasises that 'when this nightmare is over' as he puts it, he might sit and drink beer with Cromwell, but he knows that is most unlikely, since his hatred is so deeply entrenched, and since Ireland and England, Catholic and Protestant have little chance of reconciling their differences. Perhaps the nightmare will never end. Although Buffún invites Cromwell into his imagination, this does not ensure he will stop hating him. Kennelly does not pretend to solve irreconcilable differences in his poem, though he thinks it important for those differences to find expression. Perhaps hearing the voices of the other will itself increase understanding, no matter how painful it may be to hear them. As Kennelly has said in an interview, 'I don't think any Irishman is complete as an Irishman until he becomes an Englishman, imaginatively speaking'.[9] Buffún is incomplete without Cromwell, and Kennelly's poetic voice is incomplete without admitting the voice of the coloniser; indeed the voice of the coloniser may be deeply attractive to him since the colonial presence has played such an important part in the modern history of the nation, albeit as initially an unwelcome and hegemonic element within it. Kennelly writes in his introduction to the book that the Irish poet, 'to realise himself, must turn the full attention of his imagination to the English tradition'. Similarly, Yeats recorded that he owed 'half my soul' to Spenser and Shakespeare. If Spenserian epic is for Kennelly a nourishing part of that English tradition, to which he makes repeated allusion in *Cromwell*, the most egregious aspect of that English tradition is associated with the barbarism which necessarily accompanied its 'civilising' functions. Cromwell rages in the centre of that barbarism.

* * * *

For Kennelly, as I have said, poetry is a democratic locus of dialogue between contesting voices within the authorial self, a sounding box, an auditorium for polyvocal freedom. In *Cromwell* he tries to portray not only the brutality of Cromwell but also his humane kindness to friends, family members, and his soldiers. While it is partly true that *Cromwell* is, as Declan Kiberd writes, 'a contrapuntal work, pitting various "protestant" against "catholic" stereotypes', Kennelly wants to avoid merely reproducing the stereotypical, demonising portraits which centuries of legend have established.[10] Although many depictions of Cromwell in the book do indeed represent him as a pathological killer, Kennelly seeks ultimately to give expression to the complexity of the man. Therefore the book has a biographical function, and attempts to explore the character of Cromwell in the context of a general meditation on the violence of Anglo-Irish relations through the centuries, from 1641 to the present. This biographical and historical drama is mediated, as I have said, through the imagination of Buffún, in whose troubled consciousness Irish history replays its violent scenes as though in some endless, circular Joycean nightmare.

Kennelly is fascinated by Cromwell for two reasons: firstly, because he is, at least in Ireland, a moral outcast, a despotic demon of antisocial space, and Kennelly has always been interested in the marginalised figures living on the periphery of communities. Secondly, Cromwell is a figure associated with immense power, self-confidence and personal conviction, and Kennelly is attracted to such figures even as he recoils from or distrusts them. In characters like the Missionary or the Visitor he finds a boundless self-confidence which is appealing even as it is obnoxious, which is both anti-democratic and yet strangely familiar to the poet who is author of his own fictional worlds, in which he exerts absolute power and authority over the materials of his writing. Perhaps the image of worldly power is for Kennelly, as it was for Yeats, an emblem of that passionate energy which fuels imaginative world-making. These contradictions are embedded in *Cromwell*. Buffún himself invites the butcher Cromwell into his mind, only to despise him. He entertains and yet chastises him; he abhors Cromwell's example, yet his whole imagination is focussed upon him, and his dreams are filled with his memory. Perhaps Buffún recognises that Cromwell is part of himself, and that the Cromwellian will to power is not solely the agency of British colonisation but is a vital force in human relations generally, and in Anglo-Irish relations in particular. The many poems in *Cromwell* which deal with Irish violence against the English, whether in 1641, 1921, or even more recently, points to the fact that for Kennelly there is blood on everyone's hands. His poems do not imply that Cromwell made Ireland into a violent place, but suggest that violence has always been an important mode of expression, or transaction, between the Irish and her many would-be colonisers.

Brendan Kennelly has described Cromwell as:

> a paradigm of power, of an egotism hard to understand and impossible to measure; of a compulsive need to possess and control; of an unquestionable value of his own being as a model for erring humanity...of a truly passionate sense of mission and purpose.[11]

Kennelly's terms suggest that he is attracted to Cromwell even as he judges him: his unfathomable egotism is posed as a challenge to the poet who might wish to understand his inscrutable motives and his boundless confidence; his will to power is excused in the name of 'compulsion'; his brutality is understood as an expression of 'passionate' sincerity and zeal. Despite this note of admiration, however, Kennelly does portray the Lord Protector as egotistical to an absurd and humorous degree. Cromwell loves the very sound of his own name, and repeats it to himself like a mantra, which strengthens and empowers him. It makes him wise: 'I grew strong as a horse,/ Sly as a fox, wise as I am now. I/ Heard my name throb in my soul. Beautiful!' ('Oliver's Mantra', 44). The sexual undertones of the image of his name 'throbbing' within him does not detract from the impression of Cromwell's self-absorption, but rather indicates the all-encompassing power of his dedication to himself. Absorbed and hardened by self-love, Cromwell is accordingly convinced of his own capacity to shape the future, and to make

the present in his own image. He announces grimly that 'History
is when I decide to act', a tyrannical declaration which suggests
his profound sense of personal destiny ('History', 51). Of course,
Cromwell's egotism must be understood, like so much else, in the
context of his religious faith, which permitted him to believe in his
role as divinely-appointed scourge of destiny, and avenger of the
slaughtered Protestants of 1641. 'Oak' conveys the passion of his
religious conversion as a youth, but tends towards a kind of manic
hyperbole which calls into question the wisdom of such zeal:

> High in the oak, he became a God-listener,
> God-speaker, God-lover, God-doer,
> God-body, God-mind, God-spirit
> And found the wisdom of the Word. (17).

The heavy-handed repetition here raises uneasily the question whether
Cromwell's faith is not a dangerous absorption in the idea of God-
liness which might blur the boundaries between selfhood and Godhead. Is Cromwell becoming a God? Is he mad? 'But this is not mad,
this mind/ Is the mother of lightnings and splendours,/ This is
sane, this, yes, this is most sane' (17). The poem's irony registers
Kennelly's amusement at the Cromwellian definition of goodness as
revenge and mayhem ('Make men of blood account for the blood
they'd shed'). The conversational tone of the poem's last line, with
its halting caesurae and its sense of ironic certainty interrogates the
nexus between religious belief, rationality and political justice, and
argues gently but incisively that Cromwell's mystical communion
with God is achieved at the expense of his sanity. This savage
Protestant God is hungry for revenge. Indeed, Cromwell's faith
throughout Kennelly's book is couched in such avenging terms. He
is 'like God's right hand' ('According to *The Moderate Intelligencer*',
23). He is 'a ready blade' ('A Man of Faith', 41). He believes in God,
'Who believes in what I do'. Perhaps we may understand Cromwell's religious faith in *Cromwell* most clearly in relation to his
patriotism. In 'Oliver Speaks to His Countrymen', which takes the
form of a speech to friends and supporters, he gives full expression
to a love of God and country which is equal only to his hatred of
England's enemies (Spain, the Pope, Catholicism, Levellers, et al).
England is 'an emblem of Heaven' and he regards it as his solemn
duty to defend her against these enemies (64). Although he believes
himself to be 'outcast from eloquence', he also believes that he alone
'speaks the Nation's will'. The tone of self-righteousness and moral
certainty in this poem is typical of the voice of Cromwell in the
whole book: 'the love of power is noble', he avers in 'Born Kings'

(101). His sense of himself as spokesperson for the national will (oddly reminiscent of de Valera's claim that to understand the common people of Ireland he had only to look into his own heart) indicates the depth of his conviction that he is God's representative Englishman, and paradoxically replaces the much-abhorred notion of the Divine Right of Kings with that of the Divine Right of the Lord Protector. (As Christopher Hill reminds us, the English revolution effected 'the transition from divine right of monarchy to the divine right of the nation': Cromwell claims part of that right on behalf of the nation, whose supreme representative he conceives himself as.)[12] This is one of the rich ironies of this poem, and of most of the poems in which Cromwell is allowed to speak. Kennelly attempts to represent Cromwell's beliefs as accurately (and respectfully) as possible, but the effect on the modern reader is one of distaste. It is extremely difficult to square an understanding of Cromwell as a liberating agent – anti-élitist, anti-monarchical, revolutionary – with the Fundamentalism and sheer despotism of his voice in *Cromwell*.

For Cromwell, Spain is not merely one of England's most formidable enemies, but is an ally to the Irish (the English feared the Spanish would use Ireland as a base for invasion), and indeed is probably responsible for instigating the 1641 rebellion, which caused the massacre of many Protestants (20,000 Protestants, according to Cromwell in the poem). The defence of England is a categorical imperative, synonomous with the defence of Protestantism generally: 'England is Protestant/ And will be to the end' (64). In 'The Saddest News' he laments the Protestants massacred by the Duke of Savoy at Piedmont – Kennelly's knowing wink to Milton ('Let blind Milton write harrowingly well', 146). There is a gravity to Cromwell's voice in these poems, a plain, majestic conciseness and authoritative directness. The voice is indeed eloquent in its way, although Cromwell believes he lacks eloquence, and is almost apologetic for his own language: 'I speak plainly. I have no words, no wit' (65). Plain style was of course a fundamental tenet of Puritanism. Lacking in adornment (or at least claiming to be so, though often heavily metaphorical), it was the voice of absolute truth, mediated through the impure but self-abnegating channel of the humble servant. Cromwell claims he speaks 'not words, but Things', collapsing signifier and signified in one rhetorical sweep; as often with the powerful, his words make things happen. Distrusting the capacity of beautiful words to cajole and deceive, he wages war on elaborate rhetoric with his violent plainness: he says conspiratori-

ally to Buffún: 'let's butcher Rhetoric tonight' ('Speech', 140). Yet
he is not completely free of vanity about his prose style, as for example that of his own letters. In 'A Friend of the People' Cromwell
claims his letters from Ireland have a natural passion, expressive of
the rugged, unmediated truth. They are ' "The honest chronicle
of my desire,/ Rough, shaggy as the Numidian lion,/ A style like
crags, unkempt, pouring, no lie" ' (24). Of course, if Truth is English Protestantism, the language of English Protestantism is the only
appropriate medium for Truth, and the language of the colonised,
accordingly, must fail to communicate such wisdom:

> 'I must confess, Buffún' honestied Oliver
> 'Your native language strikes me as barbarous,
> Rude in the mouth, agony on the ear,
> Your very name's ridiculous
> Suggesting some aboriginal fool
> Astray where he should be most at home.
> Stones and pebbles cram every native mouth, Buffún.' (45)

For the colonising authority, the language of the colonised constitutes a threat to cultural domination, and thus is treated as uncivil-
ised, Pictish, barbaric – as the speaker puts it in another poem, the
Irish language might 'Stir the people to question what is obviously/
A satisfactory condition' ('That Word', 40). By contrast, the English language is the language of God, 'which every Christian gentleman should use' (45). It is on record that Cromwell had ambitions
to 'civilise' or 're-educate' the Irish (despite the popular belief he
wanted to kill them all).[13] One obvious agency of change would of
course be the English language itself: 'Immerse yourself in that felicitous tongue,/ Absorb its music', he tells Buffún (45). Part of its
magical properties would be to delegitimise the Irish language and
deracinate the Irish from their cultural origins. The imposition of
English on the Irish is depicted in much less 'felicitous' terms in
another poem ('An Old Murderer's Gift'), in which the English
language is transported to Ireland, along with murder, rapine and
bloodshed: ' "But out of it, for you, this/ Language I bring, blood-
born, for your convenience" ' (39). Cromwell remarks: 'I will be
remembered as a killer of language' ('Oliver's Prophecies', 104). The
short sequence of poems in *Cromwell* (pp.39-41) which focusses on
the decline and suppression of the Irish language does not concern
Cromwell directly, though they are clearly related to Cromwell's
notion of the sacred integrity of the English language, and to the
issues of political and cultural colonisation which lie at the centre
of the book. In 'A Language' the speaker complains his language

has been stolen and an alien one imposed upon him (39). His indigenous language was buried, though the lost words occasionally
emerge from their graves and are becoming 'vengefully beautiful
flowers' – a dark hint that enforced dispossession will finally produce
vengeance. (The vengeance of the Irish emerges as an important
theme in *Cromwell*.) The Irish language comes to be hated even by
the Irish: in 'What Use?' the embittered speaker complains that
Gaelic is useless in securing a job outside Ireland; English cultural
domination has marginalised the indigenous language so successfully that it becomes hated by the descendants of the colonised.

Whereas linguistic colonialism is an important minor interest in
Cromwell, Kennelly gives full imaginative treatment to the representation of military violence, a more immediate and mythologised
aspect of the Cromwellian inheritance. Kennelly's account of the
devastation visited upon Drogheda and Wexford is of course mediated
through his own vital imagination, but is indebted to Cromwell's
letters and speeches, and to the accounts by Lecky, Hill, C.H. Firth,
Denis Murphy and other historians of the period (two poems, 'That
Leg' and 'A Bad Time' are based upon anecdotes recounted by
Lecky and others).[14] Kennelly presents Cromwellian violence in two
ways, and the two kinds of presentation alternate throughout the
book. First, the violence is explained (either by Cromwell or by a
narrator) in terms of its so-called educative, civilising, healing, or
spiritually redeeming value. Second, violence is represented as an
aspect of Cromwell's pathological love of murder and rapine. Sometimes there are aspects of the second kind in the first, thus the
killing, though explicable in terms of the Cromwellian world view,
nevertheless seems insanely cruel. We find examples of the first
kind in poems like 'An Expert Teacher' – 'The sword is an expert
teacher/ Like a drowning cry or the smell of burning' (69). Cromwell characterises the sacking of Drogheda as divinely-inspired
revenge for the 1641 rebellion: 'God ordained they be avenged' he
murmurs darkly, in a famous passage (69). He argues that violence
against the native Irish and the English Catholics united under
Ormonde is ultimately for their own good. Perhaps he 'revelled in
wrecking/ And killing, hacked flesh from bone', but this was because
he 'had a part to play and played that part' ('A Part to Play', 87).
Violence is also seen as 'surgery', as the benign removal of pathological tissue by the blade: 'If I conducted a terrible Surgery/ On
some, I pity them'; of course, the hand of the surgeon-soldier was
guided by 'the Lord's hand' ('Praise the Lord', 83). Elsewhere he
proclaims with self-righteous pride: 'I came here knowing I had

Surgery to do/ That you and yours be more alive than dead...'
('Severest Friend', 54). He thinks of himself as Ireland's (toughest)
friend, whose violence is redemption, whose murder is surgical aid,
cutting out the cancerous tissue from the country's living mem-
brane. Like Margaret Thatcher's metaphor of 'carving the joint' of
the workforce, in which the removal of fatty tissue from the edible
centre of the meat is seen as life-assisting, the act of severance is
represented as benign, though painful. (In both cases, the speaker
fails to question the sinister implications of a metaphor which compares whole social groups to unwanted tissue.) Cromwell's tendency
to claim divine approval for his actions tends to suggest not only
that he is always right but that his will and God's will are identical;
since he believes his will is the nation's will, and England is God's
anointed nation, then his will is identical to God's will. If so, how
could he make a mistake? And how could he ever know if he made
a mistake? Put simply, how could Cromwell ever believe he was
wrong, if he always thought he was right?

Those poems which represent Cromwell's violence as educative,
civilising, redemptive or life-assisting provide a rationale for the
sacking of Drogheda, no matter how inhuman or cruel the rationale.
It does not excuse the actions, but it provides a meaning for it:
Cromwell believed Catholicism was a spiritual sickness; Ireland was
Catholic, thus was diseased. Heresy is erroneous, barbaric, and
deadly, thus must be rooted out. Cromwell's actions made sense
within his own terms (it wasn't madness, but politics), which were
defined by English Protestant nationalism, although this does not
make it less repulsive to the reader. His actions may have credible
motives in light of his national and religious ideas, but as Conrad
wrote of the conquest of the earth, which he considered to be 'not
a pretty thing': 'What redeems it is the idea only. An idea at the
back of it, not a sentimental pretence but an idea; and an unselfish
belief in the idea – something you can set up, and bow down before,
and offer a sacrifice to'.[15] But what values become displaced or forgotten in the act of service to a mastering idea?

There is another group of poems in *Cromwell* which paints a
less charitable picture of Cromwell as pathologically cruel, and as
sexually stimulated by murder. The poem entitled 'A Condition',
in which the representative of a besieged town agrees to surrender
on one condition, demonstrates dramatically Cromwell's egotistical
craving for complete domination. One condition is one too many:
' "What? A condition?" roared Oliver./ In the burning of an eye he
grabbed the man,/ Smashed his head against the Mass-rock' (93).

The rather heavy-handed symbolism of being killed by the emblem
of one's own religious dissidence does not detract from the effect
of representing Cromwell's diplomatic skills as considerably more
'barbaric' than anything he thought he might have found in Ireland.
This impression of the Commander of the Army as personally unstable recurs in poems like 'Such Stories' (in which Cromwell is
seen to be as ruthless on his own men as on the enemy), and in the
surreal fantasy, 'Gas', in which an absurdly schoolboyish genealogy
is mapped out between the Devil, Cromwell and the gas which
'poured from Oliver's hole'. Hitler then secured the gas for use in
his death camps: 'An ambitious Austrian corporal came and har-
nessed it/ For the good of the European, white soul' (116, 100). The
comparison between Cromwell and Hitler propounded by W.C.
Abbott lies behind this particular image, as does the notion that
Cromwell's policy of 'ethnic cleansing' foreshadowed the ideologies
of subjugation and confiscation of nineteenth-century colonialism,
and the genocidal visions of racial purity in the twentieth century.[16]
A number of poems suggest that Cromwell became sexually excited
by the murder of innocent people; his men went on a rampage in
some small town. 'They had a ball', he claims: 'Splitting the women.
Well, Buffún, they were men./ I sat astride a stallion, a little off-
stage./ He was a noble brute, throbbing. We saw it all' ('Ghouls', 45).
This misogynistic image of murder as rape, which causes amusement and vicarious sexual excitment in the mounted Cromwell, whose
stallion obscenely represents his own sexual ambitions, delivers with
full force the legend of Cromwell's lust for dehumanisation of the
Irish. Of course, the implication of sexual violation undermines the
notion expressed by Kennelly's Cromwell elsewhere in the book,
that the campaign was surgical or educative, but *Cromwell* does
nothing if it does not explore contradictory accounts of events.
Other poems explore the image of Cromwell as violent sexual per-
vert: 'Honest-to-God Oliver' and 'Performance' offer grotesque
imaginings of the Commander's sexual yearnings in the thick of
battle, among the dying and dead. 'Sex is many men storming the
walls/ Of a town before breaking and burning', he proclaims. The
libido does not serve sexual intimacy as such, but plays its part in
registering the thrill of military domination: 'Screams of surrender
tickle my balls' (106). In a surreal, anachronistic fantasy ('Performance'), Cromwell is popping Dexedrine pills throughout the nine-
month campaign, which has an extraordinary effect on his hormones:
'I could perform, part the whisker, bury the bishop, do the trick,/
Striding among those dying groans and moans...' (107). Such

obscene juxtapositioning of images suggests how his whole being thrills to scenes of murder, in which his intimate parts are touched by the emotion of conquest over an enemy whose pain is aphrodisiac to him. The shock value of these scenes conveys the effect of Cromwell's personal insanity and moral depravity. Far from being a rational, purified agent of divine or national will, Cromwell appears monstrous and perverse.

Some poems in *Cromwell* concern what Terence Brown calls 'a bizarre platoon of mythological, archetypal henchmen', namely the Giant, the Belly, the Hand, and others.[17] These figures do not bear a direct relation to Cromwell himself, any more than the poems about linguistic colonialism do, although they clearly represent in allegorical form the kind of exorbitant greed and lust which the Cromwell poems adumbrate. The Giant is a monstrous figure striding across the Irish countryside, devouring all in his path, eating the roof of a Parish Hall, gorging himself on an onion field ('Onions', 18). Introduced to Oliver Cromwell by Buffún, he announces he is hungry: what should he eat? ' "For starters" Cromwell smiled, "try twenty thousand dead" ' ('Party', 28). The Giant represents the destructive power of Cromwell's army in Ireland of 17,000 men, a gigantic number of troops, 'a formidable army, by Irish standards', wrote J. G. Simms.[18] The Giant's devouring of fields and towns also suggests the confiscations of land from the Irish which Cromwell's campaign effected, but it also personifies the cruel force of war itself, and the hatred which fuels it. The Giant might be seen as the capacity for atrocity in both Irish and English, Royalist and Parliamentarian, Nationalist and Unionist, the fragmenting power which overwhelms community: 'But now I'm into Public Libraries,/ Cathedrals, Jewellers, Antique Dealers.../ Cities offer little beyond my range' ('A New Menu', 91). In imagining the creation of the Giant, Kennelly constructs an alternative creation myth (as in Ted Hughes's *Crow* poems), which explains the origins of the Giant in violence, bloodshed, and pain. He is what philosophers call the problem of evil in the world. He represents everything which Christianity demonises, and which war manifests: '...blood groans and sighs/ And throws up out of itself a spate/ To cover the world and create me' ('Pits,' 94). In a later poem of monstrous consumption the Giant eats the character known as The Belly, who has himself distinguished himself by feeding his son to his starving pigs ('Tasty', 94; 'A Bad Winter', 144). The Belly then eats his pigs. If the poem invokes the story of Isaac ('some strange tale in the Bible'), the larger context of the poem suggests Joyce's famous remark that

Ireland is 'the old sow that eats her farrow', and thus the Belly
takes on the form of a mythologised nation which destroys its own
offspring to ensure its own perpetuity, or to maintain its own
hegemonic power. The successive moments of engorgement in
Cromwell by numerous characters suggests a nexus between individual bodily desire and the demand for economic, political and
cultural power, and spectacularly dramatises the central themes of
domination and resistance in metaphors based on the consumption
and digestion of food.

The trope of conspicuous consumption, however, is juxtaposed
with the images of starvation attaching to the famine poems which
are peppered throughout the collection, and which carry considerable emotional freight, given that *Cromwell* was first published just
two years after ten IRA hunger strikers had died in the H-Blocks;
the imaginative link between the 1847 famine and the recent hunger
strikes is strongly implied in a poem which might be considered
applicable to Bobby Sands:

> As you watch your flesh turn black and blue,
> Notice your hearing break, your eyes go stiff
> And empty, your ulcerated mouth rebel
> At water, will you know, even then,
> Us, at home, so remote from caring
> For you, we stuff our bellies full
> At nightfall, sprawl, discuss the sacrifice of one
> Who, following directions, died of daring?
>   ('Hunger', 144)

The poet castigates himself for eating while the hunger striker
deliberately and slowly dies 'of daring', as though the poem itself
can make amends for the inequities of destiny, and can assuage
the speaker's feelings of guilt. The poem is an attempt, like many
poems in *Cromwell*, to face up to the worst that can happen and
has happened, and in so doing produce a vision of suffering which
can somehow be contained and imaginatively overcome within the
aesthetic framework of the poem. In that regard the book has a
tragic dimension, and expresses a tragedian's ambition, delivered
in the sequential form of a dislocated epic.

If the hunger striker starves of his own accord however, the
famine poems concern the deleterious biological, social and cultural
effects of famine. These effects are metaphors for British misgovern-
ment in Ireland, or worse, and the sufferings of the native Irish,
whether due to war or persecution, are inscribed on their impov-
erished bodies. In 'A Green Blanket, Folded', and 'And the Curse
Assumed Power', the horror of physical death through starvation

and famine fever is rendered in terms of the clear, bold imagery so characteristic of Kennelly's style in *Cromwell*. The bones of a starving woman stick out, 'deliberate as paling-posts', and her breasts have collapsed. The speaker's compassion wells up in him as he views the scene, and he shouts out 'Let the blanket swaddle her body and mind' (90). (Does this blanket perhaps forge another link to the H-Block hunger strikes?) The curse of Cromwell is envisaged not merely as the legacy of the sword, but the insidious and fatal effects of famine and disease which his campaign caused throughout the whole region of operations. Agricultural failure contributed to the malaise: 'the children became hunger', 'And the curse assumed power over us all' (122). These poems therefore do not merely allude to the 1847 famine but also to the starvation witnessed during and after Cromwell's campaign. Enforced emigration resulted from the 1847 apocalypse, of course ('I'm a Man', 98), and disease was inevitable, due to the reproduction of blood-sucking, infected lice, which ensured the malady continued ('Famine Fever', 120). However, most of the upper classes in Dublin remain oblivious, it seems, of the extent of the suffering of the famine victims; at least they do in Kennelly's poem 'The Visit', in which they banquet with the Queen at the Viceregal Lodge, while 'the poor went on dying at their usual rate' (120). In the light of the metaphorical resonances of famine in *Cromwell*, it is highly ironical that Cromwell himself uses the metaphor of deliberate starvation in his castigation of the Catholic clergy for disseminating 'false, abominable doctrine' among their parishioners: 'You cannot feed them! Their hunger is true' ('Oliver to the Catholic Bishops of Ireland', 132).

Cromwell accepted command of the Parliamentary Army in Ireland for two reasons: to suppress the Royalist conspiracy between 'old English' Catholics, Protestant Royalists and native Irish, and to exact revenge upon the Irish for the 1641 rebellion in Ulster. As historians have pointed out, there was no logic in punishing the populations of Drogheda and Wexford, which included English Catholics, for the rebellion of Ulster Gaels, but Cromwell felt that Irish insurgency, like Catholicism, had widespread invisible allegiances.[19] In order to frame Cromwell's invasion within a historical context, and to amplify the meanings of Buffún's phantasmagoria, which is Ireland's nightmare, and to demonstrate the bloody-mindedness of Anglo-Irish relations in general during the mid-17th century, Kennelly includes a number of poems apparently concerning the violence of the rebels in 1641, some of which are presumably rooted in the harrowing accounts available in the *Depositions of 1641* housed in Trinity College Library, which Kennelly cites as a source in his introductory note to the book. Many of these poems reflect the Irish demonisation of Protestants and Englishmen which is the mirror-image of Cromwellian hatred of the Irish, and the manner of torture and murder of the Protestant victims is at least as appalling as anything the Cromwellian soldiers visited upon the inhabitants of Drogheda, as portrayed in Kennelly's poem. In this way the poem avoids constructing the narrative of the Cromwellian campaign in simplistic moral terms, for the level of victimisation on every side is deep and unspeakably tragic, although it does risk the possibility of submerging an explanation for political violence (in terms of colonisation, insurgency, counter-insurgency) in a welter of spectacular and grotesque imagery. But that's partly what night-mares are about: the reader experiences the imagery without the benefit of explanation or causal connection, as Buffún does. In 'The Dose', a woman is whipped and drowned, her sister stripped and immolated, along with a 'big Protestant house' and its owners (58). 'Repeat the dose all through the province', orders the speaker, whose medicinal metaphor relies on a self-righteousness every bit as disturbing as Cromwell's conception of his task as 'Surgery'. A Protestant landowner is tortured and killed, fire-coals stuffed into his mouth, his entrails wrapped around his neck ('Birthmark', 59). The corpse of a Kildare Protestant is exhumed and violated, for 'They must not escape just because they are dead' ('Do Good', 60). A fifteen-year old girl is half-hanged and buried alive ('Rebecca Hill', 60). In the name of God, foetuses are ripped from their mothers' wombs, because 'little lords in the womb must not escape/ Their due' ('A Holy War', 62). Protestants 'are beasts', the 'enemies of God' ('Siege', 61). As one rebel pronounces, in a line which could easily have been Cromwell's, 'All that we do is for religion' ('The Cause', 73). (As Conrad said of the conquest of the earth, 'What redeems it is the idea only.')[20] A man is killed because he has 'English eyes' ('Larribane Rock', 131). The son of a Cromwellian soldier is hanged because 'Your father grabbed our land, they said' ('Why?', 57). Some of these poems about Irish violence against English settlers or Protestants are steeped in 17th century diction, and thus imply their origins in accounts of 1641, whereas others might be images of atrocities anytime in the last three centuries, perhaps in the 1920s, thus suggesting that the fantastic memory of the dreaming subject, Buffún (in whose mind these images flicker), is an endless, non-chronological narrative of suffering, colonisation and resistance, in which it seems as if, in the words of Terence Brown, 'everything in the poem is happening at once'.[21] There are even poems about the current IRA campaign. A car bomb kills children. Lord Mountbatten is assassinated. The whole of modern Irish history is represented in violent terms, or as a series of recurrent, violent cycles, beginning in 1641 and beyond. Like famine fever itself, the violence recurs interminably: 'you too infect your own lice./ That is how the cycle begins again' ('Famine Fever', 120).

Like the dead words of the Irish language which emerge again (with a vengeance) after long burial, Irish and English hatreds in *Cromwell* sprout 'like vengefully beautiful flowers', as though in obedience to the laws of nature (39). We might argue that the naturalisation of violence which this kind of metaphor implies tends to produce a deterministic account of history, as though the violence is bound to recur ineluctably and interminably. (Indeed, Terence Brown has remarked: 'Kennelly's work assumes the determinism of Irish history, but to portray this is not his primary purpose'.)[22] In its implications, this kind of historical narrative recalls that of A.T.Q. Stewart, in his study of Ulster history, *The Narrow Ground*, in which he argues that 'violence appears to be endemic in Irish society, and this has been so as far back as history is recorded'.[23] There is nowhere in Ireland 'that has not been at some time stained with blood'.[24] The history of the country is inseparable from its history of political violence and war. Stewart rejects the argument that conflict in Ireland has been generated by 'bad colonial government', positing instead the notion that there is something intrinsically violent in the Irish character, which completely determines the nature of Irish social relations. The urge to violence is, as it were, genetically coded in the national personality. While it may be tempting to resort to such an explanation of Irish conflict, unfortunately it rests on a definition of Irish character as essentially violent and uncontrollable, and thus resembles, and indeed reinforces, so many colonialist accounts of the Irish as irrational and warmongering. It also suggests that what Stewart calls 'patterns of violence' are bound to recur, in more or less similar forms, century after century – he argues, for instance, that there is a strong formal resemblance between 19th century agrarian unrest and the violence perpetrated by the contemporary Provisional IRA. What is gained by such a reading of Irish history as a predictable (and thus oddly reassuring) recurrence must be weighed against the loss of possibility which it offers, the sense that history is indeed a nightmare from which the Irish cannot awake, because it is bound by some

internal law to repeat itself. Seamus Heaney's *North* might be said
to have offered a similar view of Irish violence, in which contemporary tarrings and featherings, killings, and bombings, are recent
echoes or repetitions of ancient bronze age conflicts. Scandinavian
raids, invasions, 'neighbourly murders' and human sacrifices are
repeated time and again, age after age, united by an atavistic tribalism, a hunger for revenge, a Northern passion for bloodshed and
power.[25] In *North*, as in *The Narrow Ground*, there appears to be
no way out of the predetermined and self-perpetuating patterns of
violence. In both cases, violence is inevitable, ever-recurrent, in a
'commodious vicus of recirculation', like Joyce's Liffey, and inescapable.[26] Kennelly's *Cromwell* has a similar feel to it. Cromwell's
violence, which was in part a response to native Irish resistance to
the Planters in 1641, is the cause of further recriminations and
revenge killings throughout the seventeenth century, and finds a
violent and disturbing echo in Irish violence against the British and
Anglo-Irish in the 1920s. It resumes again in the 1970s, and continues to the present. These instances of violence, depicted in *Cromwell* as in many cases meaningless and feral, are juxtaposed ana-
chronistically and imagistically, detaching them from the local historical contexts which gave rise to them, and promoting the sense
that they are irrational manifestations of what Seamus Heaney calls
'tribal, intimate revenge'.[27] *Cromwell* is a powerful poetic study of
the problem of violence in Anglo-Irish relations, although it offers
little in the way of a vision of how the 'patterns of violence' might
end. By tracing continuous patterns of revenge from 1641 to the
present, Kennelly does adumbrate the continuities between moments
of brutal hegemonic domination and brutal resistance, although it
is arguable that the poems suggest a predestined propensity to
violence which is eternally inescapable. But for those who live in
Ireland, this is often how it feels, and Kennelly's task has been to
render that emotion of despair, rather than to provide a blueprint
for a new political dispensation. Having said that, Kennelly does
not suggest, à la Stewart, that violence is endemic to Irish character, nor does he argue, like many nationalists have done, that Irish
violence has always been a noble response to irrational English (or
Cromwellian) brutality, but recognises that the urge to commit
violence is widespread, and that Cromwell had his reasons, as do
the Irish: 'I remember thinking, as the blood escaped/ Into the earth,
that Oliver did what Oliver did./ So did the butcher. So do I. So
do we all' ('Vintage', 147). This moment of what you could almost
call forgiveness is crucial to the book's 'argument', and to the pre-

sentation of Buffún's dream as finally a transcendence of blind hatred and despair. As recognition scenes go, it is fairly muted, but it is brave and generous in its implications.

In 'Feeling into Words' Seamus Heaney wrote that his point of view as a poet:

> involved poetry as divination, as a restoration of the culture to itself. In Ireland in this century it has involved for Yeats and many others an attempt to define and interpret the present by bringing it into significant relationship with the past, and I believe that effort in our present circumstances has to be urgently renewed.[28]

This task of seeing the present through the lens of the past involves the representation of history so that it casts light on contemporary circumstances, and helps the poet to explore his or her relationship to the past. For Heaney, the representation of history has a redeeming or healing effect, whereby the national culture can be 'restored to itself', made whole again, having been fragmented, and empowered by a clearer sense of its past. Clearly, for many writers of the Revival, including Yeats, the retrieval of narratives from the Celtic period served to deepen Irish readers' sense of their cultural origins, and to raise their consciousness of the cultural uniqueness of Ireland, as a first step towards the more daunting task of achieving political independence. For contemporary Irish writers, however, including Heaney, John Montague, Richard Murphy, and Brendan Kennelly, the representation of Irish history does not have such a simple cultural nationalist agenda. Although these poets do rehearse the inherited lore of the colonisation of Ireland in the seventeenth century, it is usually seen as a response not only to their reading of history but to the current state of Ireland, and in particular to the contemporary violence in Northern Ireland. It is a significant fact that whereas Yeats, for example, exercised his imagination in reviving Celtic legends and literature, and latterly mythologised the Anglo-Irish eighteenth century, it is seventeenth-century Ireland which has provided an imaginative focus for numerous contemporary Irish poets. In *Wintering Out*, Seamus Heaney has invoked to ironic effect the voice of Edmund Spenser, from his *A View of the Present State of Ireland*, not only in order to expose the horrific consequences for the native Irish of colonisation but also to adumbrate the roots of sectarianism in contemporary Ulster, in which the poet is indeed wintering out.[29] Murphy's *The Battle of Aughrim* and John Montague's *The Rough Field* come to mind as analogous exercises in comparing contemporary with historical conflict. The reasons for this interest in the period are unclear, although they are surely bound up with the attempt to understand the crisis in present-day Northern Ireland by reference to a historic moment of subjugation, the Ulster Plantation, which was overseen by agents of James I. It is surprising that no Irish poet before Kennelly made Cromwell the focus of a sustained poetic treatment, a fact which in itself is worth examining, and which perhaps attests to the tenacity of the curse of Cromwell, whose eyes no poet has previously dared to meet in dreams, and whose gigantic presence in the Irish national consciousness has tended to prevent rather than to enable representation.

ANTHONY ROCHE

The Book of Judas:
Parody, Double Cross and Betrayal

Most people ignore most poetry, Adrian Mitchell once wrote, because
most poetry ignores most people. The same can not be said of
Brendan Kennelly's poetry. I know many people whose deepest
concerns have been spoken to by Kennelly in his poems, often the
part that is most hurt, wounded, ashamed, afraid to come out into
the light. His poetry ventures into that place of wounding, and traces
the consequences of what happens when that private, vulnerable
self is betrayed in the cruel light of public day. That betrayed self
is the subject of Kennelly's most complete work to date, *The Book
of Judas*, addressed through a variety of voices assailing the self
from within and without. This 378-page epic poem rivals Joyce's
Ulysses and *Finnegans Wake* in length, scope and intimacy. Brendan
Kennelly refuses to fence off the public from the private domain,
seeing this as the source of so much hypocrisy. His poetry turns
public events into surreal nightmare scenarios, with a Dante-like
throng of satirised representatives. The private is viewed not as an
escape or an alternative but as the site where these communal night-
mares come to rest. In *The Book of Judas* he draws on areas which
one of the poems describes as off-limits in contemporary writing
and critical discourse: the Heaven, Hell and Purgatory of Dante
and Milton, and 'the bloodmarvel of ordinary feeling' (*BOJ* 344).

The book is in many ways a logical successor to and development of its precursor, *Cromwell*, Kennelly's first long sequence of
short poems written around a central cultural icon. In seeking out
the figure of Cromwell, Kennelly was finding the least attractive
personality in Irish history, perceiving this hate-figure as a scapegoat for the aspects of our selves which Irish people were most
reluctant to admit. This project is amplified through the figure of
Judas as not just the Irish but the Western world's favourite scape-

goat. Unlike Cromwell, Judas cannot exist in isolation but inevitably conjures up the reverse mirror-image of the Christ he has betrayed. This relationship is beautifully rendered in the book's cover, Giotto's *Betrayal of Christ*, where the two gaze deep into each other's eyes just before (or after) the fatal kiss:

> I come to him
> I kiss the tired legends in his eyes
> I kiss the pleading lepers in his face
> I kiss the mercy flowing through his skin
> I kiss his calm forgiveness of sin
> I kiss the women hovering at his side
> I kiss the men who make him their cause
> I kiss the money made and lost in his name
> I kiss the murders committed by his children
> I kiss the mob adoring him
> I kiss the treachery of men
> I kiss the ways they will remember him
> I kiss the ways they will forget him
> I kiss his words his silences
> I kiss his heart
> I kiss his caring daring love
> He seems relieved (239)

As this passage makes clear, Judas's kiss relieves Jesus temporarily of his divine burden and acknowledges his humanity. It is that rarest of occasions in the life of Christ, a moment of true drama in which he is brought face to face with his humanity by another person and forced to cede dramatic ascendancy; but Judas's triumph in his kiss also seals Christ's doom and leaves him with nothing to say. The almost two thousand years since Calvary have left his church in the hands of the consciously chosen Peter and his successors; but from the point of view of Kennelly's poem the other half of the story in the founding of Christianity is the betrayal and rejection of Judas. Much of the poem's critique is directed at institutions, and not alone the Vatican or the hierarchy, for losing touch and faith with the true sinners, the outcasts and rejects of society: 'You need to get back in the gutter, you need/ To bleed profusely' (333); and, as the second coming looms, it seems to be the poem's conclusion that the 'thief, betrayed, forced underground' (353) may well become the new messiah.

Kennelly's Judas brings with him a sense of ineradicable loneliness and isolation. He is the man who deliberately puts himself beyond the reach of God's redemption. But he also expresses the irresistible urge to embrace those forces, images and figure in society which most threaten it. There is an inevitable complicity in what

is embraced and Kennelly's poem, like its title figure, roams relentlessly through modern Irish society satirically locating where the
promises of Christ have been compromised, where only the pariah
can point the finger and unmask the deception. The great theme of
the book is betrayal, betrayal of others but ultimately of oneself.
The betrayal occurs between and among the sexes, often in the
verbal and sexual act of love; of children by parents and authority
figures; and of those of its members for whom society has least
care. A particular concern of Kennelly, developed from his earlier
poetry, is the betrayal of trust, between those who have declared
love, and by those in whom society has invested its trust: 'lawyers
teachers priests/ Doctors executives entertainers clowns bores/...
and the busy cunts of profiteering whores' (337).

   The Book of Judas gives voice to those many, usually blasphem-
ous and incongruous, occasions on which 'Jesus' comes out of one's
lips: as an expression of disgust, as a cry at the climax of sexual
intercourse, as a byword for love. Much of its language and
imagery is brutal, coarse, shocking, as the poem provides its own
commentary on the betrayal of language, insisting that we confront
on the public page the unseemly expressions, emotions and experiences we prefer to keep unrecorded. Every act of writing is an act
of betrayal, particularly when the imagery and sentiments are derived from Christian ritual. But unlike the poets who pursue the
True, the Beautiful and the Good while averting their gaze from
what is around them, the 'judaspoems' acknowledge their excre-
mental origins. They make no claims to originality or uniqueness;
they are parodies, skilful imitations: 'if poets think they sing, it is
a parody they sing' (377).

   The art of *The Book of Judas* is the art of the parodic since the
kiss between Judas and Jesus is an act of mirroring, of replication,
a moment in which Christ is forced to own, not his singularity,
but what he shares in common with fallen humanity. The language in *Judas* acknowledges its fallen condition by its fecundity,
its ability to keep spawning one poem after another, by its refusal
to stay with the high style. As Kennelly puts it in his Preface:

> In this poem I wanted to capture the relentless, pitiless anecdotalism of
> Irish life, the air swarming with nutty little sexual parables, the plati-
> tudinous bonhomie sustained by venomous undercurrents, the casual
> ferocious gossip, the local industry of rumour-making and spreading,
> always remembering that life is being parodied, that this Christian cul-
> ture itself is a parody of what once may have been a passion. (11)

Two of the main strains of verbal parody in the book imitate the
self-congratulatory, hyped-up pitches of TV show hosts and sexual

athletes or replicate the street lingo of a young Dublin tearaway.
The reader remains conscious that these are imitations, however,
since the verbal artifice does not seek to conceal itself, and the
dramatic given of the work leads us to refer such statements to the
voice of Judas speaking through these mouthpieces. But as Judas
tells us at one point, he in himself is nothing and what people
read into him is what they cannot bear to confront in themselves.
The question is finally turned upon and implicates the reader:

> What story are you? Who dares know your style?
> Who will listen when you are spoken? And
> Of those who listen, who will understand? (355)

The Book of Judas is divided into twelve sections. The short first
section 'Do it' works as a kind of overture in sounding the themes
of personal and linguistic betrayal which will be developed throughout the work. The point of connection and departure with regard
to *Cromwell* is established in the section's title poem, 'Do It', where
the Irish propensity to substitute talk for action is challenged by
the icy clarity with which a Judas or a Cromwell translates his
desires into deeds. At one level, what they perform are acts of radical individuality; but at another what they betray and reveal is the
extent to which those desires are shared with other people. This
secret sharing makes of the poems themselves an act of betrayal, a
translation into the record of written language of what is usually
whispered, roared or left unspoken in the silence.

'Do it' also establishes the dual status enjoyed by Judas, both
as an historical figure and as a resurgent force in contemporary
affairs. The voice of the Good Book protests in one poem that it
is neglected in contemporary society; but Judas reassuringly replies
that, while the Bible may not be read as frequently as it once was,
its dramatis personae are flourishing: 'I just met Cain in the murderous flush of his youth' (23). As another poem puts it, the 'weak-
ling' Cain has to murder his brother, not once but many times, in
his inability to 'banish the shadow out of his bones' (25). Judas
himself refuses to die since, no matter how many times he is ritu-
ally laid to rest, there is no killing him off: 'I break out like the
bad weather/ And sprout anew in the young and daring' (25). This
cyclical recurrence means that the past and the present are continuously read in the light of one another. The Biblical stories are re-
told with the cynical awareness and knowledge of everything that
has happened since, the present read with an awareness of its mythic
avatars. When the fall is re-imagined, the original sin is no longer
a fable about a couple in a garden but a moment whose origins are

unknown and whose consequences continue to reverberate:

> There must have been a first time.
> Something was broken, a grace lost,
> A man sidestepped himself, a woman lied.
>
> In that moment, persecution and martyrdom
> Happened, two hearts learned not to trust,
> A remarkable person was betrayed. (24)

The ubiquity of Judas allows for greater imaginative play than did the more historically determined figure of Cromwell and results in a much greater range of dramatis personae. We also meet the other apostles in their various guises, Marilyn Monroe, Adolf Hitler, Pontius Pilate (endlessly handwashing), Barabbas and such talking personifications as Church, Heaven and Hell. Irish writers are among the epic cast of characters who lurch into the poem: Brendan Behan at the last supper, Patrick Kavanagh undergoing death and resurrection, James Joyce giving up sex with Nora for Lent or dissuading the holy family from emigrating to Ireland. The contemporary focus is double, on the warring nightmare of twentieth-century history and more locally on a satiric vision of a drug-, money- and drink-addicted Ireland, driven by forces it scarcely comprehends:

> Seeing a cat crucified to a telegraph pole
> The latest fast cars gulping the highways
> I realise God created the world
> In a psychedelic haze. (21)

The poems in *The Book of Judas* are radioactive in a number of ways, not least because the experience and technique, here as in *Cromwell*, is like randomly turning the dial and switching frequencies on the radio, tuning in unexpectedly to the voices coming over the airwaves of contemporary society. The poems themselves take on different voices in different times and places. In Section Two, 'Are the poems honest, doctor?', we hear the voices of the present dispossessed, drug-addicted children and beggar-women in Dublin's inner city. Judas is now the one who will listen – and reproduce – the voices of those betrayed. Many of them raise the question and consider the implications of breaking the silence. Where silence once surrounded the issue of child abuse in Ireland, the newspapers and courts are now being filled with harrowing accounts of its frequency. In 'A Pit of Dead Men', a character called Dr Bridgeman raises the aesthetic implications of ten-year-old girls writing poems and narratives about 'their fathers' lust':

> When I was at school we did Shakespeare and Milton,
> I learned *Paradise Lost* and all its epic beauties (32)

This eerily and accurately predicts what occurred when the singer
Sinéad O'Connor published a long poem (at her own expense) in
the Irish newspapers in late 1993, recounting her experience of
abuse and seeking to retrieve the lost child within her. Her poem
provoked controversy on two counts: it broke the taboo still sur-
rounding the Irish Catholic family by claiming that she had suffered physical and psychological abuse at the hands of her dead
mother; and it suggested that what she was writing was a 'poem'.
Brendan Kennelly defended O'Connor's writing, and attracted the
derision of the high-minded by saying that her poem deserved to be
on the Leaving Certificate syllabus for schools. As Sinéad O'Connor
herself warns, on her album *I Do Not Want What I Have Not Got*
(1990), 'you must try not to be too pure'. In examining the fraught
area of child abuse, the poems in *Judas* bear witness not just to
the experience of daughters but of sons. In 'Night Air' a mother
who comes upon her sleeping twelve-year-old son's erect penis
suddenly wants it inside her. The woman who entertains while
denying such desires will act them out in other ways; and only in
later years will the legacy emerge when the damaged son requires
women to act as whores or sexually available mothers. Kennelly
goes back further into Ireland's recent past to examine the effect
of male teachers who took out their perverted sexuality on their
youthful charges under the guise of legitimate corporal punishment. He is alert, here as in his earlier poems, to what is actually
being taught in class-rooms and to the ways in which a socially
gifted child can be educated out of its experience by brutalising
acts and words. Nor are children sentimentalised; they are in turn
capable of violent acts, a theme which goes back in Kennelly's
work to a poem like 'The Stones' (*ATFV* 38-39), where children
throw stones at an old woman and derisively chant her name 'Nellie
Mulcahy' over and over.

   The strength of the sequence lies in the way it builds up a circuit of betrayals in which no one case is absolute, and in which
the encounter between Judas and each particular speaker is hinged
around the question: 'What do I care?' ('Cardboard Child', 35).
There is a strong sequence in which the persona adopted is that of
a child of the Dublin streets called ozzie, who takes the sentimental edge off Roddy Doyle even as he utters his chant of defiance
in the same four-lettered, abrasive street lingo. Again, the vexed
relation between society and aesthetic raised by narratives about
child abuse is here addressed in the poem's debate with ozzie about
language, literacy and the need 'to kummynikate' (38). But ozzie

can communicate all he wants, 'no trubbal', as he puts it himself.
And he raises one of *The Book of Judas*'s key questions when he
asks who 'dis jesus fella' was. His own unwitting example shows
the name of Jesus frequently on people's lips, more as a term of
abuse than a benediction:

> but everywun sez jesus dis an jesus dat
> pay de jesus rent by us a jesus pint
> till i get de jesus dole
>
> but who de jesus hell was he sez ossie
> i dunno sez i your jesus iggerant sez he
> shuv your iggerance up yoor bleedin hole.
>   ('skool', 42)

If the children have been taught that the traitor Judas can not 'get
within an ass's roar of heaven' (47), the evidence on ozzie's own
tongue and what he has heard on others' suggests that Jesus's heavenly
place is not so secure.

The question of 'who de jesus hell was he' leads into Section
Three, 'I hear the pages crying', which examines how in the space
of two thousand years Jesus has become a god of insult. This is the
first section of the poem to look closely at the relationship between
Jesus and Judas. The thought of Jesus splits Judas's mind 'like an
axe a tree' (53); and Section Three is similarly split between the
sacred and the profane, between the emotions of fear and love,
located in the gap between the death of Good Friday and the resurrection of Easter Sunday. The split between Jesus and Judas
assumes the dialectical shape of paradox. Samuel Beckett found
that shape most memorably expressed through the intertwined
fates of the two thieves crucified along with Christ. Beckett quotes
a sentence from St Augustine, ' "Do not despair; one of the thieves
was saved. Do not presume; one of the thieves was damned" ', and
goes on to praise it in the following terms: 'That sentence has a
wonderful shape. It is the shape that matters.' [1] The discussion of
the two thieves by Vladimir in Beckett's *Waiting For Godot* arises
out of his comparison between the account of the crucifixion in all
four gospels. Kennelly's Judas finds that all four of Jesus's biogra-
phers give equally 'mesmerising versions of the man/ But not the
man I knew'. Judas undertakes to reimagine the life of Christ by giving birth to a more fully human Jesus than any of the four evangelists offer, one who might have had brothers and sisters, who
might have had a wider range of appetites and interests. In charg-
ing the Gospels with their incompleteness, Judas is a revisionist
historian claiming that many of the vital experiences of growing

up have been edited out or are missing; he challenges the centrality
of the official received version and promotes the interest of the
apocryphal.

Judas tracks Jesus by following the language he uses and finds
in it only the merest glimpses of the man himself; and the book
he himself writes appears to write itself, as the forms of history
and mythology dictate what is recorded. At every stage by which
the language expresses what it describes, the very act of writing is
a betrayal of that experience. It is always less than adequate, since

> There is no language that is not in vain,
> No beautiful line that is not profane (61)

The betrayal of Christ's doctrine of love in and by language reduces
it to a cliché, as more than one poem observes. But this is not an
end-point for Kennelly, since no Irish poet since Louis MacNeice
has shown a greater relish for the poetic possibilities of cliché. They
are the linguistic currency in which people trade and can not be
dispensed with. The poet's aim should rather be to restore something of the currency they once possessed:

> The first cliché is love. I tore a strip of his skin.
> Look at this cliché, I said, was it for this you died?
> Was it for this you dumped yourself in the loony-bin of sin?
> Yes, he replied. (66)

For Judas 'At the heart of nothingmatters, love is born' (58) and in
such lines one hears poetic echoes of Patrick Kavanagh, who sought
to 'record love's mystery without claptrap,/[To] Snatch out of time
the passionate transitory'.[2] It is in this section that previous Irish
writers start to gather, not in the dramatic personifications which
are to follow, but through the ghostly presence of the words they
have written, transmitted from the past and modified in and through
the guts of a living poet. I have already mentioned Beckett, MacNeice
and Kavanagh. But it is the ghost of Yeats who most haunts poems
which seek to interpret the advent of Christ through the distance
of two thousand years. The 'rough beast' once more slouching
'towards Bethlehem to be born'[3] is a Jesus re-imagined through the
'tracking, trackless, shapeless, restless,/ Sleepless head' (65) of a
prophetic Judas. He asks of his saviour the same tragic, terrifying
question which recurred to Yeats: 'Was his [Jesus's] life a prepara-
tion/ For what can never happen?' (64). In the space between then
and now, history has occurred. On the Saturday between the death
and resurrection, Judas reads a history book to discover that 'Eliza-
beth the First/ Took lessons in Irish Grammar from a book/ By

Lord Devlin' (68). Most of Section Three has been in the prophetic or visionary mode. In moving to the history or 'Bunk' of Section Four, the movement is away from the mythic antinomies of Judas and Jesus towards the process of historic colonisation in Ireland.

* * * *

The central sequence in Section Four of *The Book of Judas* is in the historical mode of *Cromwell*, a series of letters about betrayal and insurrection covering the years in Ireland from 1798 to 1803. The person to whom the letters are addressed remains unnamed, a necessary third or other who provides the basis of a relationship in which secrets may be betrayed. The fawning mode of address provides a kind of parody of intimacy and is going to be re-echoed throughout Irish history: 'Your Reverence, Father,/Right Honourable, Mister, Sir,/Your Grace, Your Lordship, Your Most High,/Your Holiness, Your Majesty, Imperial or/Otherwise' (114). The letters describe in hyper-elaborate detail the movements of people under surveillance, coming and going from houses. When the writer lists a housemaid as his most frequent source of information, sexual and political betrayal are folded one over the other into a single devious act. The more he writes and records, the more other people are drawn into the web, as friends, lovers, acquaintances, and enlarge the circuit of information. As the insinuations grow, they ultimately bring the source himself under suspicion. Having thrown himself abjectly on the Godlike mercy of his addressee, he ultimately has to work harder to turn in even bigger fish. This is now more explicitly a process of Irish men betraying other Irish men in the name of some transcendent, abstract, absent power of God or government. As Edward Said remarks in his Field Day pamphlet, *Yeats and Decolonisation*, power in a colony always depends on 'an authority based elsewhere'.[4]

Increasingly the writer is unable to say what, if anything, has happened and can only report on those who failed to act. He can easily follow a suspicious person through the open thoroughfares of Georgian Dublin but loses him in 'a maze of dirty places' (99) around Fishamble Street: 'The stinking lanes of Dublin contain the secrets of the earth' (100). The sequence ends in a rapid transition from the eighteen-hundreds to present-day Dublin. The ground has been prepared for viewing Dublin as a 'city of knockers' filled with 'the streets of sneer and the pubs of mock' (101). Long after independence, the legacy of colonisation continues in the verbal forms of innuendo, malice and character asssasination, bred out of circumstance, rumour and suggestion.

The Catholic Church has intervened in this process of cultural (in)formation, has colonised and taken sides. The National Anthem and 'Faith Of Our Fathers' are anthems of hate. Christ's miracles dwindle down to a National Teacher lashing the bum of a child in a brutalising scene of classroom betrayal which is something of a *locus classicus* in Kennelly's poetry:

> Augustine Clancy,
> National Teacher, despairing of my religious knowledge and my spelling,
> Yanks me in front of the First Communion class,
> Slips down my trousers first, then my fancy
> Underpants, lashes my bum till my yelling
> Splits the parish. Miracles, my ass! (118-19)

What they have been teaching, as those who remember their classes in Irish history can attest, is the doctrine of terrorism. Going out to die in the service of a myth gradually and inevitably gives way to going out to kill with the God-like power of a bomb. If you can not decide who will live, you can at least make sure that someone dies. Nowhere is Kennelly's poetry in *The Book of Judas* more politically astute or contemporary than in locating the logic of those who plant the bombs at the centre of an entire society and in seeing it as the product of a waning, despairing religious faith. Bombs are nevertheless a force with which the contemporary Irish poet has to reckon, since 'Semtex is more powerful than disruptive prose/ Or detonating verse' (121). Much of the reckless, apparently haphazard approach to the composition of *Judas* is explained by the analogy of its writer throwing poems like bombs, having to compete with them for the audience's attention. Not every poem in the book finds its mark, by a long shot; but those which do detonate with total effect. The poems lay bare the hidden motives of those who read them, just as 'Bombs have a tricky habit of betraying/ The intentions of the bomber despite the purest/ Patriotic intentions' (109).

Judas emerges in the present as a TV chat show host, with God as interviewee. Although he wins the prize in this world of glittering awards for proving that there is no God, Judas has some tough competition from civil servants, poets and academics who all put in for it. But it is the media circus which prevails, recycling the crucifixion as a video spectacle: 'One whizzkid thought it might be a zippy idea/ To interview Jesus on the cross/ But Christ declined' (107). Despite the silence of the central character, the whizzkid manages 'to patch together/ A programme that haunted the minds/ Of millions who saw it on coloured TV'. Much of the satire in this section is directed at the 'truth of statistics' (113), the modern world's desire to place its belief in empirical evidence as proof. So the miracle of Lazarus as he emerges from the tomb is validated by a colour photograph. As the final line of Kennelly's poem entitled 'Proof' puts it, 'Proof is what I do not need' (101).

Section Five, 'The chosen few in the heavenly know', applies the contemporary arena of elitist societies and moulders of opinion to the time of Christ. In considering 'this helpless treachery of men/ In churches beds governments colleges' (129), it looks at the treacherous process by which hierarchies are formed. In 'Interview', Judas applies for a job as an apostle in the manner of a civil service exam, gives the prescribed answers and is congratulated by Jesus at the close, ' "The job is yours".' But Judas's position among the twelve apostles turns out to be neither permanent nor pensionable. He recovers his irreducible singularity by his act of betrayal; but he also consolidates the hegemony of the remaining eleven since he can now so readily be excoriated as scapegoat. The mirror image for Judas in this section is less Jesus than Peter and the Church he founded. What they share is the fact that they 'both betrayed an innocent man' (141), Judas all at once, the Church across the many centuries in which 'that passionate adventure/[Became] a bad theological lecture' (152).

The 'chosen few' suggests that many are excluded, and this section looks at categories of humankind who may not even have been called. An unruly and uninvited guest at the last supper is Brendan Behan. Judas speaks for all those who would regard a dinner party ruined by the arrival of such a guest, 'pissed out of his borstal mind,/ His trousers at half-mast, blood bubbling his face./ "Where's the fuckin' drink?" he shouted at Jesus' (136). Jesus replies to all this turbulence in the calm, accepting voice of a George Herbert poem: ' "Come in, Brendan," Jesus replied, "Take your place".' Not only are rules of social etiquette and good taste being breached by Behan splattering through the door, but also questions of literary taste and canon formation. Throughout the lives and careers of both Brendan Behan and Patrick Kavanagh, stories were told in Dublin of their public carryings-on to denigrate both the men and their work; and Kennelly himself has most often been represented in wide media coverage as the broth of a boyo from Kerry. This coverage is in almost inverse proportion to his poetry receiving serious critical attention, at least until the publication of this very necessary volume. *The Book of Judas* offers the same kind of affront as Behan and Kavanagh, since there are those who

would prefer that the poet remain sober and strait-laced in his
iambic pronouncements of a brief lyric, while keeping his angry,
ebullient, outrageous or unstoppable form for the pub. Kennelly
has honoured the ghost of Behan by transferring so much of the
private man's spirit into the public domain of poetry while repud-
iating the more questionable legacy of a life-wasting alcoholism.

A more absolute exclusion from both the Last Supper and the
literary canon is raised in Section Six: ' "How is it?" I asked Jesus,
"You haven't even/A single woman among your twelve apostles?" '
(137). Judas's question echoes, intentionally or not, the debate sur-
rounding *The Field Day Anthology of Irish Writing* and its glaring
exclusion of women not only from its contents (where there are a
few representatives) but from its editorial board of twenty-two
(where there are none). Judas asks for 'A dozen women – to be
known as the Twelve Apostlettes' (137). Jesus replies with a wintry
smile that he will bring the matter up at the next meeting. Presumably, the result may have been along the lines proposed by Field
Day, who authorised a fourth volume covering women's writing.
Is this a further betrayal of women by ghettoisation or a genuine
redress of an injustice? Since Judas is the speaker on women's
behalf, how far is he to be trusted?

The issue of women's representation is wittily addressed by
'Where Is Little Nell?' (144-45), where Judas reveals that there was
a woman present at the Last Supper, but that the Great Masters
elected to paint her out. In 'Event', the threatened confraternity
approaches Judas as 'one/Of the genuine male-chauvinist pigs in the
city' and asks him 'to do/A Norman Mailer on those intellectual/
Girls... [and] show them/ How atrocious their prose is' (146-47).
In his versions of Greek plays, Kennelly has more directly taken
on the voice of woman through such tragic heroines as Antigone,
Medea and the Trojan Women, articulating a fierce, sustained
protest at their treatment down through the ages. In *The Book of
Judas*, the voice is that of a man and is split between concern at
their exclusion and a fear at their demands. The ambivalence is the
deeper because, although Judas soon joins the women in the ranks
of the excluded, he has known what it is like to sit at the table.

Section Six, 'You', is set at the furthest remove from that quasi-
heavenly congregation. Such a place is not the traditional Hell of
the literary epic, represented in the previous section by such Dante-
esque visions as being incarcerated for eternity at the receiving
end of racist Irish and Jewish jokes. For one thing, the 'devil may
not have you, of course' (169), since 'he's very pernickety/ About

those he's willing to use his words on'. The devil's accent is 'bland, posh, with the occasional/ Descent into crude if colourful peasant dialect' and as for his favourite reading, 'Milton is his favourite poet, he thinks the Bible is crap' (170). In this account, the world of a literary epic Hell is all too reassuring and familiar, too sanctioned by centuries of literary refuge, to offer any true heart-scalding or self-confrontation. Instead, in this vision, 'Hell is not where you go to, it's where you come from' (165).

Kennelly like Beckett imagines a post-Christian world, one which takes darkness and isolation as the basic ground of its being. Like Vladimir and Estragon in *Waiting For Godot*, Judas considers hanging himself in order to get a proper perspective on the late twentieth century, its 'maimed ruins' and 'the muck beneath' (157). The lines 'Consider me/At the butt-end of hope/ Twisted' (158), with 'rope' staring out through 'hope', echoes the early remark in *Godot*: 'Hope deferred maketh the something sick.'[5] This in turn is quoting from the Bible: 'Hope deferred maketh the heart sick, but when the desire cometh, it is a tree of life' (Proverbs, 13.12). The 'heart' that Beckett can not bring himself to name is placed under erasure, and the second half of the Biblical line which promises a divine redemption is no longer available. What resounds instead of the Bible's promised consolation is the silence; and the only tree in sight is one they consider hanging themselves from at the end of each act. Judas repeatedly attempts to open a dialogue with God, but the repeated reply to his questionings is 'Silence deep as eternity' (167). Judas in a way supplies his own answer when he remarks: 'I used to be disappointed [at the silence of God] but now that I think of it/ If I'd made the world I'd keep my mouth shut too' (167).

Where Jesus achieved complete realisation in his own lifetime, Judas is only being perfected now, in a century of victims and torturers. The intimacy which the 'You' of Section Six addresses is that between the executioner and victim; the gaze which one fixes on the other is that of accusation. Here, the Christ who emerges from Judas's pain and loneliness is someone who goes on to submit yet 'another man/ To the evil scrutiny/ Of your inquisitional glare' (163). In this section of self confrontation the 'I' is always another. Each becomes the other in a Didi and Gogo double-act which stresses the callousness of Jesus and the suffering of Judas. Section Six inhabits a place of pain and self estrangement in which acquired cultural attributes are pared to the bone. Linguistically, this is the book in which silence weighs the heaviest and in which all words not only express Beckett's stain upon the silence but a devilish one at that. If God has retreated from the world he has made, then Jesus is left in the same existential dilemma as Judas. The final poem's reference to 'heart's darkness' (172) acknowledges the complicity between the two and argues that the terms of their relationship must be renegotiated.

* * * *

The next several *Books of Judas* address that renegotiation in terms of economic and sexual relationships. In 'High on silver' (Section Seven), money becomes the obsessive object of the poems and the language. This section recalls the choruses in Kennelly's classical dramas who locate much of the tragic cause in the perversion of human relations created by money rather than in any obscure or metaphysical destiny. Judas recalls Jesus in the temple reacting to the activities of the moneylenders with 'one of his rare, scattering rages' and booting 'the moneymen/Out of the temple into the street' (178). One possible source of Jesus's anger was a realisation of the direct threat posed to his godhead by Mammon's rival claims for worship. Despite Christ's admonitions, it has proved all too easy to serve both masters. Judas is as virulously satiric as James Joyce in his denunciation of simony, whether he's presenting a priest out of Dublin and *Dubliners* 'padding along College Street,/ ...steered by a mystical sense/Of direction into a bank, with a bag of money' (175) or registering the mixed message in a church where the sermon and the collection coincide: 'The priest's words mingle with the money-tinkle' (178).

Kennelly is at his most Joycean, here and throughout *The Book of Judas*, in his embrace of the entire range of human language, not only the written but the spoken, not only the pure but the profane, because for him all language is used by people as the currency of their daily exchange. So he will use it in the full declaration of its perversity, its many-sidedness, as the thirty pieces of silver in which we must trade. On the basis of the metaphor that money talks, Kennelly writes a poem for each piece of silver in the first person singular. The voice of each poem has a greater personality than the so-called individuals between whom it trades and mediates: 'money talks, they say. Wrong. I'm silent, I don't even/ Have a mind of my own. All the other minds/ Pour into my no-mind. Some will surface, many drown' (185). The bartering is most often of the dreams of the young, bought off in the guise of advancement or getting on. Words as currency are at their most angry in this section, where the language of money truly impresses 'as poetry never will'

(188). A begging letter to the editor is revealing in terms of the notional value placed by the Irish on poetry and put to the practical point:

> Mr Editor, how much do you pay
> For a moment of durable insight
> Into this perishing day?
> Enough for last month's fire? Next month's light? (186)

Even Judas, who has taken on the guise of Mammon for this section, is appalled at the sheer number of his yuppie converts and makes them drink deeply of the cup of their own damnation. By comparison with the men of money, Judas comes across as 'a cautious knacker' (188). In its fierce use of the demotic and its satiric insider's knowing view of contemporary Irish society, Kennelly's writing lines up revealingly with that of a younger feminist poet like Rita Ann Higgins in 'Poetry Doesn't Pay':

> People keep telling me
> Your poems, you know,
> You've really got something there,
> I mean really.
>
> When the rent man calls, I go
> down on my knees, and through
> the conscience box I tell him
>
> 'This is somebody speaking,
> short distance, did you know
> I have something here with my poems?
> People keep telling me.'
>
> 'All I want is fourteen pounds
> and ten pence, hold the poesy.'
>
> 'But don't you realise
> I've got something here.'
>
> 'If you don't come across
> with fourteen pounds and ten pence soon
> you'll have something at the side of the road,
> made colourful by a little snow.'[6]

The early poems in Section Eight, 'All the same in the dark', would appear to adopt a feminist perspective, as they run contemporary variations on the figure of Ireland as a woman. In answer to the visionary question, ' "And did you see the Coolun/Going down the road?" ' (203), the poems offer a series of responses in the affirmative. But the persecutions suffered by the beautiful young maid are no longer those which can be laid at the door of the traditional perfidious Albion, but rather those resulting from the systematic suppression of the rights of women in a notionally independent Ireland, the continuing colonisation of Irish women by Irish men. When the Coolun goes walking, she now does so armed with 'pen-knife, scissors, iron bar' (202); when she takes the boat to England, it is to procure an abortion; when she enters a field, it is 'To have a baby all on her own' (203). The advice offered by the collective voice of her 'friends' is the same in every case, to stay at home, just as de Valera's 1937 Constitution inscribed the home as an Irish woman's proper place. But the picture of contemporary relation-ships between men and women becomes more complicated in Sec-tion Eight when it comes to the question of finding someone to blame, the man the woman, and the woman the man. The most frequent area of betrayal for the married couple is sexual infidelity, but those layers of betrayal are complicated when the wife says that she can cope if her husband doesn't tell her, or if he leaves her in the dark, as the section title has it. The person of the bride or groom comes last on the list of priorities for the wedding. The death of a spouse may be calculated in terms of money, but that in turn casts light on the true nature of their married relationship. In the society as a whole, women are often scapegoated as the means by which men are drawn to betray themselves sexually (through being 'occasions of sin', as the old Catechism would have it); but when Judas decides to undergo a sex change and try life as a woman, he finds that sex no less adept at betrayal.

The most disturbing area of this section, and the entire book, is those poems about sexual relationships which adopt an aggressive and narrow heterosexuality, reducing the male to an erect penis and the woman to an insatiable cunt. These are charged terms and dangerous territory. There seem to me occasions when the relish is objectionable – for example, when an intellectual woman is brought to heel by a good fuck ('A Brainy Lady', 207) – and too many occasions when not only the content but the tone and imagery celebrate phallic power. The successful exceptions are those which engage with these sexual terms as a form of human and funny dialogue, as a form of sexual give-and-take or come and counter-come. James Joyce and Nora Barnacle are one such couple; he gives up sex with her for Lent in return for washing her stained bloomers. 'The Fish of Darkness' contains the phallic imagery (of rocket and fist) by having the woman draw the sleeping man's penis into her and guide the exploration under her 'dark-waking touch':

> I hear you breathe and sigh
> And utter little cries at finding

> Words beyond my reach.
> You die in me, away from me
> Not knowing what you give.
> When you wake you vanish
> When you sleep you live. (227)

And the question which applies to the nature of the sexual act is also that which has to do with the questionable style which Kennelly pushes to its limits in this section:

> If this was fake, Christ, what is the real thing? (231)

After the eros of Section Eight comes the endlessly protracted death scene of Section Nine, 'I know I've arrived, can you tell me why I'm here?' The moment of Judas's death by hanging is refracted through dozens of poems, each so many hitches on a gradually tightening noose. Walter Benjamin has said that death is the story-teller's authority, the vantage-point from which a unique authority is gained;[7] and so the poems in this section look the furthest, back to the moment of his conception, ahead to a prisoner dying of AIDS in a Dublin prison. In terms of thinking back over the events of his own life, what comes to Judas as the most crucial are the sounds of a kiss and the voice of Christ saying 'I love you'. The notion of a death-bed conversion is parodied when

> As I kicked and jigged in my hanging position,
> I decided to make a quick, mid-air
> Act of Contrition.
> Mother of Jesus, it worked like a charm.
> My soul felt scrubbed and clean
> And though assorted blood-vessels were exploding in my head
> I was free of sin (267)

What Judas does gain from becoming a spectator of his own ex-tinction is a harrowing self-awareness. His hanging at Potter's Field is the equivalent of Christ's crucifixion on Calvary; but where the latter was a temporary condition by which eternity was re-engaged, Judas's sacrifice baptises himself anew in his humanity rather than any divinity, in 'soulstink,/Bodystink, bloodstink' (269) By witness-ing the moment of his death, he can record the fright in his own heart and directly face the crowd's appetite for blood. Judas is re-born, not once but many times and can be said never to have really died. What has been unleashed in his name spreads relentlessly as a miasma of verbal and ecological pollution; but he turns that around, as money did in the previous section, by claiming that there is no part of him which the world has not penetrated and stupefied. Further, since he is the one who is blamed, he is singularly free of

the human habit of blaming others and can claim a surgical precision in operating on himself which identifies him with Cromwell.
'I prefer/ To operate on myself that I may know the man to blame/
If I should err' (267). The nature of his ending gives him a particular affinity with those like Marilyn Monroe, who chose suicide
for their style of dying. The cloak of secrecy under which suicide
is wrapped ensures that Judas will continue to have a long life, since
nothing which remains in the dark can ever be fully known and will
continue to proliferate.

* * * *

The idea of a multiple Judas gives rise to Section Ten, 'Some lads'.
This is the section of the poem where the cast of characters takes
on epic proportions, expanding to include Pontius Pilate, Herod,
Barabbas, Adolf Hitler, an Irishman, Flanagan, and others. Section
Ten also promotes the notion of literary parody as the art proper
to Judas, the art of translation in the fullest sense. When Judas
decides 'to try my hand at forging/One of the Four Evangelists,
masters of bonny prose' (285), he ends up with bad translations
but fetching versions. His art of forgery exposes the procedures of
the first four gospel writers and calls their authenticity into question. Judas notes acerbically that a fortune is to be made from
writing a preface and postscript to *Ulysses* or a life of Beckett. The
relevant text here is Joyce's *Finnegans Wake*, wherein Joyce, or
rather Shem the Penman, is described as issuing 'an epical forged
cheque on the public'. In a sequence of poems, where James Joyce
is described at dinner with the Holy Family, his last book is likened
to the Bible (286). And *Finnegans Wake* might be likened to *The
Book of Judas* whereas their earlier epics, *Cromwell* and *Ulysses*,
were both centred on a single character; for Judas is not so much
a character as a variety of poetic devices and voices. The paradox
of the real and the fake emerges again in a poem about an actor
wanting to play Judas; instead, he is encouraged to play himself as
a 'real natural' man (306) In 'The Light of Men', Judas says that
he will survive all the actors, perhaps because he is the supreme
actor and knows them all to the core. In the section's penultimate
poem, Brendan Kennelly becomes a character in his own fiction.
Since he is a 'sick man' and suffering from 'judasfatigue' (323), he
is relieved of his authorship of *The Book of Judas* by Judas himself,
who takes it over on behalf of 'the lads and I' (323). The situation
is akin to that in Flann O'Brien's *At Swim-Two-Birds*, where the
characters gang up on their sleeping author, Dermot Trellis, and

seek to wrest control of the narrative from him. The author no longer owns a privileged creation. The text of *Judas* is endlessly hijacked, in this case when Michael Collins arrives to claim the book, unaware that he has been shot and that the Civil War officially ended seventy years earlier. In *The Book of Judas*, as in *Finnegans Wake*, the text is a series of apparently random encounters across time and space with deeply rooted historical and social determinants. It should come as no surprise that the very last poem in Section Ten is called 'Time' and that it should call for 'a commercial break' (324).

Cued by the appearance of Michael Collins, the politicians move in to the poem in Section Eleven, 'He will be mist'. Many of the Biblical cast of characters from the previous section re-emerge under the colours of local Irish politicians, good party members to a man. There is much praise for Pontius Pilate and his governing of the province, but they are speaking of the late Pontius Pilate since, as Judas shrewdly observes, politicians are 'more attractive dead than alive' (332). Herod is still living and active as a party politician; when scandal about his hiring of boy prostitutes causes questions to be asked, the party faithfully closes ranks around him, declaring 'Isn't he one of us?' (326). When Judas decides to go into political retirement, the speech given in his honour describes a 'mortally misunderstood man' who has had 'his ups and downs' (334). In this valediction forbidding blame, Judas's ethically questionable political career becomes a glowing tribute to a roguish adventurer who supplied some much-needed colour to the drab political scene. Is it any wonder that Judas's best efforts to find some genuine sincerity in the Irish Free State should prove fruitless and that he is forced to resume his 'Judassmile' (327)? The politicians come on the scene after the kill (of Jesus) and are represented in terms of scabs or parasites on the dead corpse of the original. This is a more satiric version of the cultural belatedness everywhere evident in *The Book of Judas*, the postmodern difficulty in distinguishing the fake from the real thing, style from sincerity.

The focus on the church in Section Eleven is on its sexual morality. The appointment of one Christy Hannitty as castrator raises the philosophical question: 'If God gives a man balls what's he to do with them?' (329). The poem 'A Mystical Idea' is curiously prophetic of the scandal which emerged in 1992 concerning the former Bishop of Kerry, Eamon Casey, his affair with Annie Murphy and their eighteen-years-unacknowledged son:

> Christy Hannitty thought it would be a blessing
> If he cut the balls off all the Bishops of
> Ireland because debollicked Bishops are less
> Prone to the terrible temptations of love
>
> Than those who are well-hung.   (329)

The sexual hypocrisies of a bishop are not all that are being assailed here. As the context of other poems in the section makes clear, castration is being metaphorically extended to describe what the educational and pastoral practices of these godly men have brought about in the bodies, minds and hearts of young people. There is at least some hope of redemption for the church, since it has the passion and blood of Christ's sacrifice to return to for renewal. The politicians are the more deeply damned, since their ideals have been the more thoroughly corrupted and they have less of a philosophy by which to steer themselves. The churchmen locate a better life in the next world and so the more honest of them can find room to admit the deprivations of life in contemporary Ireland; the politicians are determined to preach that we live in the best of all possible worlds, either now or in the near future, and so have difficulty admitting anything in the social sphere which contradicts this (like mass unemployment or emigration). The hypocrisy of both clerics and politicians is most fully realised when the poem turns its attentions to suicide in present-day Ireland. From the Catholic Church's point of view, suicide is against the will of God and 'gravely sinful' (335); from the politicians', no other practice the more gives the lie to their lying speeches. It is left to Judas to voice his understanding of the position of a man with no prospect of work killing himself: 'We have hundreds of thousands of unemployed/ Potential suicides in our land of busy rain' (335). Section Eleven is the most relevant to contemporary Ireland and the most focussed on what does and does not get into the newspapers, setting the official stories of politicians, pundits and priests against the uncovering of unofficial stories – the social facts of emigration, the high rate of teenage suicides, the love-children of self-professed celibates. Nowhere does Kennelly's writing more vindicate Ezra Pound's dictum that poetry is the news which stays news.

The final section has the loaded title, 'The true thing'. It comes closest to establishing a normative, authoritative stance and style from which the rest of *The Book of Judas* can be assessed (and so provided many of the quotations on which my opening remarks were based). And yet in this book of paradoxes here is perhaps the greatest, since the thrust of the last section of *Judas* is to sanction

the abandonment of all styles, to achieve the articulation of nothing:
'I lock my lips on nothing and go free' (340). The author, over-
whelmed with nausea and guilt, was relieved of his responsibilities
by Judas several sections earlier. He now undergoes a death and
resurrection in relation to his own text only to re-enter it as one
of the dramatis personae rather than as the God-like manipulator
of the material. And Judas is the agent of his resurrection:

> I saw the present writer stretched face
> Down on the floor of a mucky place
> In a posture of moan-and-groan disgrace. [...]
>
> Others fled, I approached and said, 'Your health
> Is vile, your vision slanted, your style uncommon. Rise
> Up, you stinking get, and tell my story.'
>
> As from the dead, he upped. The rest is commentary. (353)

The term 'the present writer' suggests only a temporary occupa-
tion of the role, that there are others from the past and future who
will supply it. Patrick Kavanagh is one of those and makes his
own return into the poem; thrown into his beloved Grand Canal
by three Dublin businessmen, he is born again from his satiric
verses into a poet celebrating the everyday, the apparently random
and trivial. There is a glancing but loaded reference to the *fatwah*
against Salman Rushdie and his *Satanic Verses*. Where the edict
against Rushdie is literally life-threatening, Kennelly is alert to the
demonisation implicit in it and looking closer to home sees the
forces at work in Irish society which seek to crucify a writer into
a parody of his or her self. As his earlier poem *Cromwell* made
clear, these forces are as likely to be internal as external, the clam-
orous inherited voices shouting in the head.

It is only in silence and in listening that any real rebirth is possible. When you read Brendan Kennelly's *Book of Judas*, all the
words paradoxically give the sense of a great listener, of somebody
who is not only hearing the words that people say but reaching
behind the words to what the words betray: 'The small heart-
whispers they are trying to say' (341). The only way beyond 'a
story that's [...] a crafty lie/ Sucking the marrow from some bone
of truth' (370) is for the writer to treat language as the best doctor
would a sick patient. If language grows sick, clichéd and stale, the
true writerly response is not to give an official prescription but to
listen patiently to the words 'flickering at his thoughts' boundaries',
to try to 'catch the sound' of words exiled and under threat in
present day discourse. That process, as the entire poem has shown,

involves listening to the voices of others, in particular the stories
of the outcasts of society. The poem 'What's That?' starts with an
eloquently worded expression of this idea – 'What is God but
ourselves/ Hearing in eternity/ The voices we loved/ In the poor
opportunity of time?' (363) – but it soon runs out of steam, since
Judas as poet is never able 'to finish anything'. The language he
uses inevitably betrays 'the promise, the beginning'. The difficult
task of turning 'the key in the lock/Of my heart' may enable him
to listen to others but, as another poem puts it, even more crucially
to 'all the terrified strangers/ Living in me' (372).

The final task *The Book of Judas* faces is the problem posed by
gathering all these (of their very nature) random, disparate stories
into a book. For one thing, as the wickedly titled poem 'Field Day'
puts it, his endeavour 'to collect the scattered thoughts/Of the
Apostles and their apostles' (342) is bound to fail, since there is no
way everything 'people say/At guarded and unguarded moments'
can possibly be put between two covers. An enterprise which sees
itself as a chronicle of the marginalised and dispossessed is particularly, almost impossibly, vulnerable on the score of exclusion.
There is also the problem of aesthetics, which rises to a climactic
note in the very last poem, 'The True Thing' (377-78). Adorno's
dictum says 'no poetry after Auschwitz'. Kennelly's version here is
'Out of the smashed cities/ Works of art adorn the Vatican walls'
(377). And this section has a hellfire vision of poets performing 'a
dandy iambic dance' (369) and drowning in a sea of their own
abused language. In the context of late twentieth-century society, it
is no wonder that a romantic poet like the late Yeats should seek
'a theme and [seek] for it in vain',[8] clinging to a poetic ideal that
refuses to include many of the mundane elements incarnated by
Judas in the poem. The image *The Book of Judas* finds for its technique is closer to that of Stephen Dedalus in the 'Proteus' chapter
of *Ulysses*, picking through the silt and seawrack of language along
Sandymount Strand:

> If there's a way to find the nothing in the heart
> It must be a story. O I have mine but when
> I try to tell it to a man or woman
> It's all bits and pieces
> Like walking by the shore alone
> Some winter morning when the tide is out.
> I have a plastic bag to put my story in: [...]
> My bits and pieces accumulate; the story makes itself;
> There, if anywhere, I am trapped enough to belong. (366)

The Book of Judas does not claim to tell the whole truth or to offer a complete, coherent narrative. It is, as Spike Milligan once entitled a collection, *A Book of Bits or A Bit of a Book*. It does not so much demand from its reader the unflagging physical and mental concentration to get through its 378 pages: it is an arduous read because it demands of its reader the same unflinching honesty, to say 'yes' to some of its poems and 'no' to others, to admit those into our hearts which speak directly to the fears, secrets and betrayals which are lodged there. Even as we are reading *The Book of Judas*, it is reading us.

KATHLEEN McCRACKEN

Rage for a New Order:
Brendan Kennelly's Plays for Women

In the early 1970s F.E. McWilliam, one of Northern Ireland's foremost visual artists, produced a series of bronze sculptures entitled
Women of Belfast. A direct response to the Troubles, these stark,
disturbing figural works depict women besieged by civil war. Arms
and legs akimbo, dresses ripped and blown, their anguished facial
and bodily gestures are a powerful register of the physical and
psychological shock caused by bomb blast and gunfire. While *Women
of Belfast* has been regarded as an 'untypical excursion' into political
specifics on the part of an artist noted for his preoccupation with
abstract universals,[1] the series nevertheless remains among the finest,
and certainly the most mnemonically indelible, of McWilliam's
works. And however rooted these sculptures may be in personal,
emotive experience, particular place and event, they also achieve a
comprehensiveness which makes them at once prehistoric and
futuristic, emblems of Ulster in the late twentieth century and of
human suffering and endurance across time and place. It is this
quality which brings *Women of Belfast* graphically to mind when,
almost twenty years later, one encounters Brendan Kennelly's plays
about and, I would suggest, for women.

As the prologue to his version of *The Trojan Women* gives way to
the action, the prone figure of Hecuba is discovered as dawn breaks
on a battlefield before the fallen city of Troy. Hecuba's physical
attitude, her position of obvious defeat, yet of equally obvious
defiance, like that of the other women who will creep then learn to
rage their way across the stage, finds a striking visual correlative
in the postures of McWilliam's *Women of Belfast*. Both are ironic
evocations of the all-too-familiar stereotype of woman as victim
and martyr.

The point of the comparison is not simply that Kennelly's women recall McWilliam's, but to trace lines of instructive continuity between the ways in which two contemporary male artists on the island of Ireland have rendered the experience of women under different but not entirely dissimilar sets of personal, social and political pressures. Of course it is by no means unusual to find male Irish writers attempting to get 'under the skin', 'inside the heads', of women. One need look no further than Shaw, O'Casey, Joyce and Beckett or, more recently, John McGahern, Brian Friel and Paul Durcan, to discover a 'tradition' of sorts, the integrity of which continues to be a subject of critical debate. Kennelly's oeuvre is shot through with a close attention to women, from the early poems of *Let Fall No Burning Leaf* (1963) and *My Dark Fathers* (1964) through to *Cromwell* (1983) and *The Book of Judas* (1991). In the numerous public addresses and critical commentaries and, most notably, in the plays of the eighties and nineties, we find unique and varied approaches, each of which extends, yet is at the same time distinct from, those of his predecessors and contemporaries.

An inclusive study of the presences of women in Kennelly's writing, while entirely valid and much-needed, is beyond the scope of our present purposes. I wish to concentrate here on that portion of Kennelly's work in which this element registers itself most overtly. That is, in the cluster of plays or, more precisely, versions of classical Greek and, on one occasion, modern Spanish drama. There are four in all: Sophocles' *Antigone* (1984), Euripides' *Medea* (1988) and *The Trojan Women* (1990), and Lorca's *Blood Wedding* (1990).[2] The initial three form an obvious trilogy, both in terms of theme and historical framework, and are the focus of this discussion. However, the version of *Blood Wedding* is not the exception it may seem, for it continues to develop methods and concerns evident in the earlier pieces as well as to experiment with form, idiom and characterisation.

Given the condensed period of time during which these plays were composed, it is not surprising to find a certain amount of stylistic and contextual overlap with, and influences from as well as on, the poetry and prose written at about the same time, particularly the song cycle *A Girl* (1981), *Cromwell*, and several articles touching on the topic of women and violence in Irish society.[3] But before making a detailed analysis of the individual plays, it is perhaps advantageous to consider their position in Kennelly's oeuvre and in relation to his poetics, his particular *Weltanschauung*, as well as in a broader contemporary Irish context. Why the acute sensitivity to, the close identification with, the female experience? Why choose these particular plays as vehicles for exploration of that experience? What is Kennelly's understanding of a 'version' and how does it compare to those 'versions' of Greek and French drama by, for instance, Seamus Heaney, Derek Mahon or Tom Paulin? Do the plays exhibit a developing dramatic aesthetic? Is there a political agenda, a specifically 'Irish' dimension? In short, what are the personal, socio-political and archetypal implications of Kennelly's versions?

I have suggested that much of Kennelly's writing attests to an acute listening and giving voice to women. While this can be attributed to an ease and familiarity with traditional orature, with its insistence on the primacy of the spoken word, as well as to an informing dramatic tendency, it also derives from a deep personal commitment to the accurate apprehension and exact expression of female experience and identity. This is not to imply the invention of a masculine form of *écriture féminine*, but to recognise a productive surrender to what for Kennelly is a key 'obsession': women's fight, women's rage – a paradoxically empowering, creative rage – against centuries of oppression and exploitation by men. Kennelly has talked about this aspect of his writing from different angles and in different pitches, and to consider his comments is to realise that his emphasis on the feminine is bound up with what may be regarded as two fundamental aesthetic principles. The first of these he calls 'givenness' or 'going-outedness',[4] the second 'uncompromising consciousness'.[5] Givenness is a consequence of empathy, of attempting to imagine one's self as other, and thereby educating the self towards altruism and the contingent qualities of grace, humour and sympathy.

> It's about letting your imagination be enhanced by a *difference*, woman, Cromwell, Judas, others...[it is an attempt] to know that your self is not important, and that what matters is your empathising, and that paradoxically this is what creates the vitality in your nature: givenness, going-outedness, the imagination as something that makes you more alive inside, that turns your despair, your depression, your desire not to be, into vital forces of being.[6]

What Kennelly is describing, of course, is the making of personae, the adoption of dramatic masks and voices, for as he remarks elsewhere, 'For me, poetry is an entering into the lives of things and people, dreams and events, images and mindtides' (*BS* 10). And it is his attraction to 'the boundary-breakers, the limit-smashers, both in myself and in society',[7] along with his conviction that poetry 'must find its voices in the byways, laneways, backyards, nooks and crannies of self' (*ATFV* 12) which has led him to Antigone and Medea, Hecuba and Cassandra, Lorca's impassioned brides, wives and mothers – and to Cromwell and Judas. A lot of people in Ireland need to be 'contaminated' by these outcast energies. That 'contamination' might just begin to substitute humanity for hatred (*BS* 10). The irony is that much of what has been 'outcast', 'silenced', deemed 'contaminated' in Irish life is also that which is most intrinsic to human nature; the tragedy is that all too often these properties are the locus of feminine, or feminised, experience.

This displacement of the self with what is other is at the heart of Kennelly's mature identification with women. It originates in a childhood where the father's pub and later the all-male preserves of the schoolroom and the football club constituted a world of men which found its opposite in the mother's kitchen, the chat and storytelling of neighbour women, the Tarbert lessons of an esteemed teacher, Jane Agnes McKenna. In adult life it is shaped by marriage, fatherhood, the intellectual challenge of female students at Trinity, and the impact of the international women's movement on the status of women in Ireland. All these factors contributed to Kennelly's understanding of 'givenness' which he perceives predominantly in women. He defines it as 'an instructive radiance, an easy light-shedding, a weightless caressing of bewilderment into intensely lucid personal knowledge, a tenderising of rough frustrations, hastes, envies, calumnies, fatigues, futilities, felt on the skin of the body and the spirit' (*ATFV* 13). Many poems point to the absence, or at least the lack, of this quality in Irishmen (in which category Kennelly includes himself), while others expose how, when women's natural givenness is thwarted by the strictures of patriarchy, an unspoken rage expresses itself in a range of defiant, violent actions. The most powerful and moving of these poems is 'A Girl', a twenty-two part song cycle in which, as Kennelly describes it, 'I tried to enter into the mindtides of a young person who decides to drown herself' (*BS* 12). Pregnant and unable to endure the inevitable humiliation of being an unwed mother in a small Irish town, the girl delivers a series of monologues which follow an emotional logic leading to probing questions and disturbing conclusions:

Deeper darkness of the water,
Child-darkness moulding son and daughter,
Darkness of God's living air,

What will the darkness bear?

KATHLEEN McCRACKEN

118

Darkness of my father's house,
Love so sweet and perilous,
Suffering no one dares to share,

What will the darkness bear? (*BS* 146–47)

...

They gather together to pool their weaknesses,
Persuade themselves that they are strong.
There is no strength like the strength of me
Who will not belong. (*BS* 150)

Kennelly has stated that for him there is 'a connection between that girl and the enraged women, suffering their sense of betrayal and desolation, who many years later prompted me to do a version of Euripides' *Medea*' (*BS* 12). The women he refers to are women he met and observed during the summer of 1986 while undergoing treatment for chronic alcoholism in St Patrick's Psychiatric Hospital. In their sometimes inarticulate rage against the men who abandoned, betrayed or beat them into 'madness', Kennelly detected not just a profound wound, but a searing consciousness, a 'hopeless gulf between them and the men they described' (*M* 7). Medea came to epitomise Kennelly's 'devastating woman in a cell of rage' (*M* 8). But as well as being inspired by the women in St Patrick's, she is prefigured by the marginalised Kerry 'oddballs' whose public abuse and private suffering find their way into the indelible imagery and cadences of poems like 'Ella Cantillon', 'Litter', 'Miss Anne' or 'Smell'. Registered variously, the rage these women harbour is a common denominator in Kennelly's perception and record of the experience of Irish women in general. A direct line runs from the stalwart 'Trojan women' of his childhood through to the subversive anti-heroines of the dramatic versions.

'Rage' is a key concept in Kennelly's treatment of women. It is a term which invariably implies a degree of physical or psychological violence, and we should be reminded of its etymological origin in the Latin *rabia* which, rendered as 'rabies', denotes a condition of 'outcastedness'. The sources, manifestations and relation to poetry of violence, particularly the emotional violence which engenders rage, is a subject which preoccupies Kennelly. Many of his poems, from 'The Prisoner' and 'Law and Order' through to *Cromwell*, are studies in various kinds of violence, and the plays in question make extremes of emotional as well as physical violence pivotal. Kennelly regards violence as central to twentieth-century western society: 'Violence runs through education, ambition, the dream of middle-class parents for their children, the moulding of personality. Violence is basically something in us that cannot leave other people alone. The violence of the missioner, the violence of the educator, the violence of the parent.'[8] Yet he also acknowledges the obverse effect of violence, its power to inspire, liberate, transform: '...violence is very strange in that it does animate you, and there's no point adopting a bourgeois attitude, that "it doesn't exist", or that you have to educate it out of yourself. It's part of your imagination, it's part of what fuels your dreams, your nightmares, it's connected with your excitement in the presence of language...'[9] This duality generates what, in a different context, Kennelly has called 'the poetry of uncompromising consciousness'.[10]

In April 1986 Kennelly delivered the keynote lecture at the first Easter Conference on Anglo-Irish Literature at the University of Antwerp. The talk addressed the subject of poetry and violence, and is of major importance in the present context not only because it clarifies the concept of uncompromising consciousness but also because, prepared shortly after the completion of *Antigone* and just prior to the composition of *Medea*, it reflects on issues central to these and the later plays. What Kennelly appears to be interested in is not crude physical or verbal violence but transformation, the metamorphosis of that violence into something other, something creative and redemptive. He makes the case for a poetry, and a criticism, which does not sanitise, minimise or obscure the violence which enlivens good writing. Kennelly's remarks on the oppression of women in Ireland are worth quoting in full here, since they have a direct bearing on his delineation of women's situation and character in the plays:

> In Ireland, the most powerful single institution is the Roman Catholic Church... It is a predominantly *male* institution, though there are nuns everywhere. Only recently have Irish women begun to show any defiance against the Church; women were content, or *seemed* content, to go along with the fact and the implications of male domination. No divorce! No contraception! Sexual pleasure, outside of marriage, is a sin! Even *within* marriage, the purpose of sex is the begetting of children. And this *must* be the purpose – even if the mother is ill. Serious illness is no excuse. Many Irish women have died because of this kind of tyrannical, male-clerical thinking.[11]

This and similar claims were reiterated and intensified in a subsequent keynote address delivered to the Cultures of Ireland Group Conference in Dun Laoghaire in September 1991, where Kennelly again attacked the Catholic Church and the Church of Ireland as well as the State itself for the subjugation of women enforced by the patriarchal values and discriminatory sexual morality written into policies on contraception and abortion, divorce and ordination, emigration and unemployment. Kennelly's crucial point is that the uncritical, negatively-charged acceptance of these prescribed attitudes and mores, particularly on the part of Irish men, indicates one clear imperative: the 'feminisation' of Irish life:

> A lot of Irishmen would be less effeminate if they allowed their lives to be feminised. What is the word for this no-caring about women? I think it is called morality. It is also called respectability [...] Consciousness, I think, means the questing, vulnerable, promising, eager opening up of one's mind to the world of exciting alternatives. The sharpest consciousness never fully parts company with its opposite – unconsciousness. True progress is possible only between opposites. This is the flame in the dark – they need each other. But if there is no flame of sustained, developing consciousness, there is only the darkness of the closed mind...which is marked by a fierce and automatic resistance to alternatives, and by an equally fierce assertion of its own limited but ferociously held viewpoints or beliefs.[12]

Significantly, Kennelly finds one of the strongest resistances to the closed mind in the growing independence of women within the Churches, in the social and political arenas, and in the arts. The strength of these voices is twofold: they are articulating thoughts and feelings previously kept under wraps, and they are willing and well able to embrace opposites and alternatives, to speak for and about a synthetic, non-exclusive experience. *What* women are saying, and the way they are saying it, approximates to 'a new language', a language which, if we return to the 1986 address, constitutes the discourse of uncompromising consciousness, 'the poetry of hard, raw reality...of ruthless bringing-to-mind, of accusation and warning'.[13] Arguing at that time for a poetry inclusive of the violence which is the source of an enlightened and confrontational poetry, Kennelly is in fact arguing for the same cadences, the same courage and intensity, which he hears in the voices of Irish women in 1991.

Kennelly's poetics and his convictions about women, not just in Ireland but across cultures and throughout history, dovetail in the four dramatic versions he has produced during this five-year period. Givenness and uncompromising consciousness characterise each work, endowing it with personal, socio-political and archetypal meaning. All four allow for the extension of themes and techniques present in the earlier writing and pose challenges which are valuable to Kennelly both in his development as a writer and in terms of the issues he would put to a contemporary Irish audience. Indeed, Kennelly follows an established practice among modern and contemporary Irish poets. From Yeats's *King Oedipus* and *Oedipus at*

Colonus and MacNeice's *Agamemnon* through to the spate of recent versions including Paulin's *The Riot Act* and *Seize the Fire*, Aidan Carl Mathews' *Antigone*, Heaney's *The Cure at Troy*, Desmond Egan's *Medea* and Mahon's *The Bacchae*, the technical challenge of translating, adapting or, as has more often been the case, transposing or interpreting classical Greek dramatic texts has been bound up with the impulse not just to create 'parables for our times' but also with a need to re-examine precisely those binary oppositions and 'specific universals' which George Steiner, in his seminal study of the Antigone myth, identifies: 'the confrontation of justice and law, of the aura of the dead and the claims of the living...the hungry dreams of the young [and] the "realism" of the ageing'.[14]

Although a comprehensive study of the connections between these Irish versions has yet to be made, Anthony Roche's essay 'Ireland's *Antigones*: Tragedy North and South'[15] gives a detailed analysis of four versions of *Antigone* scripted in 1984: Paulin's *The Riot Act*, Mathews' *Antigone*, Kennelly's *Antigone* and Pat Murphy's film *Anne Devlin*. Roche finds Kennelly's version 'the least obviously Hibernicised' in terms of idiom and political metaphor, and certainly if we were to place Kennelly's versions alongside those of his contemporaries his would appear comparatively apolitical. If Kennelly's version of *Antigone* is less overtly political, if it is more conservative in its interpretation of the original text, this is in part because his interest lies not so much in Paulin's parabolising of certain figures and events in Irish and Northern Irish politics, or in Mathews' experimentation with postmodernist stagecraft (though both tactics are to some degree implicit in his project) as in stressing the feminist imperatives and, by extension, the broad humanist ramifications, which emerge naturally out of Sophocles' play. Roche proffers an astute feminist reading of the play, and, of the three male-authored versions he considers, concludes that Kennelly's pushes furthest in this direction, but that it too falls short of being a 'truly feminist Antigone'. 'Having brought us to the edge, Kennelly can go no further, both because his literary source does not and because that "black hole" is a woman–centred space towards which none of the three male writers...can do more than gesture'.[16] Since *Antigone*, Kennelly has gone well beyond this point. In the three plays which have followed he has moved progressively further into that 'woman-centred space' which, almost a decade ago, may well have seemed off–limits. Consequently we are able to reconsider Kennelly's *Antigone* both in its own right and as the foundation of his move into drama.

If Kennelly can be said to exhibit a developing dramatic aesthetic, then it must be regarded as part and parcel of what I have already said about the necessity for 'giving voice'. His primary motivation in turning to script adaptation would appear to have been to add scope and complexity to a poetry which has from the outset been markedly dramatic. The diversity of character types and the range of emotional intensity of the voices which animate the monologues and duologues, as well as those which inform the third-person narratives, by this stage in Kennelly's career required fuller, more dynamic representation. And this demand is linked to an independent determination to find precisely the right form through which to convey the personal and public issues relating to women discussed above, and to exercise the feminist-orientated agenda which was becoming increasingly central to his writing.

For Kennelly, then, a version is less the product of radical improvisation of the original text, less dependent upon linguistic contemporisation or contextual politicisation, than the aspiration towards what Steiner has called 'transfiguration': '...there are indeed translations which betray the original via "transfiguration", this is to say, whose verbal virtuosity, depth of sentiment, or historical impact surpass that of the primary text...For a full-length translation or adaptation to challenge its source and "stand in its way" is loving treason of a rare kind'.[17] This is much to write up to, but the enlightened humanism, and stylistic integrity, of Kennelly's approach is well-described as 'loving treason'. Kennelly works towards the articulation, and in that articulation the fusion, of the voices of Irish women today (and through them the voices of oriental, black, European and North American women) with the voices of women in fifth-century Athens and pre-civil war Spain.

However, it is equally important to recognise that Kennelly has moved steadily in the direction of more overt cultural criticism. From *Antigone*'s exploration of sisterhood and gendered responses to tradition and revolution, to *Medea*'s probing of the relationship between justifiable violence and female sexual identity, to the impassioned outcry against the victimisation of women in men's war games which provides the thrust of *The Trojan Women*, themes which also resonate in *Blood Wedding*, the mythical and historical contours come increasingly to define women's struggles in the twentieth century.

Kennelly's versions to date thus constitute on at least two levels, the syntactic and the semantic, a conscious effort to invent a language adequate to the voices of those women whose defiance of the patriarchal codes and power structures of Church and State, however silenced or ignored, he has been listening to all his life. They represent a sympathetic yet discriminating exposure of the sources and manifestations of that 'rage for a new order' on the island of Ireland. In this version of Irish life, a demythologised Mother Ireland is stripped of her status as an ironically crippling champion, whom sons must die for and daughters emulate, and understood for what she is – an empowering emblem of the collective strength, courage and potential of Ireland's women.

* * * *

The signal issue debated in Kennelly's version of Sophocles' *Antigone* is well-defined by one of his literary touchstones, Blake's dictum 'True progress is possible only between opposites'.[18] Kennelly's belief that Ireland's difficulties are rooted in the failure of 'closed minds' to embrace that which is other and opposite, whether in terms of historical reality, political and religious affiliation, gender or nationality, is concretised in the clash between the play's protagonists, Antigone and Creon. Indeed, the multitude of versions of *Antigone* produced from the sixteenth through to the present century, its fascination over and above virtually any other Greek tragedy for writers as diverse as Hegel and Hölderlin, Freud and Jung, Brecht and Anouilh, can be attributed largely to the fundamental dualities embodied in their characters. The problem, and the tragic source, in *Antigone* (as in each of the plays Kennelly has adapted) is that these opposites, however much they may reflect one another, remain irreconcilable.

Steiner contends that the excellence of Sophocles' play resides in its expression of the five major conflicts which govern the human condition. These he conveniently lists as: 'the confrontation of men and of women; of age and of youth; of society and of the individual; of the living and of the dead; of men and of god(s)', and goes on to analyse how, in their initial encounter, Antigone and Creon epitomise each category.[19] In opting to emphasise the dialectic of genders in his version, Kennelly has also chosen to highlight the drama's fundamental opposition. In doing so he is not, needless to say, breaking new ground. The subject of the play lends itself to a feminist interpretation, so it is not surprising that a number of feminist versions had appeared prior to 1984. But as Steiner is careful to note, it was not until the 1960s and the advent of 'women's liberation' that Antigone's radical feminism is championed over Ismene's generic conservatism. The prototype for subsequent stage

productions in this vein was New York's Living Theatre interpretation for German audiences of Brecht's version of Hölderlin's
translation, which instructs that 'Only women's authentic liberation,
only the utter refusal of Ismene's *notre sexe imbécile*, will break the
infernal circle...the false coupling of men and women in a traditional social order'.[20]

Kennelly adopts a comparable position in that, in his version of
Antigone, the drama becomes a site of recovery where women are
afforded expression of their 'unrestricted humanity', the male/female
confrontation is centralised, and female rights, whether to despair,
to connive, or to rage, are exposed as elemental to both the impact
of the performance and to human nature. In constructing his play
Kennelly was working out a clutch of immediate personal, cultural
and aesthetic problems in a new medium and within the confines of
a plot which, if he were to remain faithful to the original, denies
the easy resolution of the conflicts and questions the play raises. It
is perhaps best understood as a 'workshop' where the groundwork
for a developing dramaturgy and feminist aesthetic is hammered out.

The unique, double-edged love which is central to *Antigone* holds
a special fascination for Kennelly:

> In *Antigone*...I wanted to explore sisterhood, the loyalty a sister will
> show to a brother, against law, against marriage, against everything.
> There's no relationship like it; it has all the passion of your whole
> nature, this side of incest...it was a study of a girl all of whose impulses
> defied everything, in order to bury the boy, to give him dignity.[21]

Antigone's devotion to her slain brother Polyneices is blood-begotten,
unconditional. It transcends and therefore must defy the man-made
laws of the city-state; it is the root cause of the antagonism between
herself and Creon. But there is another sibling relationship whose
contours are more problematic. If the play has become an emblem-
atic feminist text, its status as such is in part due to the ramifications of the disagreement between Antigone and Ismene. Their
initial exchange summarises the issue which informs the action and
defines the two polarised responses to Creon's decree in Antigone's
radical defiance and Ismene's conservative compliance. Although
the immediate frame of reference is local and familial, the larger,
non-specific subject of their debate is, in effect, the position of
women in the governance of the city state and, by extension, the
amount of actual control they are free to exercise over their own
lives. Kennelly's diction makes it clear from the outset that Antigone
and Ismene are bound by a common 'curse'. Not only the stigma
attached to the house of Oedipus, a malaise which has brought

them 'shame, dishonour, ruin, pain' and lately left them 'robbed of
our two brothers', but their very womanhood, which renders them
powerless to counter Creon's despotism, makes them doubly afflicted.

As the children of Oedipus, and as women, the sisters appear
irrevocably fated. Yet Antigone and Ismene do not seem equally
oppressed by their femininity. For Ismene being female means (perhaps as a matter of choice, certainly as a matter of course) being
marginalised, uninformed. As her first words reveal:

> Antigone, not a single word of friends,
> Not a single happy or miserable word,
> Has reached me...
> I might as well be dead
> Because I know nothing more,
> Not, as I have said, one solitary word. (*A* 1)

Whereas Ismene has been kept, or has kept herself, well back from
the action, Antigone has been in the front lines, gathering information, weighing the meaning and the consequences of Creon's 'word'.
Antigone's visit to Ismene is designed to test the latter's 'loyalty
and love', to determine whether she is 'of noble blood' or simply
'the slavish slut/ Of a noble line' (*A* 3). If Antigone's words are hard,
they are consonant with her attitude towards Ismene from the start.
Her tone is reproachful of Ismene's isolation, and is reciprocated
in Ismene's somewhat impatient description of Antigone as having
been 'broody and wild' from childhood. Kennelly's diction con-
notes intellectual introspection, maternal anxiety and independent
action, all characteristics Antigone possesses but which offend and
inhibit Ismene's less assertive sensibility. Antigone has brought
Ismene to a neutral zone, away from the male preserve of 'that
court of sinister stone'. Here, the sisters are on 'female ground'
and Ismene is free to think for herself. Her response to Antigone's
challenge to help bury Polyneices, if not what she hopes for, is
clearly what she expects. Ismene's assertion that they are 'mere
women' who must not 'disobey the word of Creon' makes her position on the subordinate role of women, and therefore of Antigone's
threat to upset that order, perfectly apparent. For Ismene, the
authority of the state is paramount and she has neither the courage
nor the conviction to go against it. Antigone, on the other hand,
is not only unwilling but fundamentally unable to conform to the
prescriptions of what she sees as an unjust law. Her loyalty is not
to 'the ambitious living' but 'the mistreated, noble dead'. In choosing 'love' over 'frustration' she credits 'those laws/ Established in
honour by the gods' (*A* 4). The law Antigone is talking about pre-

dates and, in her view, transcends civil law: it is the law of kinship, which entails allegiance to a chthonic, intutitive, irrational but deeply religious sense of justice which is the inverse of Creon's rationalist meting of reward and punishment. Thus when Antigone speaks of her 'strength' as her most vital resource, what she means is the mental and spiritual conviction which keeps her sensitive to this knowledge. The case for civil disobedience as the 'right' reaction to self-aggrandising totalitarianism is virtually conceded in this opening exchange. Despite her departing reminder that 'Those who love you/ Will always hold you dear' (*A* 6), the majority of modern productions impress that Ismene embodies the reactionary, visionless outlook of the status quo, in especial the sensible, even-minded women upon whom the state relies for its tacit support.

Kennelly's version is not so single-minded in this respect. Without disturbing either the semantic richness or the political incisiveness of Sophocles, he manages to focus our attention first and foremost on the relationship between Antigone and Ismene as sisters and as women, and only secondarily on their function as the representatives of private and public interests, left- and right-wing thinking. We are made fully aware of the deep familial wounds which bind them, of their very different natures and, consequently, of the antagonisms which divide them. While he cannot but champion Antigone's heroic efforts, Kennelly is equally sympathetic to both sisters and is careful to emphasise that each is suppressed by Creon's strictures. Kennelly is at pains to draw out the tension between the sisters' love for one another and the difficulties they as women encounter in the political arena, and in turn to set that aspect of 'sisterhood' against Antigone's feelings about Polyneices. In seeking to define 'love', the question Kennelly asks is not which kind of love is greater – sister for sister, sister for brother – but how they are different, and what that difference tells us about human nature in general, and love in particular. He does this through a use of language which is direct and simple, yet emotive and poetically intricate. The dynamics of the sisters' relationship is conveyed through carefully modulated diction and intonation, which in turn directs us toward the issue of language and its centrality in the play.

Virginia Woolf once suggested that women experience, think and therefore write the world differently from men.[22] The relevance of this proposition to Kennelly's *Antigone* is worth pointing out: the exchange between Antigone and Ismene is essentially about correlations between language and gender, and so prepares us for Antigone's struggle towards 'articulate action'. Their debate is peppered with references to the power of language, from the initial allusion to the curse on the house of Oedipus through to Antigone's oath to make good her promise to bury her brother. The term 'word' is uttered no fewer than twenty times in the first 160 lines, and Kennelly's choice of repetition over variation is indicative of the weight he attaches to it.

While the play's primary conflict is between the power of authority invested in Creon's word and Antigone's bid to affirm that her promise is equally valid and right, the more subtle clash is between masculine and feminine discourse, between gendered ways of seeing and saying the world. Whereas Creon's language is the unequivocal and, as the chorus argues, necessarily uncompromising voice of effective government, the issue is complicated, and the drama enriched, by the fact that we are presented with at least two models of feminine discourse: Ismene's traditional posture of submissive silence and Antigone's vigorous challenge to patriarchy. The latter's 'cold words' are as rigid as Creon's, but with the difference that they involve the struggle for a language which fits her experience and her beliefs. Thus the question which becomes central to Kennelly's, as to any feminist, interpretation of the play is not simply which sister's stance is preferable, but which is in fact possible. The import of this opening section is succinctly summarised by Roche:

> The first scene between the sisters establishes a sense of woman not only taking over the moral vacuum left by men but transforming the image of heroism from violent self-assertiveness to ministering self-sacrifice.[23]

What follows is a development of this difference – the feminine alternative – via the enlargement of Kennelly's focus on gender and language. Each scene exposes the layers and ambiguities of the feminine incarnate in Antigone and her word made action.

Learning that someone has observed the rites he has outlawed, Creon is infuriated. In his ensuing tirade he twice reveals the unconscious assumption that such an act is beyond the province of any woman: 'What *man* alive would dare to do this thing?' (*A* 10) and later, 'If you don't find the *man* who buried Polyneices/...You will be slung up alive' (*A* 12, *my emphasis*). The same dramatic irony informs the vocabulary of the chorus' second ode, beginning as it does with the celebrated lines 'Wonders are many/ And none is more wonderful than man' (*A* 14). Here too Kennelly exercises stark incremental repetition to underscore that, even as a candidate for the most marginalised of creatures, woman does not qualify in the popular imagination:

> Whoever dishonours the laws of the land,
> Scorns the justice loved by the gods,
> That *man* has no city,
> That *man* must live where no one lives.
> Never may he visit my home,
> Never share my thoughts.
> That *man* must know his madness is his own
> And is not part of the people.
> *He* is a severed limb,
> A severed head
> Unacceptable to the conscious living
> And the restful dead.
>   (*A* 15, *my emphasis*)

The impact of the guard's revelation that Antigone, a 'mere girl', is the malefactor leaves the chorus stunned, Creon 'doubly-insulted'. The avian imagery which studs his report of her discovery sets Creon's curses 'Beating like the wings of maddened birds/ About to swoop and rip my brains and heart out' (*A* 16) against Antigone's maternal rage. Whereas Creon's threats carry the weight of imminent punishment, Antigone's pain renders her all but inarticulate, grasping for another means of pronouncing her sorrow:

> I saw this girl. She gave a sharp cry
> Like a wounded bird or a mother
> Brutally stripped of her children.
> When she saw the corpse deprived
> Of the covering dignity of dust,
> She cried a cry beyond all bounds of words
> And cursed whoever did that deed. (*A* 17)

The association of pathetic fallacy with Antigone's retreat from language is followed by a crucial exchange in which Creon addresses her in blatantly sexist terms. However, her immediate, subversive response marks a recovery of language and a recognition that she must learn to use it in her own way and to achieve her own ends:

> CREON. You, *girl*, staring at the earth,
>   Do you admit, or do you deny,
>   This deed?
> ANTIGONE (*looking up*). I admit it, *man*.
>   (*A* 17, *my emphasis*)

Antigone's challenge to Creon's masculine ethos is double-edged. When she asserts 'Word and deed are one in me./ That is my glory' and goes on to disclose that the people in fact support her but are silent in fear of Creon's reaction, she threatens not just to undermine the basis of his authority and power, but to equal and possibly surpass his perceived sexual superiority as well. In short,

Antigone implies that she will live as a man, something Creon fails to tolerate or understand: 'I would be no man,/ She would be the man/ If I let her go unpunished' (*A* 18).

In aligning herself with the non-secular otherworld of the gods, the underworld of the dead, Antigone seeks to counter hatred with love, to reinstate the non-patriarchal, alternative values of blood and family in place of the interventionist laws of the city-state. So complete is her commitment that she has chosen martyrdom over betrayal. As she reminds Ismene, 'I chose to die for love', 'My life is an act of service to the dead' (*A* 22-3). Yet however independent, her defiance is also an arguably self-interested gesture. For in her admonition of Ismene – 'There were two worlds, two ways./ One world approved your way,/ The other, mine' (*A* 23) – and later the chorus – 'You know all about men...power...money...But you know nothing of women' (*A* 34) – Antigone reveals what amounts to a personal religion which is prototypically feminist in premise and mode. For while she may oppose Creon on his own ground, 'as a man', she does not renounce her femininity; on the contrary, she pushes ever more deeply into that paradoxically new yet familiar territory where identity and sexuality are coterminous. Indeed, so unique is her venture that it carries her beyond the experience of either sex: 'I am a woman without fear/ In a hole in the rocks/ Where no man or woman dare venture' (*A* 35). Yet as a woman, Antigone is unaccustomed to such control and responsibility, and the prospect of self-creation is frightening, something which would choke her 'like the bone of a chicken/ Stuck in my throat...Like ivy choking a great house' (*A* 34). Trepidation, however, rapidly reverts to conviction, so much so that she can make the quasi-hubristic claim 'If I lived,/ I could change all the men of the world' (*A* 34).

The magnitude of the individual and the institution she is up against is fully exposed in Creon's treatment of Antigone and Ismene, and in particular of his own son, Haemon. His 'advice' to Haemon quickly degenerates into a diatribe in which women like Antigone are denounced as 'treacherous' and 'disobedient', and sons instructed not to think for themselves but 'Obey [their] father's will in everything' (*A* 26). This oration is symptomatic of his fear of being shamed by a woman – 'If I must fall from power/ Let it be by a man's hand,/ Never by a woman's' (*A* 27). Haemon's temperate appeal for a more democratic, pluralist, feminised form of government meets with a predictable rebuke: 'You would put a man below a woman...Go be a woman/ Since you understand the thing so well' (*A* 31). We are returned to Antigone's words to the

chorus which, in the light of Haemon's predicament, remind us of
the difficulties involved in making a place for women in established
male-centred codes:

> What man
> Knows anything of women?
>
> If he did
> He would change from being a man
> As men recognise a man. (*A* 34)

Finally imprisoned in 'the loneliest place in the world...a hole
among the rocks' (*A* 32), Antigone has made, it seems, the highest
sacrifice, exchanging marriage and children for a tomb.

The physical immediacy of her oblation links her 'body language'
to accepted notions about the necessarily corporeal, non-literate
nature of female creativity and self-expression, as well as bringing
it into line with the intuitive, emotive sphere she represents. By the
same token, however, it identifies female creativity – Antigone's
'word' – solely with female sexuality. Her individual protest is
ironically overcome by her gender, and the gap between male and
female remains unbridgeable. To see Antigone's tragic victory in
this way is to concede that because she is a 'mere woman' she
cannot, nor should she ever presume to, achieve the autonomy she
seeks, or address Creon in a language which is 'sexually pluralist'
and therefore politically effective.

Antigone's solitary courage *does* make her an exemplary woman
ahead of her time, but the 'body language' she uses to state her
case, and to achieve what measure of revenge she can, is in fact a
non-language. The audience is made to question the masculine
hierarchy Creon stands for, but at the price of Antigone's silence.
'If I lived I would change all men.' *If* she lived. Within the para-
meters of the play, however, her declamatory gesture dies with her
and she remains a victim, compelled in her death to share the silence Ismene recommends in the opening scene. Where Antigone's
language survives, of course, is in each new performance of the play.

I suggested earlier that Kennelly's *Antigone* is a 'workshop' for
both his move towards writing for the stage and the development
of a feminist aesthetic. In terms of imagery, diction and characterisation, it is obviously connected to the poetry; in terms of issues
and concerns it strikes out more forcefully than he had previously
done at the oppressive forces of patriarchy in contemporary, particularly Irish, society in the seventies and eighties. As Kennelly
shapes it, *Antigone* becomes a cautionary tale of sorts, warning both
the Creons and the Antigones (whether we understand them in

socio-political or psycho-sexual terms) in his audiences against the dangers, in the first instance, of denying the feminine, and in the second, of 'excessive love', of making 'too great a sacrifice' and an end in silence. Kennelly's *Antigone is* a play for and about women. Not only does it give Irish women a voice familiar in idiom and interest, but alongside caution it offers encouragement, finding in Antigone a model for the strength and conviction required to be 'mistress of your own fate', the author of your own language. The black hole Antigone must descend into is on one level an emblem of annihilating silence. But on another it represents the next stage on the journey towards 'articulate action' which is the destiny of all the Antigones we encounter in Kennelly's writing. Without that descent we would not have the voices of Medea and Hecuba and Cassandra or Lorca's Spanish wives and widows, for it is in this darkness that Kennelly has listened most intently to women as they learn to rage.

* * * *

In the course of her initial debate with Creon, Antigone tells him: 'Word and deed are one in me./ That is my glory' (*A* 19). Her claim of articulate action, realised in the enactment of her oath to confer burial rites on Polyneices, links Antigone to Medea, the 'heroine' of Kennelly's second version of a Greek tragedy. While Medea and Antigone are more different than alike in character and circumstance, each has been wronged, marginalised and ultimately enraged by a male-centred social order, and both have paid a high price to make good a verbal promise, in Medea's case to murder her husband's lover and her own children. As in *Antigone*, however, the status of Medea's achievement is ambiguous. Kennelly ends the play with a question, one which leaves Medea's entire enterprise provocatively open to opposing interpretations.

The chorus concludes its exode by asking: 'Is Medea's crime Medea's glory?' (*M* 75) The carry-over of the term 'glory' makes an overt connection between the two women, with the obvious difference that in Medea's case the conferment of fame and majesty is a more complex, morally-loaded affair. The importance of this line to Kennelly's *Medea* can be judged if we consider that the majority of translations, in accord with Euripides, do not end with this or any other question, instead resolving the play with the chorus' assertion that the outcome of human affairs rests in the hands of the gods. Kennelly's addition of this question signifies both the personal and the cultural importance of the key issues addressed

by his version. There are at least two possible responses to the
chorus' question, one positive, the other negative, each plausible
within a given context yet dependent for that plausibility upon the
perspective from which we view Medea's predicament and her
reaction to it. The first I will call a 'feminist' reading, the second
'socio-political'. The contrast is that whereas the first model is
about the recognition and accommodation of difference, however
painful an exercise that may prove to be, the second is about the
denial of difference and the intractability (at this stage at least) of
opposite positions.

In choosing to adapt *Medea* Kennelly has entered into the 'female
space' from which playwright and audience are excluded in *Antigone*.
The informal praise of women lauded in the Preface to *Medea*
makes a clear aesthetic statement about the role of feminine perception in Kennelly's writing:

> ...most of the insights about life and literature I've picked up from
> people, rather than my own attempts to think, have come from women...
> women have a way of saying perceptive things that is very different
> from men... Somehow or other, certain women, when they decide to do
> so, get to the core of almost any matter touching on feelings much more
> precisely, and with an astounding mixture of sensitivity and something
> approaching an unemphatic brutality, than most men are capable of
> doing, or even seem to wish to do. (*M* 6)

Not surprisingly, Kennelly attributes the impetus, and the sustenance, to prepare a version of *Medea* to women, in particular the
women in St Patrick's Hospital whose words of rage – 'savage, pitiless and precise [against] men, Irishmen like myself' – he listened
to while drafting the play (*M* 7). He is candid, too, about the personal reasons for taking on Medea at this juncture of life and career.
The product of the dual disruptions of family breakup and alcoholism, 'Medea is chaos of a kind, it's chaos in her mind; *my* mind
sympathising with *her* chaos'.[24]

The confluence of private and public pressures is transmuted in
the play into a modern Medea – 'a devastating woman in a cell of
rage' – betrayed, hurt, but above all conscious of the horror, the
fundamental wrongness of that betrayal. Kennelly's Medea differs
from Euripides' in this key aspect. While she possesses the same
'savage truthfulness' as her prototype, her aim is not purely destructive revenge, though that is undeniably part of it, but the education of her oppressor. It is her objective to raise Jason to the same
level of consciousness, and to lower him to the same depths of despair, as he has brought her. And it is in the binary ramifications
of this educative process, on the one hand benign and improving,

on the other malignant and retarding, that 'disguises are ripped away' and we are confronted with the Medeas and the Jasons beneath our own skins.

If we take the plot of *Medea* to focus on an act of revenge, then the whole of Medea's undertaking, her education and its concomitant psychological self-recovery, is rendered, according to Kennelly's views,[25] pointless and self-defeating. Yet however vengeful Medea's performance may be, this is not exclusively the angle from which Kennelly would have us read his version. The language alone is a barometer of a much broader intent. Here we are meant to understand Medea's revenge, her violent, barbaric rage, in a different and indeed positive light, one which Kennelly has summarised in a single sentence: 'At the roots of good taste lies barbarism.' He explicates this 'embrace of opposites' in remarks on Yeats's 'Easter 1916':

> Violence is the begetter of sweetness and gentleness. Murderous disorder is often the source of that beautiful, unruffled self-possession and order which are associated with style.
>
> Men with fanatical political causes embody this contradiction; they, the agents of change, are driven by a purpose that cannot change.[26]

If Medea does, in the end, achieve the kind of 'style' Kennelly is talking about, if her experience is transformative and educative and not merely destructive, it is because she has descended into the chaos and darkness of precisely this kind of fanatical conviction. Her surrender to a rage which verges on madness renders her extraordinary, the object of public condemnation, but it also puts her in touch with that source of violence which can be animating, vitalising, refreshing, which affords 'the barbarism of the truth'.

As in *Antigone*, one of the elemental oppositions in *Medea* is the confrontation of man and woman. In Kennelly's version, the dichotomy is the axis around which the entire action turns. It is possible to trace a feminist strain in the language and focus, and to determine certain lines of continuity between *Medea* and the other plays for women.

At the outset of the play Medea is cast as the archetypal victim. Betrayed by Jason's winning of another woman who can advance his position in society, her love is turned to grief and hatred, and ultimately to rage and revenge. The Nurse's immediate pity, matched later by that of the Teacher and the Chorus, however, is tempered by an awareness that Medea is perhaps not as broken as she seems. Medea is first described as lying prostrate on the earth, her eyes 'riveted on the clay, as if/ she knew that nothing lives above the grass' (*M* 13). What we initially construe as an attitude of extreme sorrow is revealed as a sign of Medea's otherness, of her association with primitive, subterranean forces deemed dangerous and evil:

> When I see her prostrate on the earth
> I know she is drinking the knowledge of the evil dead,
> the fiery strength of poisoned spirits,
> the secrets of malignant centuries. (*M* 14)

Medea's affiliation with the earth is repeatedly recognised as the source not just of her witchcraft but of the intellectual and spiritual strength which will restore her to her naturally 'fierce', 'deadly', 'upright' character. In Kennelly's version, Medea's earth-bond is identified with her femininity. Not only does this cause the archetypally feminine properties of earth (fertility, maternity, nurturance) to accrue, however ironically, to Medea; it also suggests a personal inner preserve which harbours the potential to fortify and inspire or disorient and madden. The Nurse and the Chorus fear the moment when Medea will 're-connect' with this latent energy because they know that it will free up her rage.

Throughout the opening scene Medea is perceived in terms of dualism and deception. She is 'prostrate' and 'broken' but she will be 'upright', 'fierce and deadly' (*M* 15); 'her kiss/ is deadly, her caress/ a warm poison. Her touch is/ gentle, but her will is iron' (*M* 19); she knows 'the meaning of prayer' and 'the meaning of revenge' (*M* 23); she will veil 'the deadly wandering of poison/ in the guise of irresistible beauty' (*M* 23). Kennelly makes Medea's two-facedness consistent with the double 'lives' which women have led and, in large measure, must continue to lead: the outward, public aspect of conformity, submission, propriety – the 'Ismene face' – and the inward look – the 'Antigone face' – which registers resistance, rebellion, rage against the patriarchal structures which prescribe this divided existence.

Earlier we have learned that 'Even as a girl/ Medea had a dangerous/ way of thinking about herself and others...Among women [she] has the most cunning mind of all' (*M* 14–15). As a woman, Medea's weapons against masculine intolerance have been her keen mind and her sharp tongue. Creon admits he fears her cunning mind and cutting tongue, and while Jason appears less tractable, judging Medea 'unaware/ of the infinite possibilities of...civilised language' (*M* 35), in putting his case against her confesses that even he will need 'some skill in speech/ to escape the roaring storm of your words' (*M* 38). Beneath his accusations lies an ego outraged and intimidated by her actual mastery of words.

Here, Kennelly again centralises the issue of language and gender, so that before Medea makes her first substantial speech we are apprised of the linguistic and ethical impact her words can effect. The chorus' initial utterance is more than a declaration of sympathy and loyalty; it identifies Medea's voice as her most distinctive feature, and her use of language as original with her. Her words constitute not so much a 'non-' as an alternative language which surpasses conventional communication in its articulation of acute emotion:

> Every sound she utters is such
> a cry of grief, all language could be
> drowned in it. She makes me think that
> the saddest words are only a failure to cry. (*M* 24)

Kennelly plays on the contrast between Medea's language of honesty and the language of men, which she has discovered to be riddled with lies. In a sequence of rhetorical questions and repetitions, the Nurse speculates on the effect Medea's rage will have on the contours of a language already saturated with an inherent duplicity:

> Will Medea allow
> Child-liars grow up to be
> father-liars who will beget child-liars, who will
> become father-liars to beget child-liars? Only
> the earth is true, we must shelter
> ourselves from it, protect our
> valuable lies as we protect our
> children, clothe them, teach
> them to communicate. Insure them.
> Educate them. Bless them. Send them out
> into the world to bring new children
> to the earth. The world of rage.
> Medea's world. The world of rage.
> World without lies. (*M* 19-20)

This implies that Medea's rage comprises a language of such scathing integrity that it has the power to cleanse current ways of saying ourselves and the world, a discourse atavistically couched in masculinist deceits and exclusions, with a different discourse, one which is brutally unattenuated, uncompromisingly conscious, thoroughly feminised. This is the substance of Medea's appeal to the women of Corinth, a powerful oration directed, in Kennelly's extended version, primarily to the audience.

Medea's words are more than just a plea for pity; as she herself says, they are 'a cry for justice', a sharing of the nightmare, not purely in her own interest, for her life is over and she is at best 'exiled and forsaken', but for the benefit of the women who make the city their home and must live on, generation upon generation, subject to its ways. Her address is an acute, scathing indictment of the treatment women suffer at the hands of men, an incitement to change on the part of her listeners designed ultimately to ensure their allegiance in her plan for revenge. It is a catalogue of sexual injustices – women are 'the playthings of men's bodies,/ the sensual toys of tyrants', seduced before marriage by masculine style, 'that elegant lie' – summarised by the wrenching question, 'Does a woman really exist/ apart from the "attention" a man/ pays to her?' (*M* 25). Having advised her 'sisters' of the true extent of their victimisation, she leaves it with them to act or remain passive.

As Kennelly delineates it, Medea's belief that a woman's silence is 'the most powerful', 'the most/ murderous weapon of all' (*M* 27) is an important indication of the relationship between gender and language. When women orchestrate language, and its counterpart, silence, in a conscious, specifically feminine way, then they may recover a measure of control over, and equality with, men. The efficacy of this practice can be measured by Creon's claim:

> The most difficult
> obstacle of all is a woman's silence –
> it makes a man feel that his words are less
> than the squeaking of mice in the sleeping dark. (*M* 29)

The chorus endorses this productive use of the language of rage, and through its song Kennelly, in one of the most potent declarations of feminine independence in his drama, endorses Euripides' prediction of the ascent of a 'woman's time':

> ...the time is coming when honour
> will be paid to women, when
> their feelings will not be made
> by men, when slavery will not
> masquerade as love, when
> a man's tone of voice will not
> create a tremor in a woman's
> reply, when a woman will
> not live to please
> an inferior man, when a woman
> will not sit in silence while
> her master broods in sullen
> superiority, when decisions
> are her agreement to his
> suggestions, when her hate
> can show itself, articulate
> and pure.
> ...

> There will be songs
> to celebrate the terrible truth
> of women. There will be
> womansongs in answer to the false
> songs of men. (*M* 33-34)

The vocabulary in this passage places the emphasis squarely on the role which language must play in this new order. Because of her courage and honesty in speaking out against patriarchy Medea stands as the heroic but tragic poet of 'prayer', which she defines as 'anger at what is, and a longing/for what should be' (*M* 42).

If Medea allowed Kennelly access to 'woman-centred space', that space is disclosed as essentially linguistic. Kennelly's mapping of this territory amounts not to colonisation but an empathetic release of, a giving voice to, feminine experience. The propriety and the power of such an interpretation of Euripides' play for audiences in contemporary Ireland is overt. It offers more than a recommendation: Medea's metaphoric action makes imperative the articulation of the constructive anger and the abundant creativity – the rage – which Irish women and Irish men have so successfully driven underground.

Read from this angle the answer to the play's closing question would appear to be in the affirmative. As Medea herself avows, she has gained strength and selfhood in taking revenge: 'Never before/ did I feel the fullness of womanhood...It is exhilarating, irrepressible, new,/ as though I were an army in myself./...I am at home in my own evil' (*M* 32). Yet there is a sense here that the negative connotations of her words could easily undermine the positive. An inversion of the liberating feminist reading I have proposed takes place in what follows:

> It [evil] is the only force that brings justice
> into this perfumed, jewelled, stylish world
> of absolute injustice. A little poison,
> properly administered, may restore the hope
> of that lost justice that compelled us
> to give respect to others, and dignity
> to the mind of man. A little poison
> may perform the miracle. (*M* 33)

Medea's proposal that violent revenge, in this case murder, is the only solution to injustice squares with the Old Testament, indeed pre-Christian, doctrine of 'an eye for an eye'. It is the language not of recognition and accommodation, but of entrenched difference, which for an Irish audience has an all-too-immediate historical, political and social resonance. In the nineties it is the language of bombs, assassinations, revenge-killings and corrective knee-cappings, which Kennelly describes as 'the violence of hatred'.[27]

Medea's rage is of this order. Her single-minded devotion to a 'cause' – Jason's 'education in humility' – makes her exemplary not just of a woman who has the courage of her convictions, but of a woman blinded and ironically limited and reduced by the extreme narrowness and self-absorption of those convictions. The chorus' prayer for moderation goes unheard by Medea. Instead of moderation, we witness an increasingly fanatical insistence on the execution of her plans and, ultimately, a stultifying deadlock between male and female points of view. Medea's assertion that 'From now on, words are/ useless' (M 55) is a claim that she cannot be persuaded to change her mind, but also that, like Antigone, she has not so much given up on language as gone beyond it. Although she does vacillate, momentarily shocked by the magnitude of what she is about to do, negotiation is out of the question. Action alone holds meaning, so much so that she is irrevocably convinced 'Murder is the instrument of justice' (M 55).

Rephrasing Medea's pronouncement, and the chorus' final question, Kennelly has suggested that the play principally asks: 'Is murder ever an instrument of justice?'[28] A range of political and social stalemates, from the murders carried out by Loyalist and Republican paramilitaries to the psychological and emotional assassinations which are commonplace in the public houses and private homes of Ireland, North and South, are thus brought into play. The answer which Kennelly's version appears to put forward is, in this context, a definite 'no'. However, the implication remains that in certain situations the opposite response might be valid. The opening lines point to this: 'Glory to Heaven for home and family:/ a man, woman, children' (M 13). Without the absolute reverence which society accords to the institution of marriage and family, the preservation of the species is threatened. This, the ideological reasoning which informs Medea's murders, may be the one exception to the rule; the drama is non-prescriptive. We can be more certain that the chorus' penultimate questions, however rhetorical, are fashioned to endorse a negative response:

> Why let anger poison your heart?
> How can murder so easily take the place of love?
> ...
>
> This thing called love,
> how much of the world's evil has it created? (M 71)

The words cut to the quick of the male/female, love/hate dichotomy which lies at the heart of *Medea*. Exclusive love, whether of nation or place, self or another, is ironically and paradoxically exposed as the source of bitterness, cruelty, evil. But, as we have seen, honestly-given and openly-accepted love can also be the source of knowledge, fulfilment, liberation.

The element of play and ambiguity, the possibility of at least two answers to the drama's dual concerns – the daring and sophisticated yoking of the volatile issues of feminism and nationalism – is the strength of Kennelly's version of *Medea*. Taken together, these oppositions and confrontations emphasise the Blakean touchstone: 'true progress is possible only between opposites'. The implications of such progress – language out of silence, liberation out of oppression – are as clear as the implications of its opposite – cultural stagnation, political deadlock. In adapting Euripides' *Medea*, Kennelly has created a second and possibly more urgent play for and about Irish women. He also offers a powerful and complex political parable for our times.

* * * *

When in October 1989 Kennelly gave a reading of his version of Euripides' *The Trojan Women* he prefaced his performance with the following statement:

> The play as I understand it is, very briefly, about the consequences of war, it's about the men who win and the women who lose... It's ultimately, I think, about dignity, about ultimate dignity, about the untouchable thing that remains when everything has been touched, the inviolate thing that remains when everything has been violated. The intactness of what has been broken, which I can't explain.[29]

Euripides' play is essentially an anti-war tract aimed at the perpetrators of almost sixteen years of Greco-Spartan dispute. It makes its indictment through the voices of the true victims of warfare – the women. And as in *The Bacchae* and *Medea*, Euripides warns of the consequences of suppressing the instinctive urge towards natural justice which women so ably enact. In the manner of *Antigone*, *Medea* and *Blood Wedding*, Kennelly's interpretation subverts and extends the key issues of the original in a contemporary context and idiom. In doing so he shifts the focus away from 'the men who win', directing it instead towards 'the women who lose'. Kennelly's *The Trojan Women* remains politically-charged drama: it laments and condemns the physical and psychological devastation wreaked by war and the oppression of women in general, *and* on at least two specifically Irish fronts, namely the quarter-century of civil war which continues to undermine Northern Ireland, and the ongoing struggle of women North and South to obtain equal citizenship. Building on the previous versions, Kennelly here explores that power which has made women the enemies and the victims of men, and examines with fresh and often alarming clarity their strategies for survival, their 'ultimate dignity' and inviolability, in the war against women and in the face of a grinding internecine conflict which has robbed them of daughters and sons, husbands and homes.

The Trojan Women is Kennelly's strongest work for theatre to date. The dramatic elements are finely-tuned, so that sound and sense – the varied intensity of pitch and rhythm, alternating declarations of rage and fear, defiance and despair – are in precise accord. These linguistic and ideational contours in turn constitute hymns not just to the women of Belfast and Derry, of Tarbert and Kimmage; they make equal prayers and praise for the women of Bosnia and Beirut.

Kennelly's preface to the published script serves as a 'map' of the aims set and the obstacles encountered in his making of the version: 'My problem was to convey this note of active resolution, so closely linked with seemingly utter hopelessness, in language that came in waves suggesting both the women's spirits and the sea itself' (*TW* 5). The challenge, once again, was to discover an adequate language in which to express the conflation of profound but conflicting emotions, a language which would speak not just about, but *of*, women's experience: 'A man is trapped in his own language. How could I find the words to let these women express the ever-deepening reality of their natures?' (*TW* 5) As with the previous works, the difficulty lay in being male, uncertain how to approach sympathetically, yet with accuracy and impartiality, the kernel of female sensibility. The solution (and it is an effective one) lay in fashioning an exact fit between measure and meaning. The key to Kennelly's achievement, and to our appreciation of that achievement, is the metaphor of the sea, for, on both an aural/oral and a figurative/conceptual level, the sea acts as a unifying principle serving, as Kennelly indicates, as a model for the rhythmical ebb and flow of the women's anger and surrender. It also defines a cyclical return to recurrent preoccupations: the broken city, the guilt of Helen, the treachery of men. That the sea (like the earth in *Antigone* and *Medea*) is archetypally a feminine, transitional element (associated with prime matter and intuitive wisdom, with dynamic, motivating forces, with creation and destruction, surface and abyss) which conjures both positive and negative aspects of femaleness, allows Kennelly to develop one of Euripides' primary figures along lines conducive to what in this play has become a fully-articulated feminist aesthetic.

It is fitting that the play opens with a prologue in which Poseidon, the god of the sea, delivers a soliloquy which sets the tone of defiance and the feminist agenda for what follows:

> Love will come to rule the world,
> that is, women will rule the world.
> Although what you're about to see
> might seem to say that women
> are the rags and tatters of humanity
> or, at best, the perks of war,
> women will rule the world. (*TW* 7)

That Poseidon is also the creator-god ('I make things') is equally important, for as well as embodying that life-force which drives the women to persevere, to suffer in the name of love, he is also a type for the artist, the original maker who creates, out of his dreams, cities, poems, plays, only to watch them destroyed, restored and destroyed again in a ceaseless round of blood-sharing and blood-shedding. It is also important to remember that, as a water deity, Poseidon expresses the vital struggle of the psyche to find a way of formulating a clear message comprehensible to the conscious mind. Kennelly's own voice, Prospero-like, is unmistakable in Poseidon's reminder of the direct connection between the urge to create and the inevitablity of destruction. Through this line of masculine identification we are at the same time alerted to the aesthetic dilemma which informs the action, and thus the proximity of Kennelly's position, as poet, to the women whom we are about to meet.

The symbiotic relationship between creativity and destruction is underlined by the appearance of Pallas Athena, goddess of wisdom, who demands that Poseidon make the sea 'a sea of death... mad with its own ferocity,/wild with the genius of its treachery' (*TW* 11). It will become a graveyard for the Greeks on their return home, retribution for the rape of Cassandra by Ajax in Pallas' temple. Not only does her desire for revenge point up the unpredictability of the gods; it also reveals the other side of women's love, creativity and nurturance. This is the face of acrimony and despair shaped by a constant and collective 'rape' of female identity and integrity, conditions which have made imperative and just the liberating rage so powerfully illustrated by Medea. As Poseidon observes:

> Your spirit is a knife.
> The blade is hate and love and rage.
> I see the knife in your eyes. (*TW* 10)

Together Poseidon and Pallas prefigure the gamut of binary opposites which run through the ensuing action.

The play proper opens with Hecuba waking at dawn before the smouldering ruins of Troy. Hecuba is the hub of the drama, and her soliloquy at this point introduces a constellation of central motifs. Her equation of the city with her body – 'Look at my city, look at my body' (*TW* 13) – and the complex definition of self in terms of place – 'This is not the city whose every corner is part of me' (*TW* 12) – is reiterated and developed to the point where one woman can say, 'All we know is that/ we are our city.// Our broken, fallen, ridiculed city' (*TW* 35). The women together repeat Hecuba's penultimate lamentation and invocation:

> Goodbye, goodbye, our city.
> Burnt! Lost! Gone!
> But still be in us,
> be in our blood and in our dreams. (*TW* 77)

The Greek herald Talthybius' orders are a graphic extension of the metaphor:

> Think of this city as an evil woman,
> set fire to her flesh, her hair
> rip out her heart, set fire to that,
> stand back, enjoy the flames,
> this is the best work you've ever done. (*TW* 70)

Hecuba's initial remarks describe the female body as a register of Troy's collective pain, an object to be examined, scorned, 'most savagely raped' by an aggressive, manipulative male gaze. This objectification of women, the reification of their bodies into men's adornments and playthings, is epitomised in the play's principal trope and its major complaint: women are the spoils of war. As Hecuba puts it:

> He'll win me,
> a prize, a trophy.
> He'll wear me like a medal,
> discard me like an old skin. (*TW* 13)

But her words also emphasise that the body is the only weapon left to women to protest their suffering, gain revenge, to right the balance. It is she who sets the agenda, who fires the other women to confidence and conviction:

> Women! Women! Come out! Come out!
> It is time for you to make your cry.
> Not the cry of men:
> it is time for the cry of women now.
> This is the cry that will deepen in time
> never uttered till now, but uttered once
> must be shrieked again and again.
> This is the cry of a woman's soul
> hitting the cities built by men
> rocking the world from pole to pole. (*TW* 14)

In asking herself 'Yet, may not a woman/ fight, yes, fight, here and now?/ May not a woman/ win?/ How?' (*TW* 13-14) she assumes the role of teacher and exemplar to those who are more fearful and less resourceful than she. Her strategies for 'winning' are based on self-consciousness, self-reliance and a genius for the close observation and subversion of the oppressor's tactics, combined with obedience to the body's dictates. As she advises Andromache, 'let your body teach/you how to win' (*TW* 41).

Despite her remarkable strength, Hecuba is subject to the same doubts and insecurities which she endeavours to quell in the women. She too vacillates between resignation and elation, inscribing a pattern of highs and lows which encompasses the emotional life of the other characters. Directly after likening her surrender to a devastating grief to the way men on board a sinking ship surrender to the conquering storm – 'I don't struggle, I don't curse the sea./ [...] Over me they pour, the waves, great waves of misery./ God's overwhelming waves are drowning me!' (*TW* 40) – she rallies, declaring the superiority of female intelligence over and above male action: 'My thoughts are swifter now/than any sword flashing in a man's hand!' (*TW* 41).

Comparably, her lament for her dead husband swiftly turns from a litany of sorrows to an envoi of complaint, becoming finally an outburst of sheer rage directed towards men in general:

> Who am I? I am a woman,
> I am Hecuba, Hecuba, nobody but Hecuba,
> I am not a prize, I am not a slave, not a slave
> to anyone living or dead,
> I am not a decoration or an ornament,
> I am not a bit of scandal or a piece of gossip,
> I am not something to be shown off or pointed at,
> I am not something to be used at someone's beck and call,
> I am not a thing, I am not a fuck. (*TW* 73-74)

Implicit in Hecuba's words is Kennelly's empathy with and outrage at patriarchy's inequitable perception and treatment of women.

His 'petition', however, is delivered with equal force through the other lead characters, Cassandra and Andromache, as well as the chorus of other women whose nameless, collective suffering intensifies their separate sorrows. The prophetess Cassandra veers between madness and inspiration; she is aflame with the knowledge of a horrific truth. As Hecuba describes her:

> She is driven out of herself
> Because God has breathed into her blood
> something of his own sorrow at the devastation
> caused by murderous men who want us now as prizes. (*TW* 15-16)

When she appears, Talthybius mistakes her radiant frame – 'a body all alight with the breath of God' (*TW* 21) – for the women setting fire to their own bodies in protest against being carried off by the Greek warriors. His concern is not for the suffering such an act would inflict, but for his own head should such disfigurement put their bodies 'beyond the pleasure-loving reach of men' (*TW* 21). It stands as an ironic prelude to Cassandra's equally ironic exclamation: 'I am going to be a bride. A bride!' (*TW* 21) Her celebrated 'betrothal' to Agamemnon is revealed as a vehicle for revenge: 'Whoever loves me against my will/ teaches me how to kill!' (*TW* 23) Cassandra's mystical descent into her 'ecstasy', towards the discovery of her 'special light', is akin to Antigone's 'articulate action' or Medea's 'creative rage', for it signals a tapping of the collective female psyche which in turn triggers a language of prophecy and confrontation. Her even-tempered, sagacious judgements – 'Men who win wars win nothing' (*TW* 25) – swiftly modulate into a cold rage which voices the suppressed anger of all the women:

> Randy Agamemnon! Godalmighty fucker Agamemnon!
> You are making love to a black axe
> covered in bloodstains,
> and the black axe feels like the flesh of a woman
> chosen to pay homage to your greatness.
> Her only problem is to pay that homage right. (*TW* 26)

That the meaning of her words is obscure to Talthybius, that they prompt a series of knee-jerk, misogynist responses – Cassandra is 'a mad creature,/...a perversion of woman's nature', 'a lunatic virgin', the women 'crafty bitches', 'moody' and 'treacherous' as the ocean (*TW* 27-28) – only serves to underline the unfathomable sea which, as Hecuba will conclude, divides women from men.

Kennelly's version retains the complementary arrangement of victim-protagonists of Euripides' play so that, like Hecuba and Cassandra, Andromache articulates a feminist philosophy which has been formed in a crucible of silence, reflection and bitter experience. Her discourse on the nature of masculine lust and men's calculated praise of women constitutes an all-too-familiar tale of feminine capitulation and conformity. Hector was a 'good' husband and father, but in her efforts to win his approval and maintain his affections, she forfeits her autonomy: 'I did everything to please my man...I stayed at home and walked in my own garden... I became a gifted listener, patient, sympathetic... I created the space in which his vanity might move/ like a beautiful, confident cat' (*TW* 38). Andromache's behaviour is a paradigm of the practical but compliant wife, part victim, part accomplice, whose predicament remains as common today as in 415 BC. Her revulsion at the thought of being 'fucked by his [Hector's] murderer/ in that murderer's bed' (*TW* 39), and her simultaneous acknowledgement that a widow will naturally take another lover, restates the uncertainty and vacillation experienced by each of the Trojan women. Yet her refusal to consign all to 'bondage' – 'if my body is a slave/ an untouched portion of my mind is free' (*TW* 40) – leaves her not defeated but empowered by the struggle for individuality and collective liberation: 'Somewhere, a special light/ burns for me, for you, for all lost women' (*TW* 40).

This triangle of sorrows – Cassandra's rape, the death of Hecuba's daughter Polyxena, the murder of Andromache's son Astynax – is offset by the women's rage against Helen who, though 'of their kind', is nevertheless held to be the source of all their misfortune, a schemer and a traitor, the incarnation of all that is 'an insult to women'. In her defence, Helen claims herself victim and scapegoat, and Kennelly makes it difficult to discount the kernel of truth in her challenge:

> What did any single one
> of all these thousands of young men who died
> know of me?
> That war was fought
> in furious ignorance by ignorant men!
> ...
>
> Why blame me
> for your own pride, your own bafflement,
> your need to own me? (*TW* 55)

Without allowing the audience to sympathise with Helen or to condone her actions, Kennelly alerts us to the irony inherent in the women's reactions. For although Helen, in her ability to use her physical beauty to seduce men and betray nations, typifies the kind of woman who condemns her less conniving sisters to stereotyping and exploitation, their words are not without a measure of hypocrisy. In their frenzied chant of insults – 'Tart!/ Trollop!/ Hussy!/ Doxy!/ Minx!/ Rotten fish!/ Bag o' crap!/ Witch!/ Bitch!/ Whore!/ Slave!' (*TW* 61) – the women invoke precisely that terminology which they would abolish from masculinist vocabulary. They despise her flexibility and duplicity, but their condemnation of her manipulation of men is not far removed from their own recommendations for regaining mastery and self-worth. Their strongest invective, however, is reserved for Helen's disloyalty to her husband, Menelaus. Hecuba advocates that he should 'make a law for women everywhere:/ Whatever woman betrays her husband, dies' (*TW* 59), and when he complies by promising that in punishing Helen he will make of her an example which will insure women 'will be faithful for evermore', which 'will freeze the wandering dreams of women/and keep them in the beds where they belong' (*TW* 62), it is clear how severely blind rage can limit true objectives.

Kennelly, however, is careful not to bias the argument, and this openness in turn contributes to his version's consummate range of vision. While on one level the play operates as a cautionary tale directed towards an uncritical feminism, on another it aims to deflate romantic notions about the nobility of war. The latter injects a familiar sting when Helen is figured as a malignant Mother Ireland, the old sow ravenous for her farrow:

> But you know that's what men are for:
> they fight and work and laugh and sometimes cry.
> Pick one, Helen. Pick a man. Fuck him. Let him die.
> Stick him in a grave, cold, deep, far from the sun.
> And remember always – take care of number one. (*TW* 58)

Ultimately, however, Kennelly demands that women recognise, and act on the recognition, that they possess 'a power no man can ever touch' (*TW* 78). The build-up to Hecuba's climactic declaration is precisely-paced. It begins with her apocalyptic vision of a cold, indifferent God cast in the mould of the Old Testament patriarch who has caused women to suffer 'the most unspeakable wrong'. In contrast to this pitiless destroyer is 'the music of our hearts' and 'the everlasting beauty of the song/ of earth and heaven' (*TW* 69), which give Hecuba the strength to look this male image in the eye, then turn and pray to the earth and the listening dead. Like Antigone and Medea, her appeal is to the chthonic powers of the underworld and the afterlife, those alternative, feminine regions of self and kin which are the source and the future of present sustenance. In the final moments of the play, prayer modulates into proclamation, the sea becoming a cumulative metaphor for what lies within and beyond the ken of womankind. In their conflation of conviction and ambiguity, Hecuba's closing lines constitute an apt coda to Kennelly's trilogy of Greek plays for women:

> A wave of the sea!
> Natural and fearless!
> That is what I want –
> I want to live without fear
> and I will, I will
> ...
>
> Waves waves waves waves waves
> endless unknown driven
> dreams in the hearts of women.
> Nobody can count the waves,
> nobody can count the waves,
> the waves tell more
> than the waves themselves can ever be,
> the waves outnumber every thought
> possible to you and me.
> The waves roar and moan in pain.
> The waves laugh happily.
> The waves are slaves.
> The waves are free.
> The war is over. The war begins – for me! (*TW* 79)

ÅKE PERSSON

The Critic: Towards a Literary Credo

As this anthology of critical essays illustrates, the Irish literary phenomenon of Brendan Kennelly combines several separate, though
closely interlinked, sensibilities. In accordance with his firm view
that labelling is an insult to the complexity of the self, the range of
his critical activities is scarcely captured by the label 'the critic'. His
multiple critical roles include those of university professor and
lecturer, essayist,[1] anthologist, reviewer, critic-in-poetry, author of
introductions and prefaces, judge in poetry competitions, defender
of popular culture and artists, panellist, socio-cultural commentator.
Although the focus here will be on his Ph.D. thesis, poetry, and
critical essays, it is important to bear in mind the breadth of his
critical activities and also the fact that they are frequently inseparable from his creative writing.

Borrowing Yeats's phrase, Kennelly states in his highly significant
essay 'James Joyce's Humanism', and forcefully restates it in the
arguably even more significant 'W.B. Yeats: An Experiment in
Living', that all a writer's days are essentially 'an experiment in
living'.[2] All aspects of life are confronted and explored in a self-
exploration, in a mapping of the self and the world. In the latter
essay, it is evident that Yeats comes to epitomise for Kennelly that
self-exploration which he considers essential for poetry to happen;
Yeats, he argues, 'wanted to experience it all. He wanted to say it
all. He could do this, or hope to do this only by venturing "into
the abyss of himself ", by scrutinising the darkness of his own spirit
and the spirits of others whom he ruthlessly pursued, examined
and analysed' (233). 'The light of poetry,' he further writes in the
essay 'Poetry and Violence', 'often finds its origin in the darkness
of our natures' (36). The honest poet listens to all his/her inner
voices in 'a constant dialogue with the self'. In turn, it becomes
the critic's task to listen in on the poet's listening to voices, and

for Kennelly the two activities – he has the Romantics' faith in the
availability of this 'self' – are ultimately part of the same process of
making sense. It is not a coincidence that Ibsen's dictum governs
the way in which Kennelly views literature in general, and poetry
in particular, both as a poet and as a critic: 'Ibsen called poetry "a
court of judgement on the soul": when we read poetry, really read
it, we are putting ourselves on trial' (36).[3] It is the purpose of this
essay, firstly, to demonstrate the intimate relationship in Kennelly's
work between his criticism and his poetry, and, secondly, to show
that the critical statements Kennelly makes derive from a consistent view of literature and its function in society. It will focus first
on his doctoral thesis, then on his poetry, and finally on his critical
essays exploring, for instance, the writings of Kavanagh, O'Casey,
Mahon, Yeats, and Joyce. What will emerge from this fairly broad
interpretation of 'the critic' is a sense of the literary credo on which
all his writing is founded.

* * * *

With the exception of a relatively large number of reviews, Kennelly's
first major project as a critic was his Ph.D. thesis *Modern Irish
Poets and the Irish Epic* (1966). This is a slightly misleading title:
the term 'modern' is fairly generous, since the thesis includes mid-
to late-nineteenth-century material, and the term 'poet' encompasses James Stephens as novelist. In the thesis, Kennelly explores
and assesses the creative exploitation of Irish myths by a number
of Irish writers, for instance, de Vere, Ferguson, Todhunter, Yeats
and Clarke. He is sympathetic to their efforts to create an interest
in 'a national literature', or indeed to create 'a national literature'
itself, and, in some cases, to 'present a total view of the growth of
the Irish mind and character'[4] from the early days of paganism to
Christianity. He seems to share Yeats's view of Ferguson's importance and achievement, when Yeats writes: 'Ferguson's poetry is
truly bardic, appealing to all natures alike...for it has gone deeper
than knowledge or fancy, deeper than the intelligence which knows
of difference – of the good and the evil, of the foolish and the wise...
– to the universal emotions that have not heard of aristocracies,
down to where Brahman and Sudra are not even names.'[5]
    A substantial part of his analyses of the individual writers deals
with the question whether they succeed in recreating the pagan
outlook on life found in the myths. He praises Ferguson for his
attempts to depict the violence and passion of that world, in battles
and sexual tensions, as opposed to, for example, de Vere and Clarke,

of whom the former shows an 'unwillingness to treat violent situations either of love or war',[6] and the latter is 'often repelled by what
is violent or grotesque in the sagas'.[7] Ferguson, whose 'vocation as
an epic poet' was ' "To link his present with his Country's past" ',[8]
is given by far the most thorough treatment in the thesis, and Kennelly couples him with Yeats as the most significant figures in this
context; in a somewhat sweeping, yet nevertheless arguably accurate, statement, he writes that 'They helped to lay the foundations
of a national literature'.[9]

However, to Kennelly, Yeats is important in another respect,
because his approach to the myths, as seen in his Cuchulain plays,
is far more personal than that of Ferguson or the other writers. In
Yeats's search for a poetic vision, in which the ultimate aim would
be 'intellectual freedom',[10] the myths became a way in which to
explore the many-faceted aspects of his self and to resolve his many
personal dilemmas, psychological and emotional as well as political. It is evident that Yeats's uncompromising approach impresses
Kennelly:

> Firstly, he showed that heroic myth could be used as a vehicle for the
> expression of his deepest emotions; secondly, he proved the disturbing
> relationship between the distinct heroic Gaelic past and the Ireland in
> which he lived. By re-creating an ancient heroic age, he showed the same-
> ness of all ages... He was utterly fearless in his exploration of myth;
> never repelled by what was strange, extravagant or grotesque...His plays
> show his deep understanding of the nature and function of heroism.[11]

An interesting consequence of Kennelly's exploration of pagan/
Christian tensions is his interest in the concept of heroism. His
exploration of the heroic ideal reveals a self-assertive individual as
the pagan hero, in comparison with the Christian hero in whom the
ideal is self-sacrifice, work and devotion. The pagan hero, 'the brilliant defender of his tribe, the great solitary rooted in the affections
of his people, doing fabulous deeds under the stimulus of one con-
suming aim, immortal glory', develops into a hero who is an 'outsider, leading a roving life...the rootless, wandering hero, moving
on the outskirts of society'.[12] The Christian saint-like ideal of self-
effacement is understood by Kennelly as both the antithesis and a
development of this early pagan ideal. However, he finds a kinship
between the two forms of heroism, in that the heroes 'struggle
against the limitations of their nature in such a way as to invest that
struggle with dignity and a sense of greatness of man's endeavours'.[13]
For Kennelly, vulnerability, endurance, suffering, human frailty,
courage, and nobility become key-words. There is no doubt that

his perceptions of the heroic ideal are absorbed into his own poetry, and his poetic vision of the human condition rests on these perceptions of the heroic. They become crucial to his world view and to his writing; they are intimately related to his ideas of what poetry and its function are.

Reviewing his creative work from the sixties, Kennelly seeks to articulate the aesthetic on which his poetry and criticism are based. As he comments on the art of poetry, he echoes his statement from his doctoral thesis regarding the heroes struggling against their limitations, writing in the Preface to his *Selected Poems* (1969): 'I see it [poetry] basically as a celebration of human inadequacy and failure.'[14] Time and again in his earlier as well as later poetry, people's limitations are exposed. The individual's attempts to make some sense of his/her existence are, his poems suggest, difficult enough; but when these attempts are obstructed, if the ability to speak, move or see is seriously hindered, they become even more difficult. Therefore, in his exploration of human inadequacy, physical disabilities are interlinked with the emotional states of loneliness and alienation. In 'The Blind Man', for example, the man is forced to make sense in and of his darkness, to 'Deduce what's evil, beautiful or good', being 'Awkwardly involved while still outside' (*ATFV* 16-17). Preoccupied with failure and inadequacy, many poems stress endurance rather than conventional forms of achievement. But since the outsider figures in the poems are disconnected from everyday social contact, they have to attempt to create their own reality, space and meaning; as the blind man says, 'I only see whatever I can make'. In these individuals struggling against their limitations and suffering in silence, the poet sees heroic qualities very similar to those which he points out in his doctoral study. He is in fact attempting to redefine the epic hero, a concept which becomes Miltonic in its emphasis on the power of insight, Wordsworthian in its 'levelling' social emphasis. His heroes and heroines also exist on the periphery of society, but they are not leaders, warriors, or kings, as are the traditional epic heroes; nor do they take part in battles and contests to prove their strengths. Instead, they try to make the best of their limitations in their day-to-day existence, with their physical, mental, and emotional crosses to bear. And instead of finding them on the battlefields, we find them in back streets, in back gardens, or in hospitals. But, the poet insists, their dignity and their glory are the same. In 'Lame Girl Climbing Steps',[15] for instance, the narrator makes direct references to other heroines, Marilyn Monroe, Greta Garbo, Deirdre and Joan of Arc, to emphasise his admiration for the lame girl, who has to climb the steps in an act which becomes both physical and psychological. The reference to Deirdre is a direct result of Kennelly's interpretation of Yeats's play *Deirdre* and its heroine, about whom he writes in his thesis: 'like Cuchulain, she struggles heroically against overwhelming odds and against the very limitations of her own nature'.[16] This mythologising of the marginalised can also be seen in his poems about 'the mad', particularly in 'The Fool's Rod',[17] which is a kind of hymn to the outcasts walking around the streets of Dublin. The importance of his poetry from the sixties in general, and as an illustration of his conception of heroism, has been confirmed by his inclusion of poems such as 'The Blind Man' in a four-poem manifesto in his selected poems, *A Time for Voices* (1990).

Kennelly continues his redefinition of heroism in his later poetry, most notably in *Love Cry* (1972; 1992), *Islandman* (1977; 1992), *A Small Light* (1979; 1992) and *The Book of Judas* (1991). *Islandman* (*BS* 102-26), for example, explores a psyche on the verge of disintegration, as the man struggles against his own mental and emotional limitations, being a 'Fragment in a world of fragments'. He is dislocated from his immediate environment and his history: 'My body is a wet log/ Hacked from its roots years ago...' Nevertheless, there is an anger within him, caused by 'the sight/ Of broken things', which gives him enough strength not to give in: 'I will hold. I will try to hold'. Thus, the poem represents an attempt to resist displacement and to establish a sense of belonging, a belief in the ability to reconnect to himself and the self to external forces. And there are signs that the islandman manages to do so, his eyes 'touch[ing] things as though/For the first time...' In view of later comments by Kennelly, *Islandman* undoubtedly emerges as one of his most powerful explorations of the kind of belief, and hope, which is increasingly present in his writing, as he writes in 'W.B. Yeats: An Experiment in Living':

> What is belief, for a poet?...The need for belief is an admission of the need to connect with oneself, to try to connect the energies of that self with outside energies, powerful and alien, in such a way that one has a more peaceful, convinced sense of one's own tiny, dignified place in a tumultuous world... Belief is certainly as much a demonstration of vulnerability as it can be a source of strength (*JJ* 238-39).

Later, in *Judas*, Kennelly reaffirms his deep fascination with the (socially) marginalised and alienated, and the whole sequence is arguably a dedication to them, as he writes in the Preface: 'Wherever I see men and women furiously muttering to themselves in the streets of Dublin I am saddened by their loneliness, touched by their sincerity, awed by their freedom' (*BOJ* 12).

Therefore, the integrity he looks for now is the integrity he admired in the marginalised, the mad and the disabled in the sixties and seventies, as they seem to him to have a courage and a dignity missing in the average mortal, a strong spiritual integrity despite, or because of, their limitations. There is, then, a direct relationship between his interpretation of Irish writers' handling of Irish myths, as seen in his thesis, and his own poetic vision of the human condition. His critical sensibility feeds his poetic imagination and vice versa in a constant interaction.

This is evident in his general critique of language in his later works, but even clearer in his earlier poems dealing with poets and writers, where he becomes a critic-in-poetry. A number of poets and writers come under his scrutiny: Blake, Swift, Mangan, Yeats, Pearse, MacDonagh, Plunkett, O'Connor, Kavanagh, Synge, Shelley, and, more recently, Behan and Joyce. There are clear similarities among the poems discussing the qualities of these writers, in that they articulate the need to confront a spiritual wasteland, for instance, 'dead Dublin' and 'Corroding silence' for Swift,[18] 'indifferent streets' and 'green deserts of the west' for Pearse.[19] Just as rage permeates Judas, so rage is the underlying force in most of these poems. On an immediate level, the aim is basic social change, although on a deeper level, a more far-reaching spiritual, political, and cultural re-shaping of ideas and values is sought.

The two obituary poems, 'Light Dying' (*ATFV* 126-27) and 'A Man I Knew',[20] about O'Connor and Kavanagh respectively, illustrate the poet's responsibilities in the midst of what is perceived as a stultifying environment. In the former, the narrator calls the older poet's achievement a 'heroic vision'. Central to that vision is a rage 'against the force/ That would reduce to barren silence all/ Who would articulate dark Ireland's soul', and an opposition to 'The hearts that make God pitifully small'. The implication is that the poet takes over as the true spiritual leader. Furthermore, anticipating Kennelly's deep concern about voices, this vision includes having the courage to listen to all the voices of the imagination, 'Because...all men are voices, heard/ In the pure air of the imagination', to open up to one's self and to have 'the heart to do and dare'. The critical assessment is that O'Connor is seeking a complete change of value system, with the poet as liberator, echoing Shelley's dictum that poets are the 'unacknowledged legislators of the world'.[21]

'A Man I Knew', where 'chivalry' has replaced 'heroic vision', is even more insistent. Here, Kavanagh is referred to as 'the epitome of chivalry', and the poem ends by stating that 'There is no other chivalry' than that which is found in the old poet. Chivalry is a concept deriving from a legendary past in which incorruptible and courageous warriors obeyed strict religious, social, and moral codes of conduct and defended the beautiful and the vulnerable, also demonstrating an instinctive capacity for sympathising with victims of oppression. The narrator openly comparing Kavanagh to this kind of ideal knight is a joke, but a joke which is undermined by his authentic feelings towards the dead poet's actions. The mock-epic battle in a pub, where a singing girl is defended against an 'interfering lout', thus becomes a genuine defence of the integrity of the artist. Instead of being sexually assaulted, the girl's artistic beauty is violated by the lout, and for that 'This man I knew spat in his face/ And wished him to the floor of hell'. The somewhat 'unchivalrous' act of spitting 'On every shoddy value that/ Blinded men to their true destiny' is an emotional response against 'All that distorted natural grace'. The narrator emphatically defends the old poet's behaviour and by extension his aesthetic; the code upheld by Kavanagh therefore becomes the narrator's code. When it is stated that Kavanagh 'was content to be/ Himself', it sounds simple, almost simplistic and platitudinous. But it means that Kavanagh cannot and will not allow himself to be something he is not, to be a creation of other ideologies, individual or collective. Chivalry in the traditional sense means a strict obedience to social decorum, values where the self is secondary to a code imposed within a rigid social structure. In the chivalry represented in the poem, however, the self is primary, and it breaks established rules if it has to, as the narrator-critic states: 'He lived according to *his* code/ And in *his* way was true to God' (*my emphasis*). That kind of independent self is by definition always uncontrollable, revolutionary, and subversive, as that kind of self seeks to live life to the full.

In his search for an aesthetic, Kennelly, the critic-in-poetry, continuously focusses on other writers, with whose qualities he allies himself and whose artistic efforts he finds admirable. His later production is no exception. Central to *Judas* is 'The Dinner', in which is restated the idea of the (artistic) self attempting to resist suppression and insisting on fulfilment. Joyce is invited to dinner with the Holy Family. Joseph asks him: ' "Why did you leave Ireland, James?" ' To which Joyce answers: ' "Crime...Of non-being" ' (*BOJ* 287).

* * * *

As Kennelly deploys personae in his poetry and plays in order to voice the many conflicts in the self, so the writers discussed in his critical essays become expressions of his on-going self-exploration and self-reflection. The critic and the poet, the public voice and the private, merge to produce a coherent view of the function of literature and the writer's responsibilities. The poet is the critic, the critic is the poet. The critical statements made by the public voice are also responses to the poet's own private artistic ideals and ideology. In his essay on Kavanagh he writes programmatically: 'A poet's critical judgements are always, at bottom, necessary justifications of his own most dearly held aesthetic...a poet can't be expected to advocate principles and ideas which he doesn't intend to follow' (*JJ* 112-13).

Anti-academic in that he rarely enters into a polemic with other critics, always sympathetic to the writer's efforts, uninterested in applying any critical theories, Kennelly, in 'W.B. Yeats: An Experiment in Living', gives vent despairingly, and highly polemically to his total disbelief in theory:

> As a University teacher, I am sometimes appalled at the way imagination is almost completely ousted from the teaching and study of English Literature and, instead, youngsters are expected, even compelled, to stuff their heads with boring, arid theories about poetry, theories often expressed in language that is pedantic and leaden. The actual poetry tends to get buried under all this mechanical clack. Perhaps that's the intention. In any case, it's as if some teachers no longer believe they can *enjoy* poetry. Without such belief, how can joy be communicated, shared? (*JJ* 238)

Therefore, his statements instead originate in a strong sense of conscience, individual and social. There is no doubt that Kavanagh, together with Yeats and Joyce, represents literary and artistic ideals that Kennelly is prepared fully to support: 'His was one of the most moving, coherent, and profound visions in modern poetry' (*JJ* 110), and commenting on his aesthetics, he continues: 'It is also blissfully free of all pretentiousness and obscurity. The clarity of all his statements on poetry is a mark of his confidence and clear-sightedness.' [22]

The 'comic vision' propounded by Kavanagh is, the critic argues, a result of 'man's dialogue with God, the foundation-stone of all Kavanagh's work' (*JJ* 110). This suggests a dynamic process, a journey, where the destination is 'simplicity' or, as Kennelly writes in his essay 'Louis MacNeice: An Irish Outsider', 'clarity of... self-knowledge' (*JJ* 139). The suffering and despair represented in the tragic and angry *The Great Hunger* are part of that journey, emotional states which have to be confronted in order to be exorcised, so that they can be transformed into a state of joy. Firmly claiming that 'obscurity is simply a failure of the imagination, the sanctuary of the inadequate' (*JJ* 112), Kennelly allies himself with the older poet's aims, provocatively stating that the latter 'came up with a few sentences that should be stamped on the brow of every modern poet and critic' (*JJ* 112). Central to the idea of simplicity is the concept of 'sophistication', which must be redefined as meaning 'that the poet has the courage to be utterly himself'. As Kavanagh writes: 'In the final simplicity we don't care whether we appear foolish or not. We talk of things that earlier would embarrass. We are satisfied with being ourselves, however small.'[23]

In Kennelly's final critical assessment of Kavanagh, whom he calls a 'poet-saint' (*JJ* 123) and 'one of the greatest modern poets' (*JJ* 126), he finds three significant features deriving from Kavanagh's 'liberated, independent imagination' (*JJ* 117). Firstly, and somewhat surprisingly perhaps, he finds a humility towards life, which keeps the sense of wonder and mystery alive, 'that sacred sense of mystery that is at the source of all poetry' (*JJ* 117). Secondly, because of this sense of wonder, he finds a celebration of love. '"Love's mystery" is all around us and the poet must celebrate it. Out of that sufficiency…comes the only style that matters, the style of praise' (*JJ* 123). Thirdly, he finds a sanity, stemming from the poet's rather ambitious 'attempt to understand God's mind' (*JJ* 124): '…it leads to detachment, and therefore to sanity, and therefore to the rare ability to see things as they are' (*JJ* 124).

Kennelly's praise for Kavanagh's achievement and vision sets his own agenda as a critic and helps us to understand his approach to literature. As a critic, Kennelly continually returns to the writer's attempts at mapping the self and at articulating or celebrating that 'inner conflict' (Plunkett, *JJ* 103), the 'intense and systematic exploration of his private darkness' (Yeats, *JJ* 235), that 'antithesis [which] is the foundation of human nature' (Yeats),[24] the exploration of 'the dark underworld of his mortal self' (MacNeice, *JJ* 144), the 'soul in action' (O'Flaherty, *JJ* 204), the 'emotional honesty' (O'Casey, *JJ* 210), that 'articulate contact with self' (Joyce, *JJ* 220), the 'conscience in action' (Mahon, *JJ* 130), an 'ever-deepening personal drama' (*JJ* 235) which is, to him, central to a writer's claim to greatness. It is the critic's main function to be the mediator between feeling and intellect, to listen in on the listening to the heart's voices, as he writes in the essay 'Derek Mahon's Humane Perspective', 'to define the quality of [the] voice' (*JJ* 131). When he reflects on the art of poetry in the essay 'Poetry and Violence', he is also commenting on criticism: '... I would like to say that I believe that poetry is the language of the heart, shaped, directed, controlled, moulded and ordered by its colleague, the sympathetic, vigilant and discriminating intelligence' (*JJ* 31).

In O'Casey, he finds qualities similar to Kavanagh's, and indeed similar to other Irish writers. In addition to Kavanagh, he yet again refers to Yeats and Joyce, and, in his essay 'Irish Poetry Since Yeats' (*JJ* 55-71), Austin Clarke and to some extent Paul Durcan. He writes in 'Sean O'Casey's Journey into Joy': 'There is an intriguing tendency common to some of the most interesting Irish writers. Looking at the artistic careers of these writers, we might describe this tendency as a journey into joy' (*JJ* 209). He has in mind 'the transfiguration of experience, through language, into works of art' (*JJ* 209), particularly the 'attempt to understand and express the nature of suffering', which, he argues, becomes 'images of joy' (*JJ* 209). The idea that suffering is spiritually edifying, and therefore liberating, is clearly Romantic. Romantic, too, is the stress on feelings rather than on the intellect. O'Casey, the critic claims, 'is not an intellectual; he is a celebrant' (*JJ* 210). Preoccupied with 'the humanity of people' (*JJ* 209) and urgently aware of their suffering and hardships, he was convinced that people have a right to be happy; people are at the centre of his concerns, and people are made of feelings. Therefore, Kennelly points out, O'Casey was convinced of the 'primacy and importance' of feelings in human life, and particularly the feeling of joy and compassion in the midst of cynicism and sorrow. The 'most vital' aspect of his work is comedy. O'Casey, sharing with, among others, the writers mentioned above, and also George Moore and Flann O'Brien, a comic outlook on life and art, is awarded by the critic the quality of 'comic genius' (*JJ* 213). Attempting to define that quality, Kennelly insists that we laugh at potentially destructive figures like, for example, Captain Boyle and Joxer in *Juno and the Paycock*, 'useless, mean, treacherous and irresponsible', because they produce in us a sense of empathy, or indeed catharsis, sparked by 'a strange, sympathetic humanity in us'. He continues: 'We are brought face to face with our own buried capacity for monstrous behaviour, and in one mesmeric side-splitting moment, we fall in love with our capacity for sin...we rejoice in the momentary freedom of those irresponsibles whom we normally keep caged in our hearts, manacled in cells of respectability, as we work, pay income tax...rear the children, and try to get on with or without the husband or the wife' (*JJ* 215).

Comedy, then, is set against duty, work, and commitments to various responsibilities, social and private. At the heart of that perception of comedy is the revolt against accepted norms, what Kennelly in 'James Joyce's Humanism' calls 'getting rid of a certain kind of inherited supportive morality' (*JJ* 228). The artist's search for the integrity of the imagination is by definition subversive, and Kennelly, leaning on Keats, frequently emphasises the necessary artistic aim, to be 'amoral.'[25] Again commenting on the significance of poetry, he writes in 'Poetry and Violence': '...poetry is neither moral nor immoral. It is amoral, it exists beyond conventional morality. If poetry merely reflected conventional morality, it would exist only in Christmas bards and after-dinner speeches. But poetry creates its own new fierce, vigorous code of morality' (*JJ* 42), 'recognis[ing] and demonstrat[ing] what a conventional morality will tend to outlaw and condemn' (*JJ* 44). Inherent in the true artist is an urgent longing for 'anarchy', 'irresponsibility' (*JJ* 215), 'not caring' (*JJ* 111), and 'indifference' (*JJ* 217). That is why he shares with Kavanagh the idea that 'poetry is dangerous', further stating: 'It is no wonder at all that Plato banished poets from his ideal republic' (*JJ* 36).

A good example of this attitude to art and life is Joyce, whose humanity (a recurring term in the criticism) Kennelly argues in 'James Joyce's Humanism' 'is among the bravest of the twentieth century, or indeed in the history of literature' (*JJ* 229). Impressed by the 'scrutiny of self-development' (*JJ* 217), he views the writer's life as being inseparable from his art. A difficult person to live with, he sought what the critic refers to as an 'unsupported perspective on the casual loneliness of men and women' (*JJ* 221) and an 'unsupported spiritual life' (*JJ* 221). Basically, it means that the self, in an uncompromising and ruthless refusal to give in to established norms, has to come to terms with all aspects of existence alone. Expressing the same idea, the poem 'The Dinner' once more becomes relevant (again illustrating the close relationship between Kennelly's criticism and his poetry): Joyce has an argument with Jesus about the cultural, moral, and social phenomena in Ireland and Jesus asks why Joyce cannot be like

> '...an honest-to-God
> Dubliner, go for a swim in Sandymount, spend
> Sunday afternoon in Croke Park or Dalyer,
> Boast of things you've never done...
> Miss mass, go to Knock...
> Listen to McCormack's records...
> In some strange way, James, you are,
> If you ask me, bent.'

To which Joyce significantly replies:

> 'But I didn't ask you, Jesus...
> It so happens I think things out for myself,
> I had to leave Ireland to do this
> Because no one in Ireland has a mind of his own...' (*BOJ* 287)

It is this urgent sense of not trusting any moral, political, cultural or any other authority which is, he says, central to Joyce's extreme ability to express all layers of human-ness, his 'pitiless revelations of [his characters'] hearts' habitual poverty' (*JJ* 220). The true mark of Joyce's style in *Dubliners* and *Ulysses*, Kennelly claims, is total candour in expressing the human experience. As with Kavanagh, it emanates from the candid heart, a 'total sensuous openness' (*JJ* 226), 'a set of voices mouthing acceptable contradictions, a chorus of complexity' (*JJ* 224), and 'reflects the soul's wish to be candid' (*JJ* 224).

If Joyce's life could not be separated from his art, the same, Kennelly believes, can be said about Yeats, stating that 'there is a sense in which his life is so commingled with his poetry as to be almost inseparable from it' (*JJ* 231). It is obvious that the old poet's consciously experimental approach to his whole existence fascinates Kennelly, who movingly sums up his long relationship with him in the words 'To live with his poetry is to find a friend' (*JJ* 247). There appear to be many similarities between Joyce and Yeats for the critic, in that they both searched for an absolute integrity, and they both urgently felt the heart's need and necessity to articulate their achieved integrity as lucidly and precisely as possible. 'This constant attempt,' Kennelly suggests about Yeats, 'to be accurate about what he feels and thinks has to do with the knowledge that any kind of dishonesty in poetry is ruthlessly avenged by language itself' (*JJ* 244). Neither is it a big step from Joyce's 'unsupported spiritual life' to what Kennelly refers to as Yeats's 'pursuit of isolationism, his conscious removal of himself and his art from "ordinary" people' (*JJ* 232). One difference is that Joyce left Ireland, whereas Yeats decided to stay. In order to survive artistically and emotionally in Dublin, and in order to be able to deal with 'human fragmentation, loneliness, the sense of being severed' (*JJ* 241), Kennelly implies, Yeats had to develop poetic strategies central to which is one crucial question: 'how does one not die even as one continues to breathe?' (*JJ* 236). Yeats's answer lies, Kennelly argues, in his 'defiant refusal to let vital and sparkling aspects of his spiritual, intellectual and emotional life wither away without a word of protest or a step taken to re-animate that fading life' (*JJ* 236). Two

principal ideas emerge from this stance, namely 'conflict and opposition', a sense that his poetry fluctuates between 'vulnerability and
control...risk-taking and mastery...adventure and caution' (*JJ* 235).
However, although Yeats's main concern was 'his own ever-deepening personal drama, his intense and systematic exploration of his
private darkness' (*JJ* 000), his approach did not involve a ruthless
exposure of his naked self; instead, Kennelly points out,

> He surrounded himself with characters, ghosts, spirits, creatures of leg-
> end and mythology, figures out of history and people, friends and ene-
> mies, out of his own experience, all of whom he formed into a private
> choir, a unique Yeats orchestra, to help him express both the occult and
> the obvious, the dead and the living...And he did this with a stubborn
> courage, a tough, lifelong tenacity in a frequently hostile society, an Ire-
> land so convinced of its own pietisms that every energetic alternative
> was "heretical"... (*JJ* 235)

Yeats's courage enabled him simultaneously to remain the same and
to change. Likening him to 'an ever-changing river that remains, in
spite of all the tumult, the same river', Kennelly argues that Yeats's
most fundamental aesthetic was unchanged throughout his career,
in other words, 'First poem and final play say the same thing.' Thus,
the outstanding aspect of Yeats's achievement is his extraordinary
visionary quality, which emanates from a total commitment to 'look
into the abyss of the self' (*JJ* 235). By doing so, Kennelly suggests,
Yeats managed to achieve the human spirit's highest aspiration: to
reach 'those moments of insight which, expressed, renew the tired
spirit of man and transfigure the world, if only for a moment, with
the poem's light inspired by the heart's darkness. At such moments
we know what ugliness is. We begin to remember what we have
forgotten' (*JJ* 247).

Being from a traditional Roman Catholic background, where the
authority of the local priests was the law and where 'free thinking'
was a sin, it is perhaps not surprising that Kennelly is (increasingly)
attracted to a sense of protest and revolt which he finds in all the
writers discussed, the protest in Protestantism which has to do with
conscience and a testing out of alternatives. In 'Derek Mahon's
Humane Perspective' he criticises Catholicism, which, he states,
'with its inbuilt sacramental structure of forgiveness, its absolving
paternalism, offers a certainty of pardon which can have a desensi-
tising effect on conscience because it takes, or seems to take, the
consequences for the workings of the individual conscience out of
the individual's hands' (*JJ* 127). This kind of conscience, like Joyce's
'unsupported spiritual life', relies on doubt and its own authority
and integrity, spiritual and ethical, since it does not expect any

favours from anyone, nor forgiveness. Because of this, Kennelly states, 'It does not brutalise another by anticipating too much of him or her... [It is] a conscious renunciation of emotional capitalism'. Therefore, he argues, it is 'anti-Romantic, in the purely literary sense'; yet because it insists on 'the potential of the solitary self, even the isolated self' (*JJ* 127), it is also generally 'romantic'.

Kennelly acknowledges Mahon's debt to MacNeice, whom he refers to as a 'poet of conscience' because of his 'moral honesty', and whom he sees as 'a source' of Mahon's poetry (*JJ* 128). The older poet's enormous contribution to Irish literature lies, among other things, in his ability to see and celebrate alternatives: '... his poetry points to the one thing that is absent from most Irish life and literature. He is a source of alternatives, another way of seeing, another way of experiencing. MacNeice perceives, tolerates, cherishes and celebrates difference. He proposes an alternative to prejudice in the North, an alternative to lethargy in the South' (*JJ* 128). Mahon's 'humane perspective', Kennelly claims, has this MacNeicean way of seeing and experiencing. Because it is strongly rooted in scepticism, it considers alternatives and has to come to terms with all those alternatives and different angles, showing a 'conscience in action'. In the poetry, this manifests itself in a sense of tension, 'words at war within themselves, or at least in argument with each other, ironical, loving, wild, reticent, fragile, solving' (*JJ* 129-30). However, it also gives an impression of indirectness and detachment, 'a kind of good manners' (*JJ* 133), preventing the poet from being in the centre of his poems.

In Mahon's attempts at staying on the periphery and remaining indirect, yet actually managing to 'convey a central statement' (*JJ* 133), Kennelly highlights qualities similar to his own poetic strategies, as seen in, for example, his prefaces to *Islandman* and *Judas*, that is, the use of a persona. Mahon, the critic claims, creatively exploits other poets (indeed similar to Yeats's use of different masks), in, for instance, 'The Poet in Residence (after Corbière)', in order to achieve 'exciting imaginative freedom' (*JJ* 134). The self is one step removed, yet is paradoxically in control of the Other which is allowed into the space previously occupied by the self; 'Self,' Kennelly philosophises, 'is freed from self so that self may become more comprehensively articulate' (*JJ* 134). In his self-exploration, Mahon has no scruples in taking help from other writers who become, in Kennelly's view, 'a kind of private army of conscience' (*JJ* 135); yet in the midst of this army, he says, Mahon's voice is 'uniquely his own' (*JJ* 135).

* * * *

Kennelly's critical statements emanate from his views on the art-ist's principal task: to engage in an uncompromising self-scrutiny and to find a style and a method which in an honest and a candid way express that process, or the consequences of it. 'Good poetry,' he says, 'captures consequences' (*JJ* 30). The candid expression of that process, he firmly and convincingly argues, is a great writer's most noticeable and praiseworthy quality. The self which emerges from that kind of self-scrutiny is by definition uncontrollable and subversive, as it is always different, and as it tries to break away from restrictions, individual and social, cultural and political, moral and religious. It implies a multiplicity of ideas, a destabilising of existing power structures. The poet/artist struggles to regain or colonise the self, but finds that the self is instead being colonised by external forces. Consequently, any obstacle to that process, any-thing which violates the self's right to fulfilment and growth, is a legitimate target for criticism.

The individual conscience therefore becomes the social conscience, the private voice becomes the public voice. As the artist engages in an activity in which freedom is the aim, art has a liberating func-tion, individually as well as collectively, ethically and spiritually as well as politically. Concerned about the condition of the Irish psy-che, Kennelly is consistent in his attacks on institutions and forces which have an oppressive and suffocating effect on self-expression and ultimately on the imagination. Thus his literary criticism enters the realm of cultural criticism. Although he would not explicitly speak of literature in political terms, he shows, not surprisingly, a sympathy towards that kind of protest in other writers.

Kennelly's important essay 'Poetry and Violence' is crucial to a thorough understanding of his more recent works, *Cromwell* and *The Book of Judas*, and his plays *Antigone*, *Medea* and *The Trojan Women*. Although he touches on the passionate violence inhabiting the self, and the writer's attempts to channel that inherent violence into art, his main preoccupation is the violence imposed on the self by various social and politico-religious institutions. Illustrating the oppositional nature of poetry, he gives a panorama of mental and physical abuse in Irish history, life and culture by commenting on a number of poems by Yeats, Simmons, Longley, Clarke, Stephens and Kinsella. Perhaps somewhat surprisingly – surprising since Kennelly's own (creative) writing is dominated by empathy, ten-derness, and compassion – he claims that the depiction of violence and its consequences is necessary, allying himself with Synge's powerful statement 'before verse can be human again it must learn to be brutal' (*JJ* 42).[26] Later he writes: 'Poetry, by definition, is always breaking through boundaries and categories. To try to inhibit or limit that function is to do violence to the very nature of poetry, to make it the sweet, biddable, musical slave of our expectations... It will not flatter or comfort or console; it will disturb, challenge, even threaten. Above all, it threatens our complacency' (*JJ* 44).

To Kennelly, there has existed, and still exists, in Ireland a conspiracy made up of what he now refers to as 'the respectable', who aim at controlling minds and bodies. In charge of that conspiracy is the Roman Catholic Church and the church leaders down to the local parish priest who held/holds the parishioners in a tight mental and spiritual grip. The second element of that power structure would in Kennelly's view be the teacher, who at least in past decades frequently and systematically oppressed the pupils, taking out his (occasionally her) own frustrations on them. In addition to these, there are the husband and the doctor, in all, a male power group joining together to protect its own interests, which has had devastating effects on the Irish psyche, individually and collectively. This conspiracy, and the effects of it, can be seen in Austin Clarke's poem 'The Redemptorist', to which Kennelly often returns. As the poem demonstrates, women are particularly exposed to this kind of oppression, not only in the confession box, but also in marriage, another social institution which Kennelly criticises. James Stephens, he argues, was a writer who early on understood and 'wrote about the way some women fought against the bland tyranny of men... Above all, perhaps, he is interested in how certain women fight for their *identity* in a world where so many forces combine to undermine that identity' (*JJ* 39).

Therefore the writer inevitably becomes a commentator on and critic of society, and in his attempts to 'define the quality of [the] voice', Kennelly almost without exception detects and tunes into the clear and reverberating voice of social criticism, from such earlier works as his essays on George Moore, Kavanagh, Liam O'Flaherty, Flann O'Brien and O'Casey, to more recent pieces on MacNeice and Joyce.

In Moore's stories, particularly in *The Untilled Field*, he finds a definite concern about the 'spiritual inertia' of Ireland caused by 'the stultifying influence of the Roman Catholic Church' (*JJ* 152), and claims that Moore's priests reflect a 'pious brutality' in their 'determination to smother or expel any manifestation of the individual dissenting will' (*JJ* 155). In this work, Kennelly argues, Moore examines 'a certain sickness at the very heart of Irish society'

(*JJ* 157), a state which in the critic's opinion reaches far into a multiplicity of areas:

> the atmosphere of unrelieved poverty and squalor; the frustration of all
> ideals; the suppression of individual thinking; the hysterical fear of sex
> as the supreme evil of which man is capable; the confusion of servility
> with obedience, furtive inhibition with virtuous self-denial, caution with
> wisdom; the fear of full expression and hence the distrust of the artist
> (*JJ* 152).

Kennelly finds a similar sense of rage and protest in Liam O'Flaherty's stories and Flann O'Brien's novel *The Poor Mouth*. Although his principal critical argument about O'Flaherty is the sensitive and perceptive insight that he is really 'a poet in prose' (*JJ* 198), creating with his strong energy and poetic rhythm a vivid and moving picture of the struggle between the individual and the elements, he cannot refrain from commenting on the writer's hostile attitude towards 'many of the enemies of Irish freedom' (*JJ* 206). In his *A Tourist's Guide to Ireland* O'Flaherty gives vent to an anger directed against 'priests, politicians, ignorance and various other diseases' (*JJ* 206), and in Kennelly's opinion, the same anger is brought into O'Flaherty's stories. It is particularly strong in his representation of the clergy and 'the dehumanising effects' caused by 'the single-minded money-makers, the usurers, the gombeen men, the unscrupulous dealers, the mercenary opportunists, callous and tireless' (*JJ* 207). And the satire in O'Brien's *The Poor Mouth*, Kennelly argues, mainly serves the purpose of exposing the underlying clichés inherent in the cultural and linguistic attitudes towards the Irish and the Irish language. The writer's target is 'the pretentious and the ridiculous' (*JJ* 186) who abuse language, who hide behind clichés; one of his aims is to eradicate 'the pompous and the hypocritical' (*JJ* 186) in, for example, the gentleman academic who visits the village of Corca Dorcha and who condescendingly records Gaelic phrases for his own selfish needs.

Always sensitive and open, frequently even painfully and movingly so, to the writer's efforts to come to terms with suffering and oppression, Kennelly is more readily inclined to give sympathetic rather than harsh criticism (also a feature of his many reviews). However, writing which in his opinion fails to live up to the emotional honesty and lucidity he demands is severely attacked. Thus, one of the gravest sins a writer can commit is to give in to sentimentality and emotional clichés, which to Kennelly imply mediocrity, dishonesty, and, more importantly, manipulation. Reflecting on sentimentality, he writes: 'Most forms of sentimentality are repugnant because the sentimentalist is not only committed to the cheapest form of self-deception...but also because sentimentality is usually a mask for cruelty, callousness and instinctive exploitation' (*JJ* 74). He believes, therefore, that some of O'Flaherty's stories, for example, are seriously flawed: 'if one listens carefully', he writes, 'one can hear...the heartbeat of the softie, the romantic slob' (*JJ* 201), indicating that O'Flaherty is sometimes incapable of recreating 'confused and entangled emotions' (*JJ* 201). Not even Yeats, although greatly admired by Kennelly, escapes severe criticism; referring to him as 'in certain respects repellent and impenetrable', he continues: 'For a man who talks so much about beauty, heroism and nobility, there's a forbidding emotional ugliness in his work at times, an arrogant intellectual eccentricity, a chilly hauteur, a crass distancing of himself from others, a stony self-containment...' (*JJ* 232).

* * * *

There is considerable evidence in Kennelly's critical writings that he relies heavily on the aesthetics of Romanticism in general and on the views held by individual Romantic poets: for example, his emphasis on the powers of the imagination and the importance of feelings (not to be mistaken for sentimentality, as discussed above); his view that suffering and pain are spiritually edifying; his belief that the poet is a mediator between a large (spiritual) truth and the reader; his equally strong belief in the anarchic and subversive qualities of the poet whom he sees as a liberator and an educator; his stress on poetry as amoral, not accountable to anything but itself and the imagination; his empathy with the socially marginalised; his firm conviction that there is no progress without contraries.

Furthermore, in his approach to literature he subscribes to a Romantic interpretation of the self. In categorically and consistently stating that to be true to oneself is the most admirable quality of a great writer, Kennelly shares the Romantics' conviction that it is possible to reach to all the dark corners of the self in order to get 'an insight into the nature of things',[27] or as he puts it, 'to see things as they are'. Taking this position means believing in universal truths, which in turn makes it possible and indeed permissible to make generalisations about the human condition.

But it is a position which runs counter to various recent philosophical stances and literary theories, which claim that there is no such thing as universality, no essence of anything, and that no easy generalisations can ever be made. And it must be remembered that Kennelly's critical essays focus on, and remain within, the male Irish literary canon, therefore inevitably restricting their focus to male Irish experiences. Therefore, it may well be justified, in the light of recent literary theories, to argue that Kennelly takes risks as a critic when he makes somewhat daring generalisations about, for instance, the poet as 'spokesman for all people', or myths which show 'the sameness of all ages', or asserts that Kavanagh is 'one of the greatest modern poets', or that Joyce's humanity 'is among the bravest of the twentieth century, or indeed in the history of literature'.

However, it is a measure of his self-exploration and genuine commitment to listen to voices that he continually casts his own views into doubt. He increasingly creates a space for different and arguably more radical voices, particularly women's, as seen in his plays and in *The Book of Judas*. As a critic, too, he recognises and seeks to incorporate into the Irish literary canon women writers who according to him have started, and now lead, the thorough social transformation which he insists is presently taking place in Ireland, and who all express 'difference' and previously suppressed experiences: 'Anne Hartigan, Katie Donovan, Paula Meehan, Eavan Boland, Rita Ann Higgins, Nuala Ní Dhomhnaill, Medbh McGuckian, Emma Cooke…There's a special force in the writings of these women. I find it at times quite frightening, because they are dealing with feelings that were never talked about before.' [28]

Consequently, it is not a coincidence that he in a sense has moved from Yeats to Yeats, and to Joyce. In other words, he has shifted from his early interest in Yeats's cult of a mythological Irish past and romanticised sense of Irishness, to a fascination with Yeats's continuous remaking of the self and his ruthless insistence on artistic and emotional renewal. 'The act of re-writing words on a page,' Kennelly writes in reference to Yeats, but revealing a definite tone of self-reflection, 'is inseparable from the conscious, disciplined re-moulding of the self, that interesting mess which is always capable of being shaped and re-shaped by a vigilant and vigorous imagination' (*JJ* 238). Similarly, Joyce, too, represents for Kennelly necessary and provocative aesthetic ideals, Joyce who, although aware of artistic possibilities in the exploitation of myths, instead used them to expose and explode cultural assumptions, as Kennelly himself has done in his challenging of the Cromwell and Judas myths. Kennelly's critical, and creative, writings articulate a longing for joy and peace; but they also stress that, to reach that state of mind, a thorough dismantling is necessary, of the self, of cultural clichés, and ultimately of language.

'The Roaring Storm of Your Words'

Brendan Kennelly in conversation with
RICHARD PINE

RP: You have frequently emphasised the need for the poet to address and understand the self in the search for integrity. Despite your dislike of labels and clichés, it is very necessary to know who one is and where one comes from, and what relationship one has to people and to the world. In a sense this is the poet's real task. Could you please begin by telling me who *is* Brendan Kennelly?

BK: I would have to start with the forces that made me resist the idea of labelling in the first place. You're perfectly right to say that everybody has to be described or labelled in terms of origin and relationship, but I came out of a very labelled society, where you are a member of a large family – 'one of the Kennellys' – you are Kerry, Catholic, Republican, Irish-speaking, and wild and cute. All these things *might* be true, but somehow or other I resisted, or resented, people beating you with labels and *assuming* all that to be true about you. So my engagement with the label at that level was a war against a facile understanding of the complexity I apprehended in myself and couldn't quite cope with – and yet felt vaguely insulted by being described in easily accessible ways. I fought against it unconsciously at first, simply by following the irrational call of writing, and then later by deliberately disrupting the idea of the 'great character' in myself – which, again, you could argue, is there – by choosing characters to write about, in an aesthetic sense, to write *through*, who were outside my culture or offensive to it – so that my identity became clearer to me, if that is possible, by identifying with opposites, or opponents, scapegoats

This conversation took place in Trinity College, Dublin, on Sunday 5 December 1993.

or legendarily offensive people. In Cromwell's case, for example, he was the insult, and he needn't be thought about. One of the things that has always irked me or hurt me both in myself and in my society, is the upsurge of thoughtless reaction against an idea, or against a person. It is, I think, partly due to tribalism, partly due to the notion that 'you know your enemies, you don't have to go on about them', and I think that at a broader level that is the problem of Ireland as well, of modern society – that strange mindlessness of response.

RP: When you refer to the complexity in yourself you are saying that you need to find your unique voice, the voice that can't be labelled, the need to work *through* that complexity.

BK: Yes. What I'm finding still hard is to use the word 'I', to say that this refers to this daily Brendan Kennelly who goes about his work and tries to do his job like any other person tries to. There's a logic, I think, in our looking at this 'I' – it's almost, I won't say a racial thing, but an imaginative thing, that the imagination is the expansive soul that we have. Many of us cope with it by ousting it from things like education, but for the writer it's always there, challenging and tormenting him to the point where he has to give it its voice, its say, and it keeps intruding. Sometimes I wish it would go away, and let me have the self that I'm used to. So at the moment, for example [*in his current work-in-progress*], I'm stuck into this image of an 'I' who is ageing – he would be an old poet going blind, in the streets of Dublin, he would be interested in the sad scrawled messages of humanity on walls, and he's going to have an epic response to all this, because he hears voices and he's in tune with history, with himself, with the lost, with the scrawlers.

RP: There seem to be two things here: you're talking about complexity and at the same time you're talking about opposites, in that the Cromwell who is oppositional to Irish history is someone whom you must embrace. There is an 'I' who in a sense is not you, not the self you know but the self you don't know. You once said to me that 'poets are blind men groping for light' and in Medea you say that 'manhood is deliberate blindness' (*M* 34). In a sense you're reaching out for the opposite of manhood, which is the woman, the feminine part of your own intuition, and saying that that is the part which will create the light, by which the blindness, the man-ness, in your poetry, can see. But at the same time you also have Rimbaud's problem of '*je est un autre*', that 'I' is otherness; and this is in *Judas* when Judas says 'I have never seen

him, and I have never seen anyone but him' (*BOJ* 53). Isn't that
the meaning of the complexity, the duality within you?

BK: It's very strange that you should pick out these words: a girl
stood up in my class last week and sang them as a song. I am
terrified of self-importance and of the pomposity that is in all of
us, because it is unintelligent. I'm much more interested in states
of fragmentation, because they're more likely to lead to intelligent
statements and enlightening images. Therefore I think that, as a
young man, I sought deliberate disruption. I didn't know it at the
time, but nobody could drink the way I did and not be more than
half in love with the poetic benefits of cracking up in different
ways. It is not retrospective fantasising that I'm involved in here.
I know that I was interested always in seeing things from the sky,
from the gutter, from what I took to be good and evil viewpoints,
and this seemed to be more 'me' than the me that I knew – a person who loves laughter and conversation and talk of all sorts, and
silence, long periods of solitude. Therefore blindness would be part
of that [*he recites 'The Blind Man'*, ATFV *16-17, originally published
in* Collection One: Getting Up Early]. That was back in the sixties.
It has always seemed to me that poetry is a blind art, and is written
with skill and faith. You have to believe in your blindness. Much
of the writing about poetry is not the writing of blind people, it's
the writing of people who believe they see. A lot of our critical
acumen derives from the other kind of confidence, the confidence
of perception, whereas I think a lot of poetry derives from putting
your faith in what you're going to come up with, out of your own
darkness. That's what I mean by being blind.

RP: I was very surprised to see in the Preface to *Judas*, where you
talk about poetry being a celebration of human inadequacy and
failure, that you also say that you envy certain people their blindness – that you envy them 'their loneliness, their sincerity and
their freedom' – as if those three conditions were cognate, in the
blindness of people.

BK: At some level I suffer from what every poet suffers from – I'd
like to become a poem, to become coherent and accomplished and
singing, as it were, and communicate and touch, an object that is
there, fixed and changing, according as people consider you and
experience you.

RP: Is that what you mean when you say that when you read a poem
by Yeats you are also being read by the poem (*JJ* 233-34)?

BK: Absolutely. I feel that true reading, vulnerable, open reading, which is not inquisitive or acquisitive, is a process of self-definition and this definition involves knowledge of your limitations being hoisted on you by the poem – which I think accounts for the statement we often hear, 'I get more and more out of this poem each time I read it' or 'I get a different thing out of this poem each time I read it'. That's what I mean by a poem reading the reader. It's a truly delightful experience and it goes to show, as well, that what we call the self is a very shifting entity, if it is an entity: it is permanently changing, in relation to what it tries to consider, it is always open to change and development, what the moral self might call betrayal – that you could betray a former perception, that you would change in your mind about a line, that the line might mean something to you, almost the opposite in five years' time that it does now. That's why some people have an almost terrified longing for a moral fix, where the outlook remains fixed, that, in the oldest Irish way, 'this is what God said', 'I am merely saying what God said'. And I appreciate that terror and that longing for that moral fix. But that is the opposite both of writing and of reading, which are both studies, experiences, in change that is allowed, that is permitted, because most of the changes that we undergo are 'permitted', we allow ourselves to be changed, and I think that there are some people open to that, and others not.

RP: I was interested to find that when we started talking you came very quickly to speak about Cromwell, as if you needed somehow still to 'apologise', to give an *apologia* in the technical sense of the word, for the creation of books like *Cromwell* and *Judas*. I find (and I know that I'm in a minority in this) that most people refer to your earlier work as merely leading towards *Cromwell* and *Judas* as *the* books, and in a sense that's there in your own mind, that if you had to label yourself you would identify yourself as the creator of *Cromwell* and *Judas*. Yet, those of your poems which read me come most readily from your early work. Many people have, unquestionably, found themselves in *Cromwell* and more especially in *Judas*, as you did yourself, but it's the previous work which you and your critics seem largely to be regarding principally as a prelude. Isn't there still the complexity and the faith, and the need for faith, and the need for rage, in that body of work?

BK: I didn't leap to *Cromwell* out of apology, I went to the book out of a desire to illustrate in more coherent terms what I had been saying in the early poetry. In some of the sonnets of *Love Cry* I had outcast figures. In many of the early poems, right back to Nellie Mulcahy ['*The Stones*', ATFV *38, originally published in* Dream of a Black Fox] and other poems, there were figures from outside the little parish that I was born in, and I wasn't as conscious of it, but when you saw an old woman being stoned, or a tinker beating his wife, or a teacher flogging a young fellow because he was stammering ['*The Stammer*', BS *17*] or someone actually hitting out from the parish (which is on the sea) and trying to swim to Clare, these excursions into the otherworld, whatever they were, always did attract me, and I think you are perfectly right to say that it's not a preamble. It's an abiding concern. I don't know why it is so. I live and work inside walls, as it were; I have lived in a house, I had a home once, I lived in marriage – that was a structure – but it didn't alter my interest in what seemed to me to be some kind of connecting comment on myself.

RP: The two worlds which dominate your life are the world of the village where you came from and the world of this 'village' where we are sitting now –

BK: that's one way to put it –

RP: they both have walls, they are both rigidly structural in terms of the way that relationships are organised. Aren't you saying that within a set of walls or structures, whatever it may be called, that there are these complexities and there are always people wondering what it is like to make these excursions?

BK: Yes, and there's also the sense of disintegration which is always present in oneself. And whatever the attractions are towards disintegration, it co-exists with the strong stability of the community that I find myself in. It's interesting that you point out these two worlds. A village is a world, and TCD is a world. However, I have increasingly got the same feeling about *the* World. And having learned what I did from my village and my college, the World is small, the World is knowable, and the World is connectable. One can connect with it. I no longer suffer the sense of the appalling vista or the intimidating immensity. I can more or less go anywhere, talk to anybody, and not just that, but feel that I can connect with them, by letting them come into me, whereas before, for a large part of my life, the villager or tribalist or academic was interested in getting to know them from outside. What my poetry seems to have taught me – I can't describe it as humility, or surrender, but it's 'being-at-home-in-strangeness', more than I used to be, and having the wistful capacity for surrender to life outside me, to let them into me. I suppose that as the years go by you do feel – coming up to sixty – something akin to moments of wisdom, and you begin to say in this gathering of eight young people with me, that six are brighter than me and one will be, when she reads more [*laughs*]. And yet they look at you, and have some kind of respect for you, because you've written a few books or something. And that is the same with the world, that I have grown in some kind of comic response which is rooted in the sense of inadequacy, in the sense of fragmentation, in the sense of being a bit of a human being who has a lot to do, a lot to find out. And I see that now with this new poem, it's intriguing me, this whole adventure in language that we're into. That is the difficulty now, the world of the Word.

RP: Do you worry about that a great deal? In your essay on contemporary Irish poetry ['*Irish Poetry Since Yeats*', JJ *55-71*] you mention that a playwright recently said to you that 'words are useless' –

BK: it was John B. Keane –

RP: and it's something that Stoppard and Friel have said.

BK: It co-exists with that promise that keeps us all going, that words *can* do it, that words can say it, and I think that there are moments – and it may hit you in the sixties or before it – that you are only scratching the skin of the darkness, no matter what. And I have increasingly experienced a profound sense of uselessness, and I have tried to learn to live with that too. I feel it may have a simple explanation. My response is now, more than ever, drink to the bird, drink and become ecstatic when you are visited by the sense of worthlessness, that what we do is nothing, never was anything and never will be. But I've tried to live with it, and I have written it down: words are useless, we are involved in something that is nothing in comparison with what the world faces – are we going to bomb ourselves out of existence? starve ourselves out of existence? is the whole thing poised on the edge of an indescribable abyss?

RP: And yet you have a tremendous faith in words, words are your travelling companions.

BK: I have to still assert a faith in me. I visited a man yesterday, whom I knew as a child. He taught me. He is The Swimmer that you liked the poem about [ATFV *49 – originally published in* Love

Cry, which Kennelly and I had discussed during his appearance in my
radio series, 'Music Dialogue', broadcast on RTE FM3 radio on 27
March 1992]. He's eighty-four now, and he had open-heart surgery,
and he's in great form; and he was sitting on the edge of the bed,
and the first thing he said to me was 'I'm talking with this man in
the next bed and we're describing how the small birds are vanishing out of the hedges in his county and in mine, and how very
hard it is for a hunter to find these birds' – and they were talking
about fish, birds, and leverets, and so on, and I was suddenly into
the objective world again, rid of my own neurosis, rid of my darkness, and into that objective world of the man of action which I've
always loved in him. And suddenly words took off from him, and
after his operation he was suddenly not conscious of words at all
but was describing creatures, sensations, football, a fellow in a goal
mouth with a cap, and the way his legs would go when the ball
was dropping, and this was fifty years ago – and I left him and
said to myself, 'if the writer could only always have that sense of
excitement and excited potential about words' – rather than coming, as we must, I suppose, on the dark inadequacy of the entire
enterprise. The two things should co-exist, the hope must co-exist
with the hopelessness, and I think that it's important, therefore, to
get out into communities, into, as it were, village halls, collections
of men and women in their fifties and sixties, groups of schoolboys
and schoolgirls, a bunch of businessmen who have a conception of
reason and language that is hurting them, and they don't know it.
And I think that the poet in his doubt, in his hurt, in his private
hell, can bring genuine moments of light to other people. And that,
again, is what I mean by the blind man – that you do talk out of
your blindness, you do write out of it, and out of these polar attitudes to language that you have to suffer and use.

RP: Is this why, in your plays, which are very bleak and remorse-
ful, at the moment when you are raging most for a new order, and
for justice, and for people to transcend loneliness and loss and in-
capacity, that you are at your most faithful –

BK: to people –

RP: yes, and to
something which is very deeply rooted in yourself, that you can't
quite come to terms with, that your faith is a question-mark?

BK: I do go beyond the concepts of certainty and uncertainty. The
doctors whom I've spoken to seem to have an almost naïve notion
of a nightmare or of hope. I think that at a certain point they are

intertwined. Who knows out of what moody swing or rhythm some-body decides to commit suicide or to live, who knows out of what gelling of emotional rhythms one opts for the assertion of continuity. All I can say is that when I'm in the act of writing, knowing that maybe I'm going down into a swamp, for example, I also have the desire to emerge and come up to the light and save myself. And if there is a value in these plays, I think it has to do with that genuinely fundamental and essential tension between the sinking into a bottomless darkness and the desire to rise into a civilised, shareable light, where I know the faces of my friends, where I can share their words, their laughter, where I can once again resume negotiations of friendship and connection. So as a writer I am given to beginnings. My deepest hope is that I can begin again tomorrow morning. It is connected with a depressive nature, of course, but even more than that, to have the two things in yourself, to have the longing to swoon and sink, to have the desire to rise. The language may seem melodramatic – in fact it is a most ordinary condition and it is daily and it needn't be dwelt on. The fact that I can go through a term of really difficult teaching and meetings is very important to me. I need that discipline because there is a longing in me not to do anything, but perhaps to stay drunk. I have always appreciated people who opt out, I think that sometimes it's the sign of a better intelligence, or at least an intelligent person making a better decision. It's a different kind of responsibility. I could argue from the point of view of the man or woman who says 'why go ahead with this propagation of the bour-geois stupor and greed, creating a society where our prisons are full of kids from deprived backgrounds?' and education is connected with that. What the poetry teaches you is that you *are* connected, 'the moral Christian and his laws/ Is the unbeliever and his cause'. When you perceive the connections of the world in what you are daily involved in, and you know that a lot of people are not bother-ing to make those connections, it is hard enough at times to put up with it, to understand people who opt out of it. Nor am I con-demning the contribution of people who try to opt to work and live within it.

RP: At the root of all that is what you once said to me, that the poet's ambition is 'to define love' – which of course means that you have to use words to do that. In this role – your self-defining role of defining love – do you see that there's both a public and a private side to it, almost in the Yeatsian sense of differentiating poetry and rhetoric?

BK: I would first of all say that the great poets define love. I am not a great poet, but I'm interested in love and in the stages that reach towards love. At the moment I'm not big enough, or perhaps even not skilled enough, to define love, though one day perhaps I might write the kind of poem that would do what you are suggesting poets do. I am still preparing. I am good at trying to define kinds of confusion, kinds of contradiction, kinds of turmoil, kinds of vulnerability. These are four preparatory stages to love, and I think I'm very concerned with these. The poets I love are people who seem to have got beyond that. Your point about language is absolutely true. I find that the great poems about love are utterly lucid, as if they had taken the confusion, the contradictions, the suffering and the vulnerability, gone through them all, and come out with lucidity, a statement as if, having been in a nightmare, you woke up, sat on the edge of the bed, and said – as it happened to me last night – 'Eddie is dead / He came to me in sleep / His eyes were tired and wise / He said / It's just as trivial here as there / I do hope you're enjoying your paradise'. A dead man said that to me, and he was clear. I reported what he said. And that might be a moment of contact with love, through the voice of a dead man.

RP: It is very necessary to you, isn't it, to pursue this to the uttermost. You wrote of Yeats's 'urgent need for emotional precision' [JJ 244] and in a sense it's a technical thing as well as an emotional one.

BK: The original definition of sin, from the Aramaic, is 'wide of the mark'. So the equation of the religious impulse with an aesthetic ideal of precision is to me inseparable. It is sinful to be imprecise. I am a constant sinner in that sense. I know my love of words, my attempt to know myself and others, frequently results in an imprecise mayhem of impressions. Now and then I seem to strike a line which is true and clear. The prayer for grace is a prayer for precision. If sin is 'wide of the mark' and imprecise, the state of grace is being precise, in precisely knowing a child or a friend. And it needn't be called that, but I'm only taking the idea of gracefulness, which is again lucidity or love. That one day you manage to see a thing very simply and clearly, not out of over-simplification but out of experience, out of having got through the trouble. The great poets share this with children, they have a brutal honesty which doesn't come over as brutal honesty because a child can say anything to you and it doesn't hurt you, and I think that really first class poets have the same, literally wonderful capacity for stating themselves clearly to you.

RP: Is that kind of poetry purely private, or does it have a public aspect as well? You're talking about the reader's or poet's relationship with the poem, rather than the poem's or poet's relationship with society. In that sense there's no need to create an audience other than the single reader, whereas Kavanagh and Yeats were madly anxious to create some kind of audience.

BK: I seem to have a nature that can walk into a room of seven or eight hundred people and to be able to communicate with them. Now, that's very strange to me, because when I write I feel that I'm not even writing for me, I'm writing for this person in my self that I want to apologise to, or get in touch with, or explain something to, or enter into a dialogue with. There is somebody in me who may be my father or my mother or somebody dead, or somebody perhaps unborn, that I wish to talk to. But I receive letters from people about my poems, and this leads me to think that what we call communication is never truly frontal. But in order to say whatever it is you have to say, in order to communicate with others, you have to address it to this person within, who is a private audience, who is always listening creatively, who is also a critic and comes back to you and in a sympathetic way says 'yes' or 'no'. But that strange point – that communication is not frontal – is like when you *are* talking to eight hundred people you're talking to *this* person, you are talking to one, making something clear, and what people like is the effort on your part to make something clear. This they take as referring to *them*. And it *is*; what we call communication is something quite abstract, which has also a personal, passionate dimension, which makes things happen between us. But we have to have these hidden ghosts, we have to have the hidden audience, the audience in the heart.

RP: This brings us again to the plays, and what you are trying to address in the plays, or *re*dress in the plays. Obviously, they are immensely public, in two senses: firstly they deal with themes and issues which are in the public domain and have been there for thousands of years – the historic events of ancient Greece and the way they were written about; but they are also public and political in the sense that you are putting women's issues onto our contemporary agenda. But in the sense you've just spoken about, of addressing someone within you, they are surely an attempt to speak to the Medea and the Hecuba and the Antigone within yourself?

BK: I'm not a feminist as such, in the political sense. When I wrote about Medea, I was trying to understand rage that was in myself, and Medea *was* in me, and so was Jason, and yet I could make the distinction. I could link the rage of Medea to the women in that hospital who were all around me, who were Mayo women and Clare women and Dublin women, who had landed in what they regarded as the ditch, because of men. But I seemed to be at home there, oddly enough. I liked it. It was a nice place. And to that extent it surprised me afterwards, and still does, that *some* women see it as knowledge of women. I don't feel that I know much about women, as such; I am more and more open to them, particularly since I dropped the concept of woman as purely sexual or the notion of sexual relationships always surging forward. Again, like communication, sexuality is best when it is not frontal, when it's allowed to happen, and in writing these plays I was trying to get in touch with areas of my own sexuality. Having been brought up in this passionate over-simplification which some critics have properly observed at work in me, where woman was an occasion of sin, that woman *was* sin, that is very hard to overcome. Whether you're charming, or attractive, or repulsive to a woman, under it all, at a certain level, there's this sense in an Irish catholic male of my generation, of woman as sin. How they coped with that is interesting. A lot of male tyranny over women is over sin, in conquering sin. That's an awful thing to say, but I think it is true. I've acknowledged that I share a very deep problem – that it was beaten into me, that 'company-keeping', or human relationship, was a sin. Born with this nature that I had, which is strangely joyous as well as depressive, which is celebratory, which loves, acclaims the way things assert themselves, as well as sympathy with the outcast and the defeated – given that nature, and then to be told that half of humanity is an occasion of sin, particularly when that half laughs and works and sustains you, it really fucks you up. So my plays at some level are this attempt to get at the thing in myself that is sinful, which is fragmented, which is partial vision, which is imprecise in relation to women. What I was looking for was a precise statement about the nature and consequence of sexual relationships, varying from political relationships to straightforward fucking. I have always, since youth and since I read Blake, been aware of consequences. Catholicism is not a religion of consequences, because you can go to confession and get rid of your sins every Saturday night, and walk out as if the consequences of your hurts inflicted on others did not exist. That is one of the reasons why I became interested in Protestantism, and it's one of the reasons why, as an Irishman, I became interested in England. I always thought that the English had a deeper sense of consequence – not that much in relation to Ireland – but around the world, they had a deeper sense of consequence than people of my own race.

RP: They have a sense of history in a quite different way to the Irish, because the Irish are continually having to allow for discontinuity, whereas the English 'logical' mind says 'this is the consequence of that, that is why we are a success as a nation', whereas the Irish are saying 'we know that we have been under this stone for centuries, and that is why we have to keep inventing history'.

BK: You're onto something there that hasn't been dealt with that satisfactorily. The nature of the Irish experience in historical terms has produced in a sense a deeply immoral people or society, where that special breed of corruption – rural, catholic, mindless and dynamic – a network of helping each other out in what is palpably a corrupt way, if scrutinised from outside, is being questioned at last. Two poems I read in Japan, 'The House that Jack Didn't Build' and the response 'Statement of the Former Occupant' [ATFV *150-54*] I read in a rough, rural voice, and Terence Brown said to me 'Why did you never read them like that in Dublin?' and it was a brilliant question because I suddenly had to admit that I was embarrassed or afraid, but in a foreign country I was able to show the rough experience of being in exile in language, something again which not many English poets suffer. They are very much at home in this beautifully developed language, with attendant emotions. If I were asked, for example, why there was such an upsurge of irony in the 1960s in the Movement poetry, I would be able to explain that in a way that they mightn't accept, but from the viewpoint of the man who is not at home in English even now. Sometimes I dream in Irish, but not only that – in strange accents, strange voices, so these are part of that historical feeling and that adventure of not being at home. The problem is to be at home in homelessness. As you pointed out, that goes right back to a poem like 'The Tippler' [ATFV *35, originally published in* Dream of a Black Fox] and the idea of bog-Latin; that's a chap walking into my dad's pub, an illiterate man, with his brother – I remember this – and talking in a language that wasn't English, wasn't Irish, wasn't anything; but they talked away to each other, making up this language, the O'Mahonys. I asked one of the lads, 'What's that?' and he said 'That's bog-Latin. Fellows from the bog talk bog-Latin when they come into the village.' And I can hear these things in *Finnegans Wake*. I can hear that quest for a language that is not Irish nor English, that does justice to all the consequences in oneself of history and the passing of one's own life. Living with Peggy [*his wife*] was a great experience linguistically for me, because I was into the language of explanation and psychology, the American language of highly articulate analysis of practically everything. Whereas I am prone to long moments of stupefaction, long periods of letting things sink in, as it were, and not trying to explain them. I'm not an explainer. I don't think I am.

RP: When you were writing *Antigone* and *Medea* you were bringing to the surface things that had never been spoken of before, from the women's movement, and beginning your own movement towards clarity which hadn't been expressed in this country in that way. What strikes me as very strange, in this contest of yourself with the idea of woman and the demands she makes, is that many of the women in your life have been figures of authority: the teacher, the mother, the nurse, and then later the wife and the daughter – all these are figures who exercise authority and create responsibilities. It took a long time to reach the surface in your work.

BK: I think something has to be said here which is connected with poetry, and with character, and is certainly my belief. We've often talked about the sustaining power of wonder in poetry. What is it that keeps you going from the age of eight or nine to the fifties? What is this power (although I wouldn't use that term)? I think there is something that doesn't die from childhood, and I call it 'wonder'. This means that I have never surrendered to the language of rational explanation or analysis. And even though I work in a university, where such language is the desired idiom, I do prefer, and am more at home in, the language of wonder, speculation, outrageous and often hilarious possibility, and this has stayed alive in me. I have therefore in me a child. I think in a poem [*unpublished*] about Eamonn Keane I said that he refused to murder the child in the heart. A lot of 'mature' development involves this murder; the worst murder we commit is the murder of the child in the heart. And it's often necessary, to get on in the world that we have created for ourselves. You have to appear in many parts of society like a rational, mature person, capable of judgements and balances and to look and feel OK and acceptable and without emotional problems above all, as if you had got everything solved. The sense of men in power or in positions of leadership in society is inseparable from the aura of solution and confidence and know-it-all-ness which they generate – it's false. It has to be false. But it *can* work if you kill the child and I have not done that. I think I have not done that. And therefore I do write as a child. When I wrote poems like 'Poem From a Three-Year Old' [ATFV *40, originally published in* The Visitor] I felt swingingly at home in it, and some of my more perceptive critics said that they were glad to see that I had at last publicly acknowledged my intellectual age (!) [*laughs*]. They were actually telling the truth in ways that they didn't suspect, and I approached *Medea* and the women partly from the same angle. The second thing about character is connected with that: some women – strangers – walk up to me and say they like me, and they're sincere, and I know that what they mean is that they like the child in me. Now, the child in you dies when you start talking too much about it, and we've never talked about it, and I won't talk much more about it. I think it's a bit like innocence, Richard, that innocence dies when you begin to talk of being innocent.

RP: I remember that we said once before that in a sense one never gets away from a certain *house* – it's the walls, the things that happen inside them – and I was fascinated when you said that you've carried something forward with you from childhood, because it's presumably what happens in that first house. It's one reason why I've called this book *Dark Fathers into Light*. It's something in a way that your poems are always going back to. Your first major poem, 'My Dark Fathers', is a poem which acknowledged something which still has an affective power over what you are and what you do, and I think that your writing is still going back to that first house where something indefinable or even indescribable has happened, and none of us knows what it is, but we are always trying to tear down a veil which is between us and it. I wonder how far the phenomenon of woman is concerned there. The point where you said to Gabriel Fitzmaurice 'You think I hate women: I don't, I hate myself' – it's the point where in your plays you are creating the tension between the 'you' that writes and the 'you' that you in a sense hate. Is woman the enemy, or is she merely the template?

BK: I don't think she's the enemy. There's a profound confusion between the idea that you write about somebody who hates women (you could argue that at some level Kennelly is talking about himself when he writes about Judas and this and this and this) and the idea of playing with a persona in poetry which is exploring the co-existence of hatred with attraction. I think the other thing you suggest is more interesting – the notion that something happens in a house with brothers and sisters and a father and a mother, with space itself, with the notion that there was no corner where you could go to read, to write, to think. You did love these people but you had to fight with them. There was nowhere you could hide to think things out. And you weren't ever conscious of this, and there *is* a very real sense in which talking about these women, letting Hecuba and Medea happen in me, is a search for a space that I want to open up, to enjoy their sexuality in me; I want to suffer their pain, in order to understand my own, in order to understand my original congestion, to come to terms repeatedly with the sense that women must be excluded from life, must be regarded as wrong and sinful and tempting; and to be true to my way of writing I must be them. I think that the notion of being strangled by woman is there from childhood, from the 'occasion of sin' idea. 'How many times, my child? Did you take pleasure in it, my child? Make sure you never look at a woman like that again, my child.' All that strangulation with my – I think – characteristic ebullient love of freedom, of openness, of space, I see it in me today. There are days when I want to walk out through Dublin and follow that river, I want to go out to Kilmainham, I want to see all the places. And there are times still when I want to shrivel up in the corner of a room – and I do. And I think it's true of my poetry: it has explained this passion for continuing, for trying to begin again, to fight the congested, strangulated view of the world and to open up, to experience the full range of sexuality. I think we have a right as human beings to do that, we have a duty *to be women* if our kind is to survive, to produce this human being, this man-woman, who in the future will not declare war on women, or on men, and who will save the world. I can see a creature developing, a man-woman, a woman-man, who will do that. We have to save it from ourselves. That's how I feel. I know I'm talking about a strangulated experience, but if I were to take a young Buddhist or a young English boy or girl, I'm sure they have forms of strangulation at them too, in their hearts, and that is what interests me, when I talk about space, Dublin as a city of space. It really matters to me, Richard, that I be able to experience the space offered by Dublin. You know the poem I'm talking about, 'The small hills of this city are truly surprising' [ATFV *124*, *'Clearing a Space'*] – that, to me, is my problem, clearing a space for myself in the jungle of my inhibitions and emotions and congestions.

RP: In this sense, what you so often describe as the 'abyss of the self', especially in relation to Synge and Yeats, is merely the room in which one sits or the city through which one walks –

BK: it's the chair –

RP: and it's to make the connection between them, to inhabit that room, to stretch out and reach the limits of that city, is the way of overcoming that abyss.

BK: It is. And also living in it as well. There are times when one has to carry it around with oneself. There are times when the city is an adequate vehicle, or instrument, for helping you to fight it, and the city is glorious; there are moments standing on O'Connell Bridge, looking down the river, towards that sky that can be so wonderfully coloured, with on either side the dilapidated houses – you're never long out of touch with congestion or squalor in Ireland, never. But since they're in oneself they are acceptable. And then to start walking through oneself, through the city, is to me one of the hope-making experiences. I'm sure people get it in different ways; I get it from the streets of Dublin, I get it from this strange contact with hope and from the old river. I want in this new poem to celebrate that old river and it is a beautiful old place. I know it's been done by a certain gentleman (!) but it has things to be said about its life-giving qualities – the walls and the way people throw things into it – it's a wonderful sight, a bed floating down the Liffey [*laughs*], it's so wonderful. And of course, it's such a simile – who made love in it? and where were they going?

RP: – an Irish Cleopatra?

BK: An Irish Cleopatra floating down the Liffey!!

RP: 'The bed she floated in'!

[*complete laughter*]

RP: The other thing I've noticed, while you've been talking about the emergence of the self, is that in a way you talk about the search for joy, the 'journey into joy', as really a way of coming to terms with, of making connection with, whatever is congesting or confusing us, and in a way that is the woman; that achieving this man-woman *is* the journey into joy, that it is so for us as individuals, lovers and children and parents, and it will be so for us as a society as well, if it can be achieved.

BK: If it *can* be achieved. If you could make that living relationship, which is alive – that is the hardest thing to achieve, whether it be with your poem or your words or your students, but certainly with a woman: you owe it to her to let her live and be alive in yourself. That may seem very naïve, but in fact it doesn't happen that much, it is very hard to remain giving in any relationship, and yet it is the only answer, it's the best answer, to give at the risk of in-

culcating greed in the other. I think it's the oldest thing in the world,
the oldest injunction in the world – 'give that ye may receive'. I
have a poem written after 'Let It Go' –

> I don't know if I shall be
> Speaking or silent, laughing or crying
> When it comes to me
> Out of its own distant place...
> ...if I find courage enough,
> I may speak in a manner
> Befitting this thing.
> God help me the moment
> My heart starts opening
> To comprehend and give.
> I will be born in that hour of grace
> I will begin to live.
>   ['Birth', *ATFV* 101-02]

RP: Joy, I think you said, is both sharp and deep. It's not all laughter, joy is pain at the same time as it is laughter.

BK: It is, and it includes the dull, drab task of daily living, and
togetherness.

RP: Åke Persson makes a strong point about your having the 'Romantic' faith in the sense that you believe in certain universal truths.
Would it be true to say that that is also what ultimately reconciles
you with catholicism, that it deals in universals rather than specifics?

BK: Well, that's an interesting question. I'm appalled by certain
personalities and attitudes. It's almost inseparable from the Irish
thing – Articles 2 and 3 [*of the Irish Constitution*] remind me of the
claims for Infallibility for some reason. The thing about being Irish
is that, as if to compensate for our inherited mindlessness, we are
driven to make absolute claims on others. That is the thing we
must stop – being possessors of truth, owning other people. At a
very deep level I would disagree and say that I am resisting the
absolutes. The kind of catholicism that interests me is ragged,
irrational, probably unjustifiable, but full of interesting little sentences, of faces, of a myth that is, to me, pleasing. The most pleasing thing about it is something like the idea of the communion of
saints, where you can actually talk to your dead. I like it psycho-
logically, poetically, and if there's a religious strain in me I would
like it in that sense: I would like to talk to my father, and I would
sit there and talk to the people I've lost, including the living I have
lost. That's what it means to me. My interest in it is as mythical as
it is religious. If you take, for example, the seven sacraments, they
are good in teaching – I like to renew my students, I like them to

commune with each other, with me: at a purely educational level *it makes sense* to do these things and to prepare yourself for the journey. So, the words 'journey into joy' have a vaguely sacramental touch to them, that it is a journey and it is more a hope, a journey into the daily hope of joy. It is not an ultimate joy, and in that sense, too, I disagree with the 'Romantic' label. My concept of joy is work, trying to make myself clear to you, now, and that is where something like the sacraments, with their insistence on constant renewal, of the self, come in, if they were properly applied – I'm not even a practitioner, but I can see what the old men and women dreamed of, they were dreaming of what the psychiatrists were dreaming of, the psychologists, they were dreaming of renewal. You know that little poem 'Begin', at the end of *Good Souls to Survive* –

> Though we live in a world that dreams of ending
> That always seems about to give in,
> Something that will not acknowledge conclusion
> Insists that we for ever begin

– I have heard that these four lines have helped a lot of people, even though it was a poem specifically about Pembroke Road, about that bridge [*Baggot Street Bridge*]: it's Kavanagh territory, but I myself lived in Raglan Road. It's the most normal thing in the world, this strange life-giving quality of Dublin, co-existing with the crushing narcissism and the assassins among us and the begrudgery, the knockery, the refusal to let hope live, as if up from the very streets themselves came the opposite of all that. *That* quality, that is sacramental to me. And it's also the most 'romantic'. I like the outrageously irrational assertion of hope where there doesn't seem to be much. If I didn't do that, I wouldn't live, if I didn't fly in the face of myself, in the face of my own depression, if I were not a rebel against myself.

RP: I worried when I read in your essay on Yeats the picture of utter devastation in imagining 'Lear, deprived *even* of the presence of the fool' [JJ 232], that you could conjure something as empty as that. Full of nothing but madness which had lost the way of redeeming itself. It's presumably against that sort of picture – which is bleaker even than anything in Beckett –

BK: – when you're deprived of the factor that could drive you mad, you're truly alone then. And I'm also imagining being robbed of the babble, of the accusers, begrudgers, of all the 'maddening' things – nothing left but that state – a terrible state, isn't it?

RP: In *Judas* you make Joyce say 'no one in Ireland has a mind of his own'.

BK: I was talking about myself. I relate to my country reasonably well, I see it as in an unphilosophical tradition. I see a lot of people liking to be told what to think, whether it is the Church or the Leaving Cert. or the hoisting of responsibility onto political figures, to be oracles of revelation, when they are commonplace men and women, *that* is what I meant, the pedestallisation of mindlessness. Also I had in mind, I have to admit, that original idea of free-thinking, the sin of freedom − here again, the sin of thinking, intellectually. I remember devastating comments on Shaw, for example, the idea that people who indulged in certain kinds of thinking − that this was wrong. People who chased after magic. No exploratory sexual relationships, no exploratory freedom of thinking, no opening up to challenging differences in religion, in culture. Even the Irish language − sometimes a feeling was given to you that if you didn't talk it and write it and sing it, that you weren't fully Irish. That's dangerous rubbish. All that was part of what I have in mind when I fight myself. I love Irish, and I translate the poems. But I will not now confuse that love with the venomous ambitions of men who associate speaking Irish with *being* Irish. I want a world, and will fight for a world, that is free of these strictures. If you want a poetry that relates to everyone potentially (while exercising whatever discriminations are necessary to make it a human act) and think to the utmost edges of your personal abyss, and go into *every* difference, and survive, that's the world that the poet has to offer. And it's the world that accepts his own depression, alcoholism or madness. And their possible return, their ironic reconquest of hope. I live with that possibility. I dream of it.

NOTES

RICHARD PINE: Introduction

1. Richard Pine, 'Brendan Kennelly: Q&A', *Irish Literary Supplement*, Spring 1990, pp.21-23; all otherwise unattributed quotations by Brendan Kennelly in this Introduction are derived from this source.

2. Åke Persson, Introduction to Brendan Kennelly, *Journey into Joy: Selected Prose* (Newcastle upon Tyne: Bloodaxe Books, 1994) p.15.

3. Brendan Kennelly, Introduction to *Penguin Book of Irish Verse* (Harmondsworth: Penguin, 1970) p.30; *JJ*, p.46.

4. 'a mortaller': in 'The Sin' (*ATFV* 129-32) F.X. Skinner 'committed a sin ...a mortaller', i.e. a mortal sin.

5. In the Introduction to the *Penguin Book of Irish Verse*.

6. On frequent occasions in his *Essays and Introductions*.

7. 'Brendan Kennelly: Q&A': Kennelly is specifically referring to the life of words: 'One of my favourite pastimes is reading the Oxford English Dictionary, and I'll take a word and trace its joyous history. It reminds me of my own life, the struggle of a word to survive its own stages, to stay alive, to serve a young boy or girl who's encountering that word for the first time, and behind it are centuries of experience, and it's in the mouth of that child, and that's joy to me, the word as survivor.'

8. cf. Austin Clarke, introduction to *Plays of George Fitzmaurice: Dramatic Fantasies* (Dublin: Dolmen, 1967), p.viii.

9. In a television documentary 'State of the Art', produced by Sean O Mordha, broadcast by Radio Telefís Éireann 6 January 1993 (*my emphasis*).

10. 'Almost fifty years ago, I heard women in the village where I grew up say of another woman, "She's a Trojan", meaning she had tremendous powers of endurance and survival, was determined to overcome different forms of disappointment and distress, was dogged but never insensitive, obstinate but never blackscowling, and seemed eternally capable of renewing herself' (*TW* 2).

11. 'Brendan Kennelly: Q&A': 'The woman who kills her children is unbelievable, the mind cannot grasp it, it's killing the future, it's killing the one thing on which my poetry rests: hope.'

12. In a letter to Thomas Moore in 1821, quoted by James Fenton in his 1992 Ronald Duncan Lecture, South Bank Centre, London, November 1992.

13. cf. *ATFV* 11: 'behind everything I write is the story/ballad culture of my youth'.

14. In 'Satire in Flann O'Brien's *The Poor Mouth*', in *Journey into Joy*, p.184.

15. *Shelley in Dublin* (Dublin: Beaver Row Press, 1982), p.5.

16. 'Brendan Kennelly: Q&A': 'letting your imagination be enhanced by a *difference*... my own attempt to know what this thing is in you, to know that your self is not important, and that what matters is your empathising, and that paradoxically is what creates the vitality in your nature: givenness, going-outness, the imagination as something that makes you more alive inside, that turns your despair, your depression, your desire not to be, into vital forces of being.'

17. 'The Watcher in the Shadow', *Irish Times*, 16 April 1971.

18. cf. Anthony Roche, 'Ireland's Antigones: Tragedy North and South' in *Cultural Contexts and Literary Idioms in Contemporary Irish Literature*, edited by M. Kenneally (Gerrards Cross: Colin Smythe, 1988) pp. 221-50.

19. 'Modern Irish Poets and the Irish Epic', unpublished Ph.D. thesis, Trinity College, Dublin, 1966; in the introduction to the *Penguin Book of Irish Verse* Kennelly particularly emphasised the importance of Mangan and Ferguson as transitional nineteenth-century figures.

20. cf. Donncha Dall O Laoghaire: 'Loss of learning/brought darkness, weakness and woe/ on me and mine', *An Duanaire: 1600-1900, Poems of the Dispossessed*, edited by Sean O Tuama & Thomas Kinsella (Dublin: Dolmen, 1981), p.195.

21. *A Kind of Trust* (Dublin: Gallery Press, 1975), pp.16-17; cf. Ferguson, 'No rootless colonist of alien earth,/ Proud but of patient lungs and pliant limb/ A stranger in the land that gave him birth,/ The land a stranger to itself and him', *Mesgedra* (*The Poems of Samuel Ferguson*, edited by Padraic Colum, Dublin: Allen Figgis, 1963).

22. *Shelley in Dublin*, pp.22-25; cf. Yeats, 'Too long a sacrifice/ Can make a stone of the heart' ('Easter 1916').

23. *Penguin Book of Irish Verse*, p.42.

24. I am thinking particularly of Kennelly's 'The Gift' (*ATFV* 12): 'It was a gift that took me unawares/ And I accepted it'; cf. Seamus Heaney: 'Between my finger and my thumb/ The squat pen sits./ I'll dig with it', 'Digging', *Selected Poems 1965-1975* (London: Faber, 1980) pp.10-11.

25. W.B. Yeats, 'Anima Hominis', *Mythologies* (London: Macmillan, 1959), p.331.

26. Not least in the sense that it is structurally rooted in the dialogic style typical of the nineteenth century imagination.

27. *Moloney Up and At It* (Cork: Mercier, 1984) p.43.

28. *Antigone*, typescript, p.34.

GABRIEL FITZMAURICE: 'Becoming Song': The Translated Village

1. John Liddy, *The Angling Cot* (Dublin: Beaver Row Press, 1991), p.22.

2. Seán Ó Ríordáin, *Línte Liombó* (Dublin: Sáirséal agus Dill, 1971), p.14.

3. Review in *The Kerryman*, 30 December 1983.

4. Peter Levi, *The Lamentation of the Dead* (London: Anvil Press Poetry, 1984).

5. Seán Ó Ríordáin, *Éireaball Spideoige* (Dublin: Sáirséal agus Dill, 1952). Réamhra [Introduction].

6. Robert Leslie Boland, *Thistles and Docks* (Tralee: Kerry's Eye, 1993).

AUGUSTINE MARTIN: Technique and Territory in Brendan Kennelly's Early Work

1. *The Rain the Moon*, p.39

2. 'Sonnet', *The Rain the Moon*, p.57.

3. *Collection One: Getting up Early*, p.48.

4. Bryan MacMahon, *The Lion Tamer* (London: Macmillan, 1948) p.134.

5. *Selected Poems* (1969), p.33.

6. *Good Souls to Survive*, p.22.

7. 'Very Tragical Mirth, the Poetry of Brendan Kennelly', *Ireland Today*, September/October 1987.

8. *Shelley in Dublin*, p.10.

9. *Irish Writing*, no.3, 1947.

10. *Dream of a Black Fox* p.60.
11. *Dream of a Black Fox*, p.168-69.

GERALD DAWE: 'And Then – The Spring!': *Breathing Spaces*

1. Patrick Kavanagh, *Self Portrait* (Dublin: Dolmen Press, 1964) p.14.
2. *Self Portrait*, p.10-11.
3. *Self Portrait*, p.7.
4. *Self Portrait*, p.18.

JONATHAN ALLISON: *Cromwell:* Hosting the Ghosts

1. W.B. Yeats, 'The Curse of Cromwell'. *W.B. Yeats: The Poems*, edited by Richard Finneran (New York: Macmillan, 1983), p.304.
2. W.E.H. Lecky, *History of Ireland in the Eighteenth Century*, 1 (London: Longmans, Green, and Co., 1913), p.103.
3. Christopher Hill, *God's Englishman* (London: Penguin, 1970, 1990), p.266.
4. Hill, p.265.
5. Hill, p.262.
6. Supposedly, official figures for casualties at the siege of Drogheda are: 3552 fatalities among Cromwell's enemies, which included the English Royalist garrison held by Sir Arthur Aston (an English Catholic), and, most controversially, a large number of Irish civilian inhabitants of Drogheda. Cromwell is said to have lost 64 men in the siege. (See J. G. Simms, *War and Politics in Ireland, 1649-1730*, edited by D. W. Hayton and Gerard O'Brien (London & Ronceverte: Hambledon Press, 1986, p.9).
7. R.S. Paul, cited in Hill, p.112. J.G. Simms points out that Cromwell gave no quarter to anyone in Drogheda bearing arms, but that this was an acceptable convention of war, 'if a summons to surrender had been rejected', which it had. Where Cromwell appears to have been criminal is in offering no quarter to unarmed priests and civilians (Simms, pp.8-9). Corish writes that 'the massacre was not confined to the garrison, but became quite indiscriminate': Patrick J. Corish, 'The Cromwellian Conquest, 1649-53', *A New History of Ireland, III: Early Modern Ireland, 1534-1691*, edited by T.W. Moody, F.X. Martin and F.J. Byrne (Oxford: Clarendon Press, 1976), p.340.
8. Lecky, p.101.
9. Richard Pine, 'Brendan Kennelly: Q&A', *Irish Literary Supplement*, Spring 1990, pp.21-23.
10. Declan Kiberd, 'Contemporary Poetry: Introduction', *Field Day Anthology of Irish Writing*, 3 (Derry: Field Day, 1991), p.1362.
11. Kennelly, cited in Terence Brown, 'Awakening From the Nightmare: History and Contemporary Literature', *Ireland's Literature: Selected Essays* (Dublin: Lilliput Press, 1988), p.255.
12. Hill, p.256.
13. Hill notes Cromwell's 'conscientious enthusiasm for conferring the benefits of English civilisation on the natives, whether they liked it or not' (p.117).
14. See 'That Leg' and 'A Bad Time' (*C*, pp.52, 53), and Lecky, p.103.
15. Joseph Conrad, *Heart of Darkness*, edited by Robert Kimbrough, third edition (New York: Norton, 1988), p.10.
16. W.C. Abbott, cited in Hill, p.260.
17. Brown, p.254.

18. Simms, p.2.

19. Simms writes: 'It was a travesty to hold the garrison and citizens of Drogheda responsible for the actions of Ulster Gaels' (p.9). Corish writes of Cromwell's justification for the massacre of Drogheda by reference to the 1641 rebellion: 'That this justification could be advanced for the massacre of the inhabitants of a town that had never at any time been in the hands of the confederate catholics was a sombre indication of how far the guilt for "innocent blood" was now presumed to extend' (p.340).

20. Conrad, p.10.

21. Brown, p.253.

22. Brown, pp.255-56.

23. A.T.Q. Stewart, *The Narrow Ground: Aspects of Ulster, 1609-1969* (London: Faber, 1977), p.113.

24. Stewart, p.113.

25. Seamus Heaney, 'Funeral Rites', *North* (London: Faber, 1975), p.16.

26. James Joyce, *Finnegans Wake* (Harmondsworth: Penguin, 1983), p.3.

27. Seamus Heaney, 'Punishment', *North* (London: Faber, 1975), p.38.

28. Seamus Heaney, 'Feeling into Words,' *Preoccupations: Selected Prose 1968-1978* (London: Faber, 1980), p.60.

29. Seamus Heaney, 'Bog Oak', *Wintering Out* (London: Faber, 1972, p.15.

ANTHONY ROCHE: *The Book of Judas:*
Parody, Double Cross and Betrayal

1. Quoted by Alan Schneider, 'Waiting for Beckett,' in *Beckett at 60: A Festschrift* (London: Calder and Boyars, 1967), p.34.

2. Patrick Kavanagh, 'The Hospital', *Collected Poems* (London: MacGibbon and Kee, 1968), p.153.

3. *The Collected Poems of W B Yeats* (London: Macmillan, 1950), p.210.

4. Edward W. Said, *Nationalism, Colonialism and Literature: Yeats and Decolonisation* (Derry: Field Day, 1988), p.9. The material is reprinted in revised form in Edward W. Said, *Culture and Imperialism* (London: Vintage, 1994), pp.265-88.

5. Samuel Beckett, *The Complete Dramatic Works* (London: Faber and Faber, 1986), p.11.

6. Rita Ann Higgins, *Goddess on the Mervue Bus* (Galway: Salmon, 1986), p.20.

7. 'Death is the sanction of everything that the storyteller can tell. He has borrowed his authority from death.' Walter Benjamin,'The Storyteller', *Illuminations*, translated by Harry Zohn, edited with an introduction by Hannah Arendt (London: Collins Fontana, 1975), p. 94.

8. 'The Circus Animals' Desertion', *The Collected Poems of W B Yeats*, p.391. Compare 'A Beautiful Mind': 'Recently I met/One of the unacknowledged legislators of mankind. (...) He said: "I can't find a theme."' (373).

KATHLEEN McCRACKEN: **Rage for a New Order:**
Brendan Kennelly's Plays for Women

1. Judy Marle and T.P. Flanagan, *F.E. McWilliam* (Arts Council of Northern Ireland and Arts Council of the Republic of Ireland, nd), p.9.

2. Brendan Kennelly, *Antigone*, unpublished typescript (Dublin, 1984); first performed at the Peacock Theatre, Dublin, May 1986. *Medea* (Newcastle upon

Tyne: Bloodaxe Books, 1988); first performed at the Royal Dublin Society
Concert Hall, Dublin, October 1988; *Blood Wedding*, unpublished typescript
(Dublin, 1990); unperformed. *The Trojan Women* (Newcastle upon Tyne:
Bloodaxe Books, 1993); first performed at the Peacock Theatre, Dublin, June
1993. All further references to these works, and to *A Time For Voices: Selected
Poems 1960-1990* (Newcastle upon Tyne: Bloodaxe Books, 1990) and *Breathing
Spaces: Early Poems* (Newcastle upon Tyne: Bloodaxe Books, 1992) will be
made within the text as *A* (*Antigone*), *M* (*Medea*), *TW* (*The Trojan Women*),
BS (*Breathing Spaces*) and *ATFV* (*A Time For Voices*).

3. These include Kennelly's keynote address at the Conference on Anglo-Irish
Literature at the University of Antwerp on 9 April, 1986, subsequently published as 'Poetry and Violence' in his *Journey into Joy: Selected Prose*, edited
by Åke Persson (Newcastle upon Tyne: Bloodaxe Books, 1994), pp.23-45; his
address at the Annual Conference of the Ireland Funds in Kilkenny, 22-24
June 1990, published as 'Learning From Our Contradictions', *Ireland: Look,
The Land Is Bright* (Ireland Funds Conference Proceedings, 1990), pp.23-32;
'Q. & A. with Brendan Kennelly', with Richard Pine, *Irish Literary Supplement*,
9.1 (Spring 1991), pp.21-23; and his keynote address at the Cultures of Ireland
Group Conference in Dun Laoghaire, 27-28 September 1991, published in
Culture in Ireland: Division or Diversity? edited by Edna Longley (Belfast:
Institute of Irish Studies, 1991), pp.19-27.

4. Kennelly, 'Q. & A.', p.22.
5. Kennelly, 'Poetry and Violence', *JJ*, p.45
6. Kennelly, 'Q. & A.', p.22.
7. Kennelly, 'Q. & A.', p.22.
8. Kennelly, 'Q. & A.', p.21.
9. Kennelly, 'Q. & A.', p.21.
10. Kennelly, 'Poetry and Violence,' *JJ*, p.45.
11. Kennelly, 'Poetry and Violence', *JJ*, p.36.
12. Kennelly, 'Keynote Address', *Culture in Ireland*, p.21.
13. Kennelly, 'Poetry and Violence', *JJ*, p.45.
14. George Steiner, *Antigones* (Oxford: Clarendon Press, 1984), p.138.
15. Anthony Roche, 'Ireland's *Antigones*: Tragedy North and South', *Cultural
Contexts and Literary Idioms in Contemporary Irish Literature*, edited by Michael
Kenneally (Gerrards Cross: Colin Smythe, 1988), pp.221-50.
16. Roche, p.246.
17. Steiner, pp.104-05.
18. Kennelly, 'Learning From Our Contradictions', p.23.
19. Steiner, p.231 ff.
20. Steiner, p.150.
21. Kennelly, 'Q. & A.', p.22.
22. Virginia Woolf, *A Room of One's Own* (1929; New York: Harcourt, Brace,
Jovanovich, 1981), pp.97-104.
23. Roche, p.242.
24. Kennelly, 'Q. & A.', p.22.
25. In his address to the Cultures of Ireland Group Conference, Kennelly
began by posing a question and positing a partial response: 'But how is it
possible to speak of Ireland without using language of judgement, and therefore of blame? Blame is *useless* – it's like *revenge* or cynicism. It probably does
more damage to the person who lays it than to the person on whom it is laid.'
Kennelly, 'Keynote Address', *Culture in Ireland*, p.19.

26. Kennelly, 'Poetry and Violence', *JJ*, p.32.
27. 'Hatred is a dynamic force, a stimulating, animating power. Hatred hates indifference. Hatred loves its own annihilating expression, wiping out distinctions between innocent and guilty, adult and child, man and woman. Hatred tolerates no humane hierarchies of kindness, gentleness, affection, considerateness. Hatred sneers at the futility of intellectual subtlety. And hatred is, above all, a devoted servant to a cause. In serving that cause, whatever it be, hatred is exemplary in its attention to its own unshakeable purpose.' Kennelly, 'Poetry and Violence', *JJ*, p.30.
28. Kennelly, 'Q. & A.', p.22.
29. Brendan Kennelly, Introduction, *The Trojan Women*, Project Arts Centre, Dublin, 15 October 1989.

ÅKE PERSSON: The Critic: Towards a Literary Credo

I am indebted to Antoinette Quinn, Britta Olinder, Paul Keen, and Gilbert Carr for helpful comments on earlier versions of this essay.

1. With the exception of essays from the sixties and early seventies, essay-writing is not a major genre of Kennelly's. The majority of his published essays were originally lectures, which helps to explain the tone of the spoken word conveyed in them.
2. Brendan Kennelly, *Journey into Joy: Selected Prose*, edited by Åke Persson (Newcastle upon Tyne: Bloodaxe Books, 1994), p.217. All quotations are from this edition, unless otherwise indicated.
3. Henrik Ibsen, 'Epilogue', in *Lyrical Poems*, selected and translated by R.A. Streatfield (London: Elkin Mathews, 1902), p.38.
4. *Modern Irish Poets and the Irish Epic*, unpublished Ph.D. thesis submitted at Trinity College, Dublin, 1966, p.48.
5. *Modern Irish Poets and the Irish Epic*, p.91.
6. *Modern Irish Poets and the Irish Epic*, p.52.
7. *Modern Irish Poets and the Irish Epic*, p.314.
8. *Modern Irish Poets and the Irish Epic*, p.135. Samuel Ferguson, 'Mesgedra', *Poems* (Dublin: William McGee; London: George Bell and Sons, 1880), p.42.
9. *Modern Irish Poets and the Irish Epic*, p.166.
10. *Modern Irish Poets and the Irish Epic*, p.220.
11. *Modern Irish Poets and the Irish Epic*, p.262.
12. *Modern Irish Poets and the Irish Epic*, p.30.
13. *Modern Irish Poets and the Irish Epic*, p.37.
14. *Selected Poems* (New York: E.P. Dutton & Co, 1969; enlarged edition 1971), p.viii.
15. *Good Souls to Survive* (Dublin: Allen Figgis & Co, 1967), p.39.
16. *Modern Irish Poets and the Irish Epic*, p.261.
17. *My Dark Fathers* (Dublin: New Square Publications, 1964), pp.9-11.
18. 'Swift', *Let Fall No Burning Leaf* (Dublin: New Square Publications, 1963), p.14; 'The Fool's Rod', *My Dark Fathers*, pp.9-11.
19. 'Three Men', *Good Souls to Survive*, pp.54-55.
20. *Dream of a Black Fox* (Dublin: Allen Figgis, 1968), pp.55-56.
21. Percy Bysshe Shelley, 'A Defence of Poetry', *Shelley's Prose, or The Trumpet of Prophecy*, edited by D. L. Clark (London: Fourth Estate, 1988), p.297.
22. *Irish Poets in English: The Thomas Davis Lectures on Anglo-Irish Poetry*, edited by Seán Lucy (Cork: Mercier Press, 1973), p.161.

23. Patrick Kavanagh, *Collected Pruse* (London: MacGibbon and Kee, 1964), pp.20–21.

24. *Modern Irish Poets and the Irish Epic*, p.253.

25. John Keats, cf. Letter to Richard Woodhouse, 22 October 1818, where he says that the poet 'has as much delight in conceiving an Iago as an Imogen'.

26. John Millington Synge, 'Preface' to *The Poems, Collected Works*, 1, edited by Robin Skelton (Oxford: Oxford University Press, 1962), p.xxxvi.

27. C.M. Bowra, 'The Romantic Imagination', *The Romantic Imagination: A Selection of Critical Essays*, edited by J.S. Hill (London: Macmillan Press, 1977), p.93.

28. 'Keynote Address', *Culture in Ireland: Division or Diversity? Proceedings of the Cultures of Ireland Group Conference*, edited by Edna Longley (Belfast: Institute of Irish Studies, The Queen's University of Belfast, 1991), p.23.

ÅKE PERSSON

Select Bibliography of Works
by and on Brendan Kennelly

1. *Works by Brendan Kennelly*

1. POETRY

Cast a Cold Eye (with Rudi Holzapfel). Dublin: Dolmen Press, 1959 (CACE).

The Rain, the Moon (with Rudi Holzapfel). Dublin: Dolmen Press, 1961 (TRTM).

The Dark about Our Loves (with Rudi Holzapfel). Dublin: John Augustine and Co, 1962 (TDAOL).

Green Townlands: Poems (with Rudi Holzapfel). Leeds: University Bibliography Press, 1963 (GT).

Let Fall No Burning Leaf. Dublin: New Square Publications, 1963 (LFNBL).

My Dark Fathers. Dublin: New Square Publications, 1964 (MDF).

Up and At It. Dublin: New Square Publications, 1965 (UAAI).

Collection One: Getting up Early. Dublin: Allen Figgis, 1966 (COGUE).

Good Souls to Survive. Dublin: Allen Figgis, 1967 (GSTS).

Dream of a Black Fox. Dublin: Allen Figgis, 1968 (DOABF).

Selected Poems. Dublin: Allen Figgis, 1969 (SP69).

A Drinking Cup: Poems from the Irish. Dublin: Allen Figgis, 1970 (ADC).

Bread. Dublin: Tara Telephone Publications, 1971 (B).

Selected Poems, enlarged edition. New York: Dutton, 1971 (SP71).

Love Cry. Dublin: Allen Figgis, 1972 (LC).

Salvation, the Stranger. Dublin: Tara Telephone Publications, 1972 (STS).

The Voices. Dublin: Gallery Books, 1973 (TV).

Shelley in Dublin. Dublin: Anna Livia Books, 1974; Dublin: Egotist Press, 1977 (SID74).

A Kind of Trust. Dublin: Gallery Books, 1975 (AKOT).

New and Selected Poems, edited by Peter Fallon. Dublin: Gallery Books, 1976 (NASP).

Islandman. Dublin: Profile Press, 1977 (IM).

The Visitor. Dublin: St Bueno's Press, 1978 (TVR).

A Girl: 22 Songs,. 1978. Song cycle sung by Bernadette Greevy. Music: Seoirse Bodley to poems by Brendan Kennelly. Fully published in *BS* (AG). Recorded by Gael-Linn, Dublin, 1981.

A Small Light. Dublin: Gallery Books, 1979 (ASL).

In Spite of the Wise (also entitled *Evasions*). Dublin: Trinity Closet Press, 1979 (ISOTW).

The Boats Are Home. Dublin: Gallery Books, 1980 (TBAH).

Shelley in Dublin, revised edition. Dublin: Beaver Row Press, 1982 (SID82).

The House That Jack Didn't Build. Dublin: Beaver Row Press, 1982 (THTJDB).

Cromwell: A Poem. Dublin: Beaver Row Press, 1983; corrected edition, Newcastle upon Tyne: Bloodaxe Books, 1987 (C).

Moloney up and At It. Cork and Dublin: Mercier Press, 1984 (MUAAI).

Selected Poems, edited by Kevin Byrne. Dublin: Kerrymount Publications, 1985 (SP85).

Mary: From the Irish. Dublin: Aisling Press, 1987 (M).

Love of Ireland: Poems from the Irish. Cork and Dublin: Mercier Press, 1989 (LOI).

A Time for Voices: Selected Poems 1960-1990. Newcastle upon Tyne: Bloodaxe Books, 1990 (ATFV).

The Book of Judas: A Poem. Newcastle upon Tyne: Bloodaxe Books, 1991 (BOJ).

Breathing Spaces: Early Poems. Newcastle upon Tyne: Bloodaxe Books, 1992 (BS).

2. NOVELS

The Crooked Cross. Dublin: Allen Figgis, 1963; Dublin: Moytura Press, 1989.

The Florentines. Dublin: Allen Figgis, 1967.

3. PLAYS

Irishmen Make Lousy Lovers. Unpublished. Performed at the Eblana Theatre, Dublin, 1973.

Antigone. Unpublished. First performed at the Peacock Theatre, Dublin, 1986.

Cromwell. Staged version. First performed at the Damer Hall, Dublin, 1986.

Medea. Newcastle upon Tyne: Bloodaxe Books, 1991. First performed at the Royal Dublin Society, Dublin, 1988.

The Trojan Women. Newcastle upon Tyne: Bloodaxe Books, 1993. First performed at the Peacock Theatre, Dublin, 1993.

Blood Wedding. Unpublished, not yet performed.

4. CRITICISM

Modern Irish Poets and the Irish Epic. Unpublished Ph.D. thesis presented at Trinity College, Dublin, 1966.

Journey into Joy: Selected Prose, edited by Åke Persson. Newcastle upon Tyne: Bloodaxe Books, 1994.

5. ANTHOLOGIES

The Penguin Book of Irish Verse. Harmondsworth: Penguin Books, 1970; second and enlarged edition, 1981.

Landmarks of Irish Drama. London: Methuen, 1988.

Joycechoyce. The Poems in Verse and Prose of James Joyce (with A. Norman Jeffares). Schull, West Cork: Roberts Rinehart Publishers, 1992.

Irish Prose Writings: Swift to the Literary Renaissance (with Terence Brown). Tokyo: Hon-No Tomasha, 1992.

Between Innocence and Peace: Favourite Poems of Ireland. Cork and Dublin: Mercier Press, 1993.

Dublines (with Katie Donovan). Newcastle upon Tyne: Bloodaxe Books, 1994.

Ireland's Women: Writings Past and Present (with Katie Donovan and A. Norman Jeffares). London: Kyle Kathie; Dublin: Gill & Macmillan, 1994.

6. OTHER BOOKS

Real Ireland (photographs: Liam Blake, text: Brendan Kennelly). Belfast: Appletree Press, 1984.

Ireland Past and Present, edited by Brendan Kennelly. London: Multimedia Publications & New Jersey: Chartwell Books, 1985; Dublin: Gill and Macmillan & London: Multimedia Publications, 1992.

7. TRANSLATIONS OF BRENDAN KENNELLY'S WORK

Vásnivy Tichy Hlas, translation into Czech by Jana Kantorová-Báliková. Bratislava: Slovenský Spisovatel, 1985.

Brendan Kennelly's Stone, collective translation into Greek. Final elaboration and introduction by Liana Sakelliou. Poets at Thira Series. Athens: Erato Publishers, 1992.

8. RECORDINGS ON AUDIO CASSETTES

Living Ghosts: 23 Poems by Brendan Kennelly. Dublin: Livia Records, 1982.

What Happens All the People? Selected Poems. Dublin: Dermot Moynihan, 1991.

9. COLLECTED POEMS IN ALPHABETICAL ORDER

(r) indicates substantial revision since original publication, (e) indicates substantially extended version, (s) indicates substantially shorter version. (I) and (II) indicate same title but different poem. For reasons of space, the sequences *A Girl, Cromwell* and *The Book of Judas* are here treated as individual poems.

TITLE OF POEM	FIRST COLLECTED IN:	SUBSEQUENTLY APPEARED IN:
A Beetle's Back	ATFV	
A Branch	GSTS	
A Cow's Jawbone	GSTS	
A Cry for Art O'Leary	SP85	LOI
A Drama	DOABF	SP69, SP71
A Drowned Girl	TDAOL	COGUE, SP69, SP71, SP85
A Farmer Thinks of His Daft Son	COGUE	
A Girl	AG	BS
A Glimpse of Starlings	SP85	ATFV
A Greasy Pole	TBAH	ATFV
A Great Day	BS	
A Half-Finished Garden	SP85	ATFV
A Kerry Christmas	DOABF	SP69, SP71, BS
A Kind of Trust	AKOT	NASP, SP85, ATFV
A Leather Apron	TBAH	ATFV
A Love-Song	ADC	LOI
A Mad Woman	GSTS	
A Man I Knew	DOABF	SP69, SP71
A Man in Smoke Remembered	TVR	ATFV
A Man with the Good Word	TVR	
A Man, But Rarely Mentioned	TVR	ATFV
A Music	STS	NASP, ATFV
A One-Legged Man	TDAOL	
A Passionate and Gentle Voice	STS	SP85, ATFV
A Peering Boy	BS	
A Pool	DOABF	
A Restoration	SP85	ATFV
A Return	TBAH	BS
A Short Story	GSTS	BS

A Small Light	ASL	SP85, BS
A Special Odour	DOABF	SP69, SP71
A Tale for Tourists	SP85	BS
A Viable Odyssey	STS	SP85, ATFV
A Visit	DOABF	SP69, SP71, SP85, ATFV
A Winter Rose	SP85	ATFV
Actaeon	AKOT	NASP, SP85, BS
Adam	LFNBL	SP85
Admonition	CACE	
After School (sonnet 15)	LC	ATFV, BS
Ahavallin Churchyard	DOABF	
All the Time in the World (sonnet 21)	LC	BS
Ambulance	GSTS	ATFV
And November	TRTM	
And Who Will Judge the Judges in Their Time?	THTJDB	
Any Image	CACE	
Apostles of Possibility	DOABF	
Ardmore	TRTM	
Assassin	B	
At a Gate	TRTM	
At Kelly's Corner	DOABF	
At Table	GSTS	
At the Party	DOABF	SP69, SP71, BS
Attention	STS	
Baby	SP85	ATFV
Ballad for a Dreamer	TRTM	
Beatings	TBAH	
Before Leaving	TRTM	COGUE
Begin	GSTS	SP69, SP71
Between Sky and Stone	TBAH	BS
Beyond Knowledge	SP85	ATFV
Birth	STS	NASP, ATFV
Birthdays and Farewells	DOABF	SP69, SP71
Blackbird (I)	GSTS	SP69, SP71, BS
Blackbird (II)	ADC	LOI
Blame	ATFV	
Blind Girl	TDAOL	
Blood (I)	SP85	BS
Book	TV	ATFV
Boor	ADC	LOI
Bread	B	SP71, TV, NASP, SP85, ATFV

Breath	STS	
bridge	ATFV	
Calling the Shots	THTJDB ATFV	
Carrig	NASP	
Cat	TDAOL	
Catechism (sonnet 14)	LC	ATFV, BS
Certain Old Women	MDF	COGUE
Changes of Rule	COGUE	
Cheated	BS	
Children's Hospital	GT	COGUE
Christ's Bounty	ADC	LOI
Clearing a Space	SP85	ATFV
Cock (sonnet 39)	LC	BS
Connection	TV	ATFV
County Mayo	ADC	LOI
Cromwell	C	SP85, ATFV (in part)
Cry	DOABF	SP71
Curse (sonnet 12)	LC	BS
Daring	B	
Death of a Strong Man	DOABF	BS
Design (sonnet 41)	LC	BS
De Valera at Ninety-Two	THTJDB SP85, ATFV	
Dream and Daylight	SP85	
1. Runners of the Dark		
2. Limping		
Dream of a Black Fox	DOABF	SP69, SP71, NASP, SP85, ATFV
Dublin: A Portrait	DOABF	SP85, ATFV
Easter	TRTM	
Ella Cantillon	TBAH	BS
Elopement (sonnet 24)	LC	BS
End	DOABF	
End Friend	CACE	
Entering	TBAH	ATFV, BS(r)
Escape	GSTS	
Etain	ADC	LOI
Evensong	TDAOL	
Eyes (I) (sonnet 40)	LC	BS
Failure	BS	
Fang and Claw	MDF	
Farmer	TDAOL	COGUE
Fascinated Waters	MDF	COGUE
Fionn's Generosity	ADC	LOI
Flash	DOABF	

Flight	B	
Flood	ADC	LOI
Fool (sonnet 5)	LC	BS
Four Portraits	TDAOL	
Red Biddy		
Burke		
A Mad Woman		
Night Watchman		
Fragments	BS	
Free (sonnet 11)	LC	BS
Freedom Fighter	THTJDB	BS
From the Throat of a Dancer	B	
Gestures	DOABF	SP69, SP71, NASP, ATFV
Getting up Early	COGUE	SP69, SP71
Ghosts	DOABF	SP69, SP71
Giants	SP85	
Girl in a Rope	DOABF	SP69, SP71, BS
Girl on a Tightrope	SP85	ATFV
God Bless Munster	ADC	LOI
God's Eagle	STS	
God's Praises	ADC	LOI
Gold Grains	GSTS	
Good Souls, to Survive	GSTS	SP69, SP71, ATFV
Goodbye	CACE	
Grass	TV	
Happy the Man	ADC	LOI
Harvester	CACE	
Harvesters	BS	
Hate Goes Just as Far as Love	ADC	LOI
Heart	TV	
Heat (sonnet 29)	LC	BS
Her Face	ATFV	
Her Head	ADC	LOI
High Planes	NASP	ATFV
Honey (sonnet 36)	LC	ATFV, BS
Hope	ADC	LOI
Horsechestnuts	SP85	ATFV
Hospitality in Ancient Ireland	ADC	LOI
House	SP85	BS
How Glad Are the Small Birds	ADC	LOI
Hunchback	GSTS	SP69, SP71, ATFV
Hy-Brasil	THTJDB	
I Hear	CACE	
I See	TVR	

I See You Dancing, Father	SP85	ATFV
Ice and Light	MDF	
Ice	DOABF	SP69, SP71
Ice-Flower	TRTM	
If You Were Bold Enough	BS	
Image (I)	TRTM	COGUE
Image (II)	STS	
Immediate Man	BS	
Innocent (sonnet 37)	LC	ATFV, BS
In Spite of the Wise	ISOTW	
In the Barony of O'Connor	GT	
In Thomas Street	MDF	
Interrogation	GSTS	
Is It Possible I Shall See You?	SP85	
Islandman	IM	SP85, BS(r)
It Was Indeed Love	SP85	BS
It Was No Crushing Terror	TBAH	BS
Jack, Ageing, Labours to Assuage the Rage of the Appalling Off-spring of the Former Occupant	THTJDB	
James Clarence Mangan	MDF	
James Joyce's Death Mask	TDAOL	
Jesus at School	ADC	LOI
Jesus on the Sabbath	ADC	LOI
Jet (I)	CACE	
Jet (II)	DOABF	
John Bradburn	SP85	BS
John Keane's Field	TVR	
Johnny Gobless	MDF	COGUE
Justice	B	
Kate of Gornavilla	ADC	LOI
Keep in Touch	AKOT	ATFV
Killing the Winter (sonnet 22)	LC	BS
Killybegs	TBAH	SP85, ATFV
Kings that Stare	GSTS	
Kisses	ADC	LOI
Knives	ATFV	
Knockmealdown	ADC	LOI
Lame Girl Climbing Steps	GSTS	
Law and Order	THTJDB	BS
Lear in Africa	ATFV	
Leaving	SP85	BS
Let It Go	STS	NASP, ATFV
Light Dying	COGUE	SP69, SP71, SP85, ATFV

Light Seed	TRTM	
Light	STS	SP85
Lightness (sonnet 2)	LC	BS
Lightning	STS	TV, NASP, ATFV
Lily Lynch	LFNBL	
Lime (sonnet 16)	LC	BS
Lislaughtin Abbey	COGUE	SP69, SP71
Listening to the Man Who Made the Neutron Bomb	THTJDB	
Litter	BS	
Living Ghosts	ISOTW	TBAH, BS
Local History	TBAH	BS
Loss (sonnet 32)	LC	BS
Lost	TBAH	ATFV
Love-child (sonnet 6)	LC	BS
Love Cry (sonnet 1)	LC	SP85, ATFV, BS
Love of Ireland	LOI	
Mad Boy's Song	LFNBL	
Man Making Fire	LFNBL	SP85
Man with Fifty Myths	TVR	
Marlowe	COGUE	
Mary	M	LOI
Mary Magdalene (I)	TDAOL	
Mary Magdalene (II)	BS	
Mastery	AKOT	SP85, BS
May the Silence Break	AKOT	SP85, ATFV
Meddling	B	
Midnight City	DOABF	
Milk	SID74	SID82, BS
Miss Anne (sonnet 7)	LC	BS
Moloney and the Dust	MUAAI	
Moloney at the Wake	LFNBL	UAAI, COGUE, MUAAI(r)
Moloney Cures the Curse	MUAAI	
Moloney Discovers the Winter	UAAI	
Moloney Enters into a Dialogue Concerning the Listowel Water Supply	MUAAI	
Moloney Meets Miss Immaculata Mullally	MUAAI	
Moloney Recalls the Marriage of the Barrell Muldoon	MUAAI	
Moloney Recalls the Transfiguration of the Pooka Mullane	UAAI	

Moloney Remembers the Resurrection of Kate Finucane	MDF	UAAI, COGUE, SP69, SP71, MUAAI
Moloney Remembers Timmy Thankgod	MUAAI	
Moloney Sees Through a Blind Eye	UAAI	
Moloney's Revenge	MUAAI	
Moloney Up and At It	UAAI	COGUE, SP69, SP71, MUAAI
Moment	CACE	
Moments When the Light	GSTS	SP69, SP71, SP85, ATFV
Money	DOABF	
More Dust	SP85	ATFV
Moth and Candle Flame	TDAOL	
My Dark Fathers	MDF	COGUE, SP69, SP71, NASP, SP85, ATFV
My Story	ADC	LOI
Needles (sonnet 30)	LC	BS
New (sonnet 48)	LC	SP85, BS
Night–Drive	DOABF	SP69, SP71, BS
Nightmare	DOABF	
Now	STS	
O'Neill's Letter to Sir John McCoughleyn	ADC	LOI
October, Six O'Clock	TRTM	
Of a Flower's Mother	TRTM	
Old Man	CACE	
Old Men	LFNBL	COGUE
Old Year Out	GSTS	
On a Change in Literary Fashions	LOI	
On Mael Mhuru the Poet	ADC	LOI
On the Death of William Gould	ADC	LOI
On the Murder of David Gleeson, Bailiff	ADC	LOI
On Wandering	CACE	
Orphan	B	
Osnagh at the Graveside	CACE	
Outside the Church	NASP	
Packy	NASP	
Pain (sonnet 20)	LC	BS
Pattern	TRTM	
Peace	TV	
Permission	STS	
Phone Call	ATFV	
Play	TBAH	BS

Playground	STS	
Poem	TV	
Poem from a Three Year Old	TVR	SP85, ATFV
Points of View	THTJDB	ATFV
Portrait	B	
Portrait of a Little Old Lady	GSTS	
Prayer to Venus	SP85	
Preservation	LFNBL	
Prodigal	SP85	
Proof	B	NASP, ATFV
Queen in Exile	LFNBL	
Question	SP71	
'Ran-Dancers	GSTS	
Realisation	GSTS	
Rebuke (sonnet 19)	LC	BS
Reconciliation	ADC	LOI
Remember What Marina Said?	BS	
Rialto	MDF	
Ritual (sonnet 23)	LC	BS
Rock	B	
Rome	ADC	LOI
Sacrifice	NASP	ATFV
Saint, Bird, Angel	ADC	LOI
Saint Brigid's Prayer	LOI	
Samain	GT	
Santorini	BS	
Schoolboy	THTJDB	
Sculpted from Darkness	TBAH	BS
Sea	TV	SP85, ATFV
Sebastian	GSTS	
Secrets	B	SP71, SP85
Separation	STS	SP85, ATFV
She	ADC	LOI
She Sees Her Own Distance	SP85	ATFV
Shell	TV	NASP, ATFV
Shelley in Dublin	SID74	SID82(r), SP85, BS
Shock (sonnet 33)	LC	BS
Shy (sonnet 18)	LC	BS
Silence	TV	NASP, SP85, ATFV
Sing and Be Damned to It	SP85	BS
Sister (sonnet 28)	LC	BS
Six of One	TBAH	ATFV
1. The Barbarian		
2. The Expert		

3. The Warriors
4. The Missionary
5. The Convert
6. The Savage Ego
   Is a Circus Tent

Small Black Stars	DOABF	
Smell (sonnet 9)	LC	BS
Smoke	STS	NASP
Snow	TV	
So	SP71	
Song of a Man Incapable of Self-Government	THTJDB	
Song of Summer	LOI	
Sonnet	TRTM	COGUE, SP69, SP71
Special Thunder (sonnet 10)	LC	BS
Spring (sonnet 27)	LC	BS
Spring in Kerry	COGUE	
Spring's Tiger	MDF	
Star	NASP	ATFV
Statement of the Former Occupant	THTJDB	SP85, ATFV
Steps	DOABF	
Straying	ATFV	
Such a Silence	DOABF	
Sufficiency	TDAOL	
Survival	MDF	
Swanning (sonnet 4)	LC	SP85, ATFV, BS
Swift	GT	LFNBL
Synge	B	SP71
Tail-End Charlie	THTJDB	ATFV
Talking to Coats	TRTM	
Telemachus	LFNBL	
Ten Bob	SP85	BS
That Look	TBAH	ATFV
That Room	SP85	
The After-Child	TRTM	COGUE
The Bell (I)	ADC	LOI
The Bell (II)	TBAH	
The Big House	TBAH	BS
The Big Words	SP85	ATFV
The Birds	LFNBL	COGUE, SP69, SP71
The Blackbird's Song	ADC	LOI
The Black Cliffs, Ballybunion	DOABF	BS
The Black Fox, Again	SP85	ATFV
The Blackthorn Pin	ADC	LOI

The Blind Man	COGUE	SP69, SP71, ATFV
The Boiler	SP85	
The Book of Judas	BOJ	
The Brightest of All	TBAH	SP85, ATFV
The Brown Man's Woman	GT	COGUE
The Bulls	B	
The Burning of Her Hair	ATFV	
The Cause of Palm Trees	THTJDB	
The Celtic Twilight	GSTS	SP85, ATFV
The Cherrytrees	SID74	SID82(r), SP85
The Child and the Wind	TRTM	
The Children	GSTS	
The Cliff of Alteran	ADC	LOI
The Crossed Country	GSTS	
The Dancer	SP71	
The Dead	LFNBL	
The Dead Wife	SP85	LOI
The Devils	AKOT	
The Dogs	DOABF	
The Dummies	LFNBL	COGUE, SP69, SP71
The Exhibition	TBAH	ATFV
The Fall (sonnet 3)	LC	SP85, BS
The Falling	CACE	
The Feeding Dark	NASP	
The Fire Is Crying	SP85	ATFV
The Fool's Rod	MDF	SP85
The Furies	STS	ATFV
The Gift	TRTM	COGUE, SP69, SP71, NASP, ATFV
The Gift Returned	TBAH	ATFV
The Girl Next Door	DOABF	
The Good	COGUE	SP69, SP71, SP85, BS
The Grip	DOABF	SP69, SP71, ATFV
The Habit of Redemption	STS	SP85, ATFV
The Hammers	DOABF	
The Happy Grass	ISOTW	TBAH, BS
The Harrowing of Hell	SP85	LOI
The Hill of Fire	LFNBL	
The Hole	SP85	
The Holy Man	ADC	LOI
The Hope of Wings	SP85	BS
The Horse's Head	TBAH	SP85, ATFV
The House	TRTM	COGUE, SP69, SP71 SP85

The House That Jack Didn't Build	THTJDB	SP85, ATFV
The Hurt	AKOT	NASP, SP85, ATFV
The Image of God	GSTS	SP69, SP71
The Indifferent Mistress	ADC	LOI
The Innocents	DOABF	
The Island (I)	TV	SP85, ATFV
The Island (II)(eight sections from)	AKOT	NASP(s), IM(e), SP85(e), BS(e)
The Islandman	NASP	IM(e), SP85(e), BS(e)
The Island Protected by a Bridge of Glass	SP85	LOI
The Joke	THTJDB	SP85, ATFV
The Kill	GSTS	
The King (I)	GT	
The King (II) (sonnet 8)	LC	BS
The King of Ireland's Son	THTJDB	
The Kiss	NASP	ATFV
The Learning	SP85	ATFV
The Limerick Train	GSTS	SP69, SP71
The Lislaughtin Cross	NASP	ATFV
The Loud Men	SID74	SID82(r), SP85, ATFV
The Love of God	SP85	BS
The Man I Saw To-day	GSTS	
The Moment of Letlive	STS	ATFV
The Mother	TRTM	
The Names of the Dead Are Lightning	TBAH	ATFV
The Nature of the Dark	MDF	
The Old Woman of Beare	ADC	SP71, SP85(r), LOI
The Ovens	BS	
The Pig	SID74	SID82, ATFV
The Pig-Killer	DOABF	SP69, SP71, NASP, SP85, ATFV
The Pilgrim	TBAH	
The Prisoner	SP85	BS
The Prodigal Son	DOABF	
The Queen Bee	B	
The Runner	B	NASP, SP85, ATFV
The Sandwoman	ATFV	
The Scarf	SP85	ATFV
The Scholar's Retreat	AKOT	
The Seapigs	GSTS	
The Second Tree	SP85	BS
The Shannon (I)	LFNBL	COGUE, SP71

The Shannon (II)	LOI	
The Sin	THTJDB	SP85, ATFV
The Singers	DOABF	
The Singing Girl Is Easy in Her Skill	ISOTW	TBAH, BS
The Smell	TBAH	SP85, ATFV
The Sneer	BS	
The Son of the King of Moy	ADC	LOI
The Song Inside	DOABF	SP69, SP71
The Speech of Trees	ATFV	
The Stallion	GSTS	SP69, SP71
The Stammer	SP85	BS
The Stick	TBAH	ATFV
The Stonebreaker	AKOT	
The Stones	DOABF	SP69, SP71, NASP, SP85, ATFV
The Storm	ADC	LOI
The Story	TBAH	ATFV
The Struggle	GSTS	
The Swimmer	B	NASP, SP85, ATFV
The Tamer	COGUE	
The Teachers	GSTS	SP69, SP71
The Thatcher	DOABF	SP69, SP71, NASP, ATFV
The Third Force	SP85	ATFV
The Throw	SP85	BS
The Tinker Man	CACE	
The Tippler	DOABF	SP69, SP71, NASP, SP85, ATFV
The Traveller	TRTM	
The Tree of Life	ADC	LOI
The Tree's Voice	MDF	GSTS
The Trembling Man	LFNBL	
The Vikings	ADC	LOI
The Visitor	TVR	TBAH, SP85, ATFV
The Wake	BS	
The Waking-Pageant	CACE	SP85
The Way of Waves	LFNBL	COGUE
The Wayside Fountain	ADC	LOI
The Whispering Blood	TBAH	BS
The Whistler	GT	
The Whiteness	STS	NASP, ATFV
The Wild Man and the Church	ADC	LOI
The Wild Man of the Woods	ADC	LOI
The Wind	ADC	LOI

The Work Was Coming Out Right	SP85	
The Wren-Boy	MDF	GSTS
There Are Women	SP85	
There	CACE	
This One Word	CACE	
Thoughts Astray	SP85	LOI
Thorn (sonnet 13)	LC	BS
Three Men	GSTS	SP69, SP71
Pearse		
Plunkett		
MacDonagh		
Throwaway (sonnet 26)	LC	SP85, BS
Tide (sonnet 34)	LC	BS
Timber (sonnet 17)	LC	BS
Time	TV	
Time for the Knife	AKOT	ATFV
Tinker Camp	DOABF	
To Learn	TBAH	ATFV
To Marina Tsetaeva	SP85	
To Rembrandt	SP85	
Tomorrow	GSTS	
Tonight You Cry	AKOT	
Tonight's Dream	B	NASP
Too Near	AKOT	
To You	STS	ATFV
Traffic Lights, Merrion Road, Dublin	SID74	SID82
Treasure	THTJDB	BS
Tree	TV	
Uncertainty (I)	ADC	LOI
Uncertainty (II)	LOI	
Union	DOABF	SP69, SP71, NASP, BS
Valentine Brown	ADC	LOI
Village	CACE	
Warning	B	
Water	B	
We Are Living	TBAH	SP85, ATFV
Westland Row	TRTM	COGUE, ATFV
Wet Grass	CACE	
What Else? (sonnet 42)	LC	BS
Who Killed the Man?	THTJDB	
Who Will Buy a Poem?	LOI	
Willow	STS	ATFV
Wings	SP85	ATFV

Winter Night	COGUE	
Wish	ATFV	
Withered Hands	LOI	
Witnesses	BS	
Word	TV	BS
Work (I) (sonnet 38)	LC	BS
Yeats	TRTM	
Yes	TBAH	ATFV

Although *Cromwell* is considered by the poet to be one poem, the following individual poems appear in later volumes (in order of appearance in sequence):

A Host of Ghosts	SP85
Oak	SP85
Balloons	SP85, ATFV
Oliver to His Brother	SP85
A Friend of the People	SP85, ATFV
Manager, Perhaps?	SP85, ATFV
Magic	SP85
Oliver Writes to the Speaker of the Parliament of England	SP85
Rebecca Hill	SP85, ATFV
Some People	ATFV
Oliver Speaks to His Countrymen	SP85
Wine	ATFV
A Bit of a Swap	ATFV
An Example	ATFV
A Condition	ATFV
Pits	SP85
Reading Aloud	SP85
Gas	SP85
Discipline	ATFV
Oliver's Prophecies	ATFV
Ass	SP85
A Relationship	SP85, ATFV
Oliver to a Friend	SP85
Nails	ATFV
'Therefore, I Smile'	SP85, ATFV
A Running Battle	ATFV
The Traps Are True	SP85
Home	SP85
Am	SP85, ATFV
A Soft Amen	SP85

The following untitled sonnets (numbers and first lines indicated below), originally published in *Love Cry*, are omitted in *Breathing Spaces*:

Sonnet 25: Vision is knowing that I cannot see.
Sonnet 31: Do you mind if I say now, at this stage,
Sonnet 35: Drops of blood
Sonnet 43: They are killing the field at the back of our house.
Sonnet 44: Dear Autumn girl, these helter-skelter days
Sonnet 45: 'Speaking of mystery,' you said, 'look at that slug,
Sonnet 46: I know that in a twinkling knowledge might undo
Sonnet 47: You. A word on the lips of the infinite dead,

10. UNCOLLECTED POEMS PUBLISHED IN PERIODICALS, MAGAZINES, NEWSPAPERS & OTHER PUBLICATIONS (IN CHRONOLOGICAL ORDER)

'Poem'. *Icarus*, No.28, June 1959, p.21.

'The Journey'. *Icarus*, No.29, December 1959, p.12.

'The Walker'. *Icarus*, No.30, March 1960, p.14; 'Man in an Archway', p.15.

'The Swans'. *Icarus*, No.32, December, 1960, p.21.

'Head'. *Icarus*, No.33, March 1961, p.10; 'Red', p.43.

'Elegy for a Shadow'. *Kilkenny Magazine*, No.3, Spring 1961, p.7.

'Swift's Hospital'. *Icarus*, No.36, March 1962, p.28.

'Good Friday'. *Icarus*, No.37, June 1962, p.21; 'Woman', p.53.

'Owen Roe O'Sullivan'. *Icarus*, No.39, March 1963, p.6.

'Road Accident'. *Icarus*, No.41, December 1963, p.23.

'The Builders'. *Dubliner*, No.1, Spring 1964, p.42.

'Jacob Boehme'. *Hermathena*, No.XCIX, Autumn 1964, p.92.

'Lazarus'. *Icarus*, No.44, December 1964, p.3.

'October'. *Icarus*, No.45, March 1965, p.5; 'The Wind at My Door', pp.16–17.

'Modes of Departure: I. Genesis. II. The Innocents. III. Earth. IV. Sea. V. Fire. VI. Air. VII. Profit in Loss. VIII. Dance after Dark'. *Kilkenny Magazine*, No.14, Spring/Summer 1966, pp.20–24.

'Each Man His Madness'. *Dublin Magazine*, No.2, Summer 1966, p.49.

'The Girls'. *St Stephens* (University College Dublin), Series II, No.10, 1966, p.7.

'The Land'. *Hermathena*, No.CIV, Spring 1967, p.82.

'A Man in a Yellow Oilskin'. *Honest Ulsterman*, No.1, 1968, p.10.

'A Couple: He; She'. *Honest Ulsterman*, No.4, 1968, p.17.

'Nightcolour'. *Capella* 3. Dublin: Tara Telephone Publications, December 1969, p.23; 'Tears', p.23.

'Small Murders'; 'Brave New World'. *Icarus*, No.58, Michelmas
Term 1969, no page numbers.
'The Virgin Rock, Ballybunion'. *Ariel: A Review of International
English Literature*, No.3, July 1970, p.58; 'The Given Days', p.79.
'Old Poet's Late-Night Story'. *Honest Ulsterman*, No.22, 1970, p.33.
'Granny Twomey'. Broadsheet 7, edited by Hayden Murphy, 1970
(Trinity College Old Library).
'Seeds'. *Capella* 5/6. Dublin: Tara Telephone Publications, Autumn
1970, p.9.
'W.H. Auden's Face'. *The Book of Invasions*, No.4 (Broadsheet).
Dublin: Tara Telephone Publications 1970, no page number.
'Journey'. *Dublin Magazine*, No.6, Winter 1970/71, p.68.
'The High Places, the Secret Places'; 'It Needs the Wind'.
Broadsheet 10, edited by Hayden Murphy, 1971 (Trinity College
Old Library).
'The Leap'. *Capella* 8. Dublin: Tara Telephone Publications 1971,
pp.8-9; 'A Scarecrow', p.9; 'The Diver', p.10.
'Four Poems': I. 'Justice'; II. 'Return'; III. 'Cries'; IV. 'The Failure
of Darkness'. *Year of Dog*, edited by K. Lee. Putney, Vermont:
Year of Dog Press, No.1, 1972, pp.35-41.
'Something Would Be Understood'. *Journal of Irish Literature: A
Listowel Writers Number* (Delaware), No.2, May 1972, p 27;
'Cliché', p.29.
'In Praise of Stumblers'; 'The Door'. *Swarthmore College Bulletin:
Alumni Issue*, May 1972, no page numbers.
'Poems from the Irish': I. 'Things'; II. 'The Maker'; III. 'There';
IV. 'Trust No Man'; V. 'The Guest House at the Monastery of
Cork'; VI. 'A Prayer'; VII. 'The Poet to His Old Cloak'; VIII.
'Writing in the Open Air'; IX. 'And So We Made a City Robed
in Light'. Topic: 24. *Themes in Irish Culture* (Washington and
Jefferson College, Washington and Pennsylvania), Fall 1972, pp.
54-59. (II, V, VII, and VIII also in *Lines Review*, No.62 1977,
pp.22-23.)
'When the Flesh Opens'. *Broadsheet* 17, edited by Hayden Murphy,
1973 (Trinity College Old Library).
'The Cry in Things'. *Irish Times*, 3 February 1973.
'Meat'. *Icarus* 64 (Trinity College Dublin), Summer 1973, pp.14-
15.
'Talk'. *Icarus* 66 (Trinity College Dublin), Winter 1973, no page
number.
'This Night'. *Broadsheet* 20, edited by Hayden Murphy, 1973 (Trinity College Old Library).

'First Time'; 'Father to Son'. *T.C.D. Miscellany* (Trinity College Dublin), Michelmas term 1973, no page numbers.

'Shells and Stones'; 'Steel'. *T.C.D. Miscellany* (Trinity College Dublin), No.1403, 1973, no page numbers.

'Whatever The Sparrow'. *T.C.D. Miscellany* (Trinity College Dublin), No.1404, 1973, no page number.

'Bones'; 'Tides'. *T.C.D. Miscellany* (Trinity College Dublin), No. 1405, 1973, no page number.

'Seascape'. *T.C.D. Miscellany* (Trinity College Dublin), No.1405, 1973, no page number. (Also in Broadsheet 20 above.)

'Drops'; 'Greeting'; 'Street Singer'. *T.C.D. Miscellany* (Trinity College Dublin), No.1406, 1973, no page numbers.

'The Bombed Angel'. *Moderna Språk*, No.3, 1973, pp.225-26. (Also in *T.C.D. Miscellany*, No.1390, 1973, no page number.)

'Something Is Missing'. *Choice: An Anthology of Irish Poetry Selected by the Poets Themselves with a Comment on Their Choice*, edited by Desmond Egan and Michael Hartnett. Dublin: Goldsmith Press 1973, pp.52-53.

'The Kite'. *Irish Times*, 12 January 1974.

'Herbert Park'. *Irish Times*, 28 December 1974.

'There Are Walls Everywhere'. Poem-Sheet 2, edited by G. O'Brien, Kincora Poetry (Athlone, Ireland) 1975, p.5.

'Courage'. *Trinity Trust News* (Trinity College Dublin), No.1, 1975, p.4. (Also in *Broadsheet* 21, edited by Hayden Murphy, 1974.)

'Touch and Go'; *Études Irlandaises: Revue Française d'Histoire, Civilisation et Littérature de l'Irlande* (University of Lille, France), No.4, 1974, pp.9-10; 'The Old Criticism', p.10; 'The Fort of Rathangan', p.10.

'The Grudge'. *Broadsheet* 23, edited by Hayden Murphy, 1975 (Trinity College Old Library).

'No'. *Irish Press*, 3 May 1975.

'The Harpies'. *Lines Review*, No.62, 1977, pp.19-20. (Also in *Cahiers du Centre de Recherches sur Les Pays du Nord et du Nord-Quest*, p.78.). 'Parnassus', p.22.

'Outside'. *Broadsheet* 30, edited by Hayden Murphy, 1978 (Trinity College Old Library).

'The Good Hours'. *Cahiers du Centre de Recherches sur Les Pays du Nord et du Nord-Quest*, No.1, 1978 (Caen, France), p.76; 'Epitaph for a Politician', pp.79-80.

'Critic'. *Irish Press*, 29 April 1978.

'An Examination of Conscience'. *The First Ten Years: Dublin Arts Festival*, edited by Peter Fallon and Dennis O'Driscoll. Dublin:

E. & T. O'Brien 1979, pp.28-29.

'A Picture'. *Image and Illusion: Anglo-Irish Literature and Its Contexts. A Festschrift for Roger McHugh*, edited by Maurice Harmon. Portmarnock: Wolfhound Press 1979, pp.11-12. (Also in *Irish University Review*, No.1, Spring 1979, pp.11-12.)

'Always'. The Writers: A Sense of Ireland, edited by Andrew Carpenter and Peter Fallon. Dublin: O'Brien Press 1980, p.83; 'Goddess', p.84.

'One O' Them'. *Quarryman*, December 1980, p.11.

'Ceól (Symphony No.3)': Music by Seoirse Bodley to ten poems by Brendan Kennelly. I. 'Nil fearann, nil tíos agam; Nil fionta na ceól'; II. 'Nil clagar is binne na ceól a'mhala'; III. 'Mo Cheól Thu'; IV. 'An Ceól agus an Náire'; V. '...ag ceartú ceóil is ag cumadh rann...'; VI. 'Laoithe Dochais'; VII. 'Ceól na mBréag'; VIII. 'Nil sa cheól uile ach gaoth'; IX. 'Ceól Na Farraige'; X. 'Ceól An Cheóil'. Published in the Programme on the occasion of the State Opening of the National Concert Hall, Dublin, 9-10 September 1981.

'The Lie'; 'Eyes'; 'Tidiness'. *Guth agus Tuairim. Association of Principals and Vice-Principals of Community and Comprehensive Schools*, Vol. 3, Autumn 1982, p.63.

'Looking: I. Fair Enough. II. From What I See'. *Irish Times*, 22 January 1983.

'The Despair of Whales'. *Ireland and the Arts: A Special Issue of Literary Review*, edited by Tim Pat Coogan. London: Namara Press, 1983, p.117; 'Folk', p.117; 'When the Game Is Over', p.118; 'The Field of Cries', pp.118-19.

'Grattan'. *Aquarius*, Nos 15&16, 1983/84, p.59.

'Nora O'Donnell'. *Irish Times*, 28 July 1984.

'The Trouble'. *Poetry Ireland Choice*, November 1984.

'To an Ex-Feminist'. *Irish Times*, 9 November 1985.

'From Bleedin' Christ: The Death of David Kilroy'. *Poetry Ireland Review*, No.14, Autumn 1985, p.33.

'To a Book' (translated from the Irish). *Irish Independent*, 26 October 1985.

'The Ten Commandments. A Selection of poems from 'Bleedin' Christ': I. Modern Sculpture; II. Coca-Cola; III. Lifestyle; IV. A conference on Women; V. 'Pologise; VI. Liver; VII. Glof, Bor, Flovver; VIII. Rohan; IX. True Love; X. Centres'. *Sunday Tribune*, 22 December 1985.

'What the Sea Brings'. *Poetry Ireland Review*, No.15, Winter 1985/ 86, p.49. (Also in *Thalatta: Hommage à la Mer*. Luxembourg:

Euroeditor 1985, p.168.). 'Joy', p.50. (Also in *Thalatta*, p.166.)

'Challenges'. *Beyond the Shore: The Irish within Us*. Northampton: Northampton Connolly Association, 1985, p.27; 'Up There', p.28.

'On the Flightiness of Thought' (translated from the Irish). *The Deer's Cry: A Treasury of Irish Religious Verse*, edited by P. Murray. Blackrock, Co. Dublin: Four Courts Press 1986, pp.39-40.

'The Growing Game'. *Irish Times*, 4 October 1986.

'A Small Success'. *Hermathena*, No.CXLI, Winter 1986, p.65.

'Lines for Derry Jeffares'. *Literature and the Art of Creation. Essays and Poems in honour of A. Norman Jeffares*, edited by Robert Welch and S.B. Bushrui. Gerrards Cross: Colin Smythe, and Totowa, New Jersey: Barnes and Noble Books 1988, pp.253-54.

'Blood' (II). *New Nation*, No.4, February 1989, pp.19-21.

'Work' (II). *Irish Independent*, 23 December 1989.

'Vital Ireland'. Allied Irish Bank Calendar for 1990: 'Aspects of Europe' (January); 'Our Own Style' (February); 'To Dante' (March); 'This Listening Moment' (April); 'La Freia's Hall' (May); 'The Cup' (June); 'Portugal – the Sea' (July); 'Figures in a Field' (August); 'Truly Mine' (September); 'I Saw Them Passing' (October); 'The Peaceful Kingdom' (November); 'In Gratitude, Old Masters' (December).

'Poem for Charles Haughey'. *Irish Press*, 30 November 1991.

'Healer'. *Under the Weather. Alcohol Abuse and Alcoholism: How to Cope*, by J.G. Cooney. Dublin: Gill and Macmillan, 1991, p.xi.

'Saint Augustine on God'. Special limited edition on the occasion of a charity evening for Christine Bourke, 26 February 1992.

'There Came a Pleasant Rain'. *Krino*, No.14, Winter 1993, p.29.

11. SELECTED REVIEWS AND JOURNALISM
(IN CHRONOLOGICAL ORDER)

'*Twice Round the Black Church* by Austin Clarke'. *Dubliner*, No.3, May/June 1962.

'*Thy Tears Might Cease* by Michael Farrell'. *Hermathena*, No.XCIX, Autumn 1964.

'*Collected Poems* by Patrick Kavanagh'. *Dubliner*, No.4, Winter 1964.

'*Collected Poems* by Denis Devlin'. *Dublin Magazine*, No.1, Spring 1965.

'*Nationalism in Modern Anglo-Irish Poetry* by Richard J. Loftus'. *Dublin Magazine*, Nos 3 & 4, Autumn/Winter 1965.

'Frank O'Connor, the critic and scholar' (*The Backward Look* by Frank O'Connor). *Sunday Independent* (Dublin), 30 April 1967.

'*William Blake* by Raymond Lister; *Blake's Songs of Innocence and*

Experience, edited by Geoffrey Keynes'. *Hibernia*, No.5, May 1968.
'Mary Lavin's most exciting collection' (*Happiness and Other Stories*). *Sunday Independent* (Dublin), 7 December 1969.
'*Blake and Tradition* by Kathleen Raine, 2 vols.'. *Dublin Magazine*, No.3, Spring 1970.
'Choosing an Anthology' (*The Penguin Book of Irish Verse*). *Irish Times*, 28 April 1970.
'Yeats Ltd.' (*The Circus Animals* by A. Norman Jeffares). *Hibernia*, No.19, October 1970.
'The Watcher in the Shadow' (J.M. Synge). *Irish Times*, 16 April 1971.
'The Poet Kavanagh, complete...' (*The Complete Poems of Patrick Kavanagh*, edited by Peter Kavanagh). *Sunday Independent* (Dublin), 12 March 1972.
'Yeats without his mask' (*Memoirs* by W.B. Yeats). *Irish Independent*, 13 January 1973.
'A little more passion would help' (*Gradual Wars* by Seamus Deane). *Sunday Independent* (Dublin), 21 January 1973.
'Austin Clarke 1896-1974'. *Irish Independent*, 23 March 1974.
'Burying Shelley's "angel" image' (*Shelley: The Pursuit* by Richard Holmes). *Irish Independent*, 10 August 1974.
'*Thieves of Fire* by Denis Donoghue'. *Studies*, Vol. LXIII, Winter 1974.
'*High Talk: The Philosophical Poetry* of W.B. Yeats by Robert Snukal'. *Review of English Studies*, new series, No.101, February 1975.
'How Pleasant to Meet Mr Eliot' (*Eliot* by Stephen Spender). *Hibernia*, No.9, May 1975.
'Tough-minded poet of our stark human scene' (*Site of Ambush* by Eiléan Ní Chuilleanáin; *Kicking* by Gregory O'Donoghue). *Sunday Independent* (Dublin), 22 February 1976.
'Abnormally Normal' (*William Blake: A New Kind of Man* by M. Davis). *Hibernia*, No.7, April 1977.
'Passion's Asses' (*The Oxford Book of Welsh Verse in English*, edited by Gwyn Jones; *Laboratories of the Spirit* by R. S. Thomas). *Hibernia*, No.9, April 1977.
'Voyage into the Interior' (*Sing Me Creation* by Desmond O'Grady). *The Stony Thursday Book*, No.6 1978.
'Eiroticism' (*Some Irish Loving: A Selection* by Edna O'Brien). *Hibernia*, No.26, July 1979.
'Lyric Wit' (*Poems 1962-1978* by Derek Mahon). *Irish Times*, 22 December 1979.
'A Work of Desolation and Despair' (*Flesh: The Greatest Sin* by

Eithne Strong). *Irish Independent*, 12 July 1980.

'The poet as conscience of his people' (*Austin Clarke: A Study of His Writing* by G. Craig Tapping). *Sunday Independent* (Dublin), 22 February 1981.

'A homage to other poets' (*Courtyards in Delft* by Derek Mahon). *Sunday Independent* (Dublin), 31 May 1981.

'What Heaney thinks of other poets' (*Preoccupations: Selected Prose 1968-1978* by Seamus Heaney). *Sunday Independent* (Dublin), 21 December 1981.

'The danger in admiring women from afar' (*Thomas Hardy: A Biography* by Michael Millgate). *Sunday Independent* (Dublin), 20 June 1982.

'Putting Montague to the test' (*Selected Poems* by John Montague). *Sunday Independent* (Dublin), 10 October 1982.

'Guinness, football and God...' (Gaelic football). *Irish Independent*, 23 September 1983.

'F.S.L. Lyons, masterly historian'. *Irish Press*, 24 September 1983.

'Whetting a poetic appetite' (*Edible Anecdotes* by Julie O'Callaghan). *Sunday Independent* (Dublin), 6 November 1983.

'The Lives of Four Great Irishmen' (*W.B. Yeats* by Augustine Martin; *Jonathan Swift* by Bernard Tucker; *G.B. Shaw* by John O'Donovan; *Oscar Wilde* by Richard Pine). *Evening Press*, 11 November 1983.

'From one story-teller to another...' (Eamon Kelly). *Sunday Independent* (Dublin), 22 January 1984.

'Rules are there to promote the rich rhythm of football' (Gaelic Athletic Association). *Irish Independent*, 15 March 1984.

'How time and place shaped some of our greatest writers' (*A Writer's Ireland: Landscape in Literature* by William Trevor). *Irish Independent*, 24 March 1984.

'Soaring from the Treetops' (*Sweeney Astray* by Seamus Heaney). *New York Times Book Review*, 27 May 1984.

'A House on a Hill' (Kerry). *Irish Times*, 1 July 1985.

'*Collected Poems, Volume 1* by Michael Hartnett'. *Poetry Ireland Review*, No.15, Winter 1986.

'Eavan Boland: The complex humanity of a happy woman' (*The Journey and Other Poems* by Eavan Boland). *Irish Times*, 6 December 1986.

'Patrick Kavanagh: 20 years on'. *Irish Times*, 30 November 1987.

'A capital place for a culchie' (Dublin). *Irish Independent*, 1 and 2 January 1988.

'Calm passion for literature' (*An Appetite for Poetry* by Frank Kermode). *Sunday Tribune*, 26 November 1989.

'An astute dreamer' (*The Yeats Companion. With a Bibliographical Portrait* by Ulick O'Connor). *Sunday Independent* (Dublin), 11 February 1990.

'Unleashing the "crack"' (Irishness). *Irish Independent*, 23 June 1990.

'Figures of the father' (*Daddy, Daddy* by Paul Durcan). *Irish Times*, 18 August 1990.

'New life in the arts'. *Irish Independent*, 17 April 1991.

'Dublin's First Nights' (*The Power of Darkness* by John McGahern). *Irish Times*, 2 November 1991.

'Bringing Irish writing to Europe and beyond'. *Irish Independent*, 25, 26, 27 December 1991.

'Long live Charlie' (Charles Haughey). *Irish Independent*, 1 February 1992.

'Man of the Kingdom' (Kerry). *Irish Independent*, 8 February 1992.

'If you're Irish' (St Patrick's Day). *Irish Independent*, 14 March 1992.

'Willie and Maud...' (*Always Your Friend: The Gonne-Yeats Letters, 1893-1938*, edited by A. MacBride and A. Norman Jeffares). *Irish Independent*, 17 and 18 April 1992.

'Sex and the real test of strength'. *Irish Independent*, 29 May 1993.

'Why we're lucky to have Sinéad' (Sinéad O'Connor). *Irish Independent*, 12 June 1993.

'Roddy Doyle! He'd make a cat laugh' (*Paddy Clarke Ha Ha Ha*, and Doyle winning Booker Prize). *Irish Independent*, 30 October 1993.

2. *Selected Broadcasts with RTE, Dublin*
(*with RTE Reference Numbers*)

1. RADIO

'Focus' (Kennelly on *The Penguin Book of Irish Verse*). S AA3297, 28 April 1970.

'Arts: Poetry Anthology. Basil Payne, Brendan Kennelly, Michael Longley, Maire MacEntee, W.H. Auden'. S AA3053, 2 October 1973.

'Arts: Brendan Kennelly on new collection [*A Kind of Trust*]'. S BB2276, 15 July 1975

'Pleasures of Gaelic Literature, No.7' (Kennelly lecture on Brian O'Nuallain's [Flann O'Brien's] *An Beal Bocht* [*The Poor Mouth*]). S AA2913, 17 January 1976.

'Austin Clarke: Poet on the Air. 50 Years of Irish Radio' (Kennelly presenter of programme). S 170/76, 18 April 1976.

'A Girl' (Song cycle sung by Bernadette Greevy. Music: Seoirse Bodley to poems by Kennelly). S AA586, 17 October 1978.

'The O'Casey Enigma, No.8' (Kennelly's Thomas Davis Lecture on 'Sean O'Casey's Journey into Joy'). S BB3432, 18 May 1980.

'Personally Speaking: Brendan Kennelly'. S AA2075, 8 July 1981.

'Poetry Patterns: Brendan Kennelly'. S BB2234, 3 March 1984.

'Conversations in Pluralism: Brendan Kennelly'. S BB1826, 20 May 1984.

'Poems Old, Poems New' (Kennelly presenting series on various themes in poetry 19 parts, once a week). RTP03117, 10 January – 23 May 1987.

'*Medea*' (Kennelly play). S AA 4285/6. 'Kennelly interviewed before radio performance'. S BB3301, 21 July 1989.

'The Arts Show' (Kennelly on story-telling). S AA4671, 28 February 1990.

'The Arts Show' (Kennelly interviews Jack Hanna). S AA4564, 15 May 1991.

'Music Dialogue' (Kennelly interviewed by Richard Pine). 27 March 1992.

'Trinity 400' (Kennelly presenting series on various aspects of Trinity College, Dublin, 10 parts, once a week). S D00969-S D00978, 27 April–29 June 1992.

'My Education: Brendan Kennelly'. RTP09140, 12 August 1993.

'Words and Music'. S AA9962, 30 October 1993.

2. TELEVISION

'Telefís Scoile' (Kennelly's lecture on Gerard Manley Hopkins: 'The Quest for Essence'). A30/899, 23 January 1975.

'Writer in Profile' (Kennelly interviewed). LB102, 17 October 1976.

'The Late Late Show' (Kennelly discussing *Cromwell*). B90/1390, 17 December 1983.

'Folio' (Kennelly and Jennifer Johnston discussing three novels). B30/745, 14 February 1984.

'The Late Late Show' (Kennelly interviewed). B60/2401, 17 November 1984.

'The Late Late Show' (Kennelly in studio discussion). B90/1991, 9 February 1985.

'Poet's Eye' (Kennelly introduces and reads a selection of his poetry). B30/751, 13 December 1987.

'Kenny Live' (Kennelly on poet Davoren Hanna). B90/3369, 22 April 1989.

'Questions and Answers' (Kennelly on panel). B90/347 19 February 1990.

'The Late Late Show' (Kennelly discussing *The Book of Judas*). HX90/2198, 27 September 1991.
'Writer in Profile' (Kennelly interviewed). BX31/4, 26 May 1993.

3. *Works on Brendan Kennelly*

1. POSTGRADUATE THESES

Jennifer Belshaw. *Form; The Artistic Nightmare: An Analysis of the Sonnet Form in Brendan Kennelly's* Cromwell. Unpublished M.Phil. thesis presented at Trinity College, Dublin, 1988.

Frances Gwynn. *Theme and Craft in the Poetry of Brendan Kennelly: 1959-1968*. Unpublished M.Litt. thesis presented at Trinity College, Dublin, 1976.

John McDonagh. *An Exploration of the Themes of Childhood and Education in the Poetry of Brendan Kennelly with Specific Reference to* The Boats Are Home. Unpublished M.A. thesis presented at the University of Warwick, 1991.

Erwin Otto. *Das lyrische Werk Brendan Kennellys. Eine Beschreibung der Gedichte auf dem Hintergrund des Dichtungsverständnisses und der spezifisch irischen Erfahrungen des Autors sowie der Tradition irisch-englischer Dichtung*. Dr.Phil. thesis presented at Justus Liebig Universität, Giessen, 1975.

Noel Twomey. *Confessions of a Casual Addict: A Profile for Radio of Brendan Kennelly*. Thesis project for M.A. at Dublin City University, 1991.

2. SELECTED ESSAYS

Terence Brown. 'Awakening from the Nightmare: History and Contemporary Literature'. *Ireland's Literature. Selected Essays*. Mullingar: Lilliput Press & Totowa, New Jersey: Barnes & Noble Books, 1988.

Carla De Petris. 'Brendan Kennelly's Cromwell, or the Comic Hero'. *Le Forme del Comico. Atti dell' VIII Convegno dell' Associazione Italiana di Anglistica*, Torino, 28-30 ottobre 1985, edited by C. Marengo Vaglio et al. Alessandria: Edizioni Dell' Orso, 1990.

Frank Kinahan. 'Brendan Kennelly'. *Dictionary of Literary Biography, Vol. 40: Poets of Great Britain and Ireland Since 1960. Part 1: A-L*, edited by Vincent Sherry. Detroit: Gale Research Company, 1985.

Christopher Murray. 'Three Irish Antigones'. *Perspectives of Irish Drama and Theatre*, edited by J. Genet. Savage, Md: Barnes and Noble Books, 1991.

Erwin Otto. 'Poetry and Social Perspectives. Brendan Kennelly's *Shelley in Dublin*'. *Études Irlandaises*, new series, No.1, December 1976.

Åke Persson. 'Mapping the Kennelly Space'. *Poetry Ireland Review*, No.37, Winter 1992/1993.

Bernadetta Quinn. 'Brendan Kennelly, Instrument of Peace'. *Antigonish Review*, No.83, 1990.

Gerard Quinn. 'Brendan Kennelly: Victors and Victims'. *Irish Review*, No.9, Autumn 1990.

Anthony Roche. 'Ireland's *Antigones*: Tragedy North and South'. *Cultural Contexts and Literary Idioms in Contemporary Irish Literature. Studies in Contemporary Irish Literature 1, Irish Literary Studies 31*, edited by Michael Kenneally. Gerrards Cross: Colin Smythe, 1988.

3. SELECTED REVIEWS

Bruce Arnold. 'Two young poets in a different vein' (*Good Souls to Survive*). *Sunday Independent* (Dublin), 23 July 1967.

Eileen Battersby. 'Womanpower' (Performance of *The Trojan Women*). *Fortnight*, No.319, July/August 1993.

Eavan Boland. 'Books' (*My Dark Fathers*). *Dubliner*, No.3, Autumn 1964.

Eavan Boland. 'Kerry Monologues' (*Up and At It*). *Irish Times*, 26 February 1966.

Dermot Bolger. 'A poetic cause for celebration in cynical times' (*The Book of Judas*). *Sunday Tribune*, 10 November 1991.

Bono [Paul Hewson]. 'Nothing compares to you...' (*The Book of Judas*). *Sunday Press (Living)*, 8 December 1991.

Sigerson Clifford. 'Ballylongford up and at It' (*Collection One: Getting Up Early*). *Kerryman*, 17 September 1966.

Gerry Colgan. '*Medea* at the Gate' (Performance of *Medea*). *Irish Times*, 7 July 1989.

John Devitt. 'The treachery of language' (*The Book of Judas*). *Sunday Independent (Living and Leisure)* (Dublin), 27 October 1991.

David Fitzgerald. 'Books' (*Collection One: Getting Up Early*). *Dublin Magazine*, Nos 3 & 4, Autumn/Winter 1966.

Gabriel Fitzmaurice. 'Sympathy for all creation' (*Mary*). *Kerryman/Corkman*, 25 March 1988.

John Goodby. 'Reviews' (*The Book of Judas*). *Irish Review*, Spring/Summer 1992.

Frances Gwynn. 'Book Review' (*The Voices*). *IASAIL Newsletter*, No.8, 1974.

Tim Harding. 'Return of Antigone' (Performance of *Antigone*). *Sunday Press*, 4 May 1986.

Michael Hartnett. 'Irish Poetry' (*A Drinking Cup*). *Hibernia*, No.20, 1970.

Mark Patrick Hederman. 'The Monster in the Irish Psyche' (*Cromwell*). *Irish Literary Supplement*, No.2, Fall 1984.

Robert Johnstone. 'Brendan Speaks to Oliver's Countrymen' (*Cromwell*). *Krino*, No.5, Spring 1988.

Conor Kelly. 'Waking from History's Nightmare' (*Cromwell*). *Sunday Tribune (Inside Tribune)*, 22 January 1984.

Declan Kiberd. 'Translating O Rathaille into Kennelly' (*Love of Ireland*). *Alpha*, No.4, 1989.

Jeremy Kingston. 'A candle held to brutality' (Performance of *Cromwell*). *Times*, 4 March 1991.

Peter Levi. 'On fire over Cromwell' (*A Time for Voices*). *Independent*, 26 December 1990.

James Liddy. 'A line must be drawn...even with poets' (*The Rain, the Moon*). *Hibernia*, No.6, 1961.

Edna Longley. 'Beyond the Incestuous Irish Anger' (*Cromwell*). *Fortnight*, No.204, 1984.

Sean Lucy. 'Cromwell's curse' (*Cromwell*). *Tablet*, 29 September 1984.

Augustine Martin. 'Kennelly: cheerful, desolate' (*A Time for Voices*). *Irish Independent*, 21 July 1990.

Augustine Martin. 'No one is forgiven' (*The Book of Judas*). *Irish Independent*, 7 December 1991.

Peter McDonald. 'Permanent Beginning' (*Selected Poems*). *Irish Review*, No.1, 1986.

Peter McDonald. 'Poetry of sustenance and suffering' (*A Time for Voices*). *Irish Times (Weekend)*, 23 June 1990.

Hayden Murphy. 'Book Reviews' (*The Penguin Book of Irish Verse*). *Dublin Magazine*, No.4, Winter 1970/1971.

Christopher Murray. 'Reviews' (*A Time for Voices*). *Studies*, No.316, Winter 1990.

Christopher Murray. 'Spancelled in a Place' (*The Boats Are Home*). *Irish Literary Supplement*, No.1, Spring 1982.

David Nowlan. 'Subverting ancient Tragedy' (Performance of *The Trojan Women*). *Irish Times*, 3 June 1993.

David Nowlan. '*Antigone* at the Peacock' (Performance of *Antigone*). *Irish Times*, 29 April 1986.

Robert Nye. 'The voice of uncommon sense' (*A Time for Voices*). *Scotsman*, 9 June 1990.

Erwin Otto. 'Reviews' (*Shelley in Dublin* and *A Kind of Trust*). *Moderna Språk*, No.2, 1976.

Åke Persson. 'Kennelly Nails the Reader' (*The Book of Judas*). *Krino*, No.12, Winter 1991.

Richard Pine. 'No Answers, Only Questions' (*The Book of Judas*). *Irish Literary Supplement*, No.2, Fall 1992.

Maurice Riordan. 'Striking sparks' (*Cromwell*). *Irish Press*, 25 February 1984.

Anthony Roche. 'Joycean joust with Jesus and Judas' (*The Book of Judas*). *Sunday Business Post*, 10 November 1991.

Jonathan Sawday. 'Lord Protect Us' (*Cromwell*). *Poetry Ireland Review*, No.10, Summer 1984.

Peter Sirr. 'A laneway packed with shadows' (*The Book of Judas*). *Irish Times (Weekend)*, 21 December 1991.

Michael Smith. 'Editorial. Irish Poetry and Penguin Verse' (*The Penguin Book of Irish Verse*). *Lace Curtain*, No.3, 1970.

Charles Spencer. 'True to Medea' (Performance of *Medea*). *Daily Telegraph*, 20 July 1989.

Oliver Taplin. 'Tongue-lashing' (Performance of *Medea*). *Times Literary Supplement*, 28 July–3 August 1989.

Colm Toibin. 'Brendan Kennelly finds a big theme' (Performance of *Cromwell*). *Sunday Independent (Dublin)*, 1 February 1987.

W.H. Van Voris. 'Good bet becomes better' (*Good Souls to Survive*). *Irish Press*, 22 July 1967.

4. SELECTED INTERVIEWS & PROFILES

Alpha. 'Kennelly: Returning the compliment. Brendan Kennelly on God'. *Alpha*, 28 September 1989.

Melanie Boast. 'Star Interview. The world according to Brendan Kennelly'. *Woman's Way*, 28 February 1992.

Ciaran Carty. 'Perspectives. The Mightiest Power in the World. Politicians Betrayed by Their Own Words Says Poet Brendan Kennelly'. *Sunday Independent* (Dublin), 30 January 1977.

Ciaran Carty. 'Why sensuality is not a dirty word'. *Sunday Independent* (Dublin), 6 February 1977.

Ciaran Carty. 'The enemies of learning...and the tyranny of commonsense. Brendan Kennelly: "It's very hard to be educated coming through the Irish system"'. *Sunday Independent* (Dublin), 8 February 1981.

Ciaran Carty. 'Bleedin' Christ'. *Sunday Tribune*, 22 December 1985.

Damian Corless. 'Rhymes & Reason'. *In Dublin*, No.12, 1993.

Katie Donovan. 'Blaming it all on Judas'. *Irish Times* 19 December 1991.

Irish Independent. 'Women and love. Brendan Kennelly returns to his favourite subject'. *Irish Independent*, 8 July 1989.

Literary Review. 'On Language and Invention: Interview with Brendan Kennelly'. *Literary Review*, No.22, Winter 1979.

Michael Murphy. 'Brendan's Voyage'. *Hot Press*, 1 February 1985.

Tom O'Dea. 'Passionate Particularity. A profile of Brendan Kennelly'. *Magill*, October 1988.

Richard Pine. 'Q. & A. with Brendan Kennelly'. *Irish Literary Supplement*, No.1, Spring 1990.

Deirdre Purcell. 'The Brendan Voyage'. *Sunday Tribune (People)*, 3 July 1988.

Lorcan Roche. 'Women and me'. *Irish Independent*, 27 September 1988.